What Makes Teachers U
and What Can You Do A

GW00750969

Many teachers, support staff and school leaders are tired, stressed and overstretched. And even though this frequently makes the headlines, it isn't a new problem. In this book, Mark Solomons and Fran Abrams argue staff wellbeing should be rooted in the culture and climate of our schools. They provide a roadmap to recovery for struggling schools which should lead to improvements in staff morale, workload management and mental wellbeing.

With a range of real-life examples, this book focuses on how school leaders can build workplace wellbeing in even the most challenging environments. It includes clear links to research evidence and summaries of the key steps necessary to deal with common issues such as:

- Identifying and mapping issues in your school

- Leading for wellbeing

- Creating and maintaining a happy workforce

- Developing a culture of everyday wellbeing

- Overseeing change.

Written in an entertaining yet informative manner, this is the go-to guide for school leaders who want to support staff by building a more positive and supportive workplace.

Mark Solomons, former Sainsbury's Bank operating board member, has more than 12 years' experience developing leadership and culture in education. A school governor and trustee for more than 20 years, he founded Welbee, a multi-award winning edtech start-up supporting schools to measure and systematically improve staff wellbeing. This is his second book.

Fran Abrams is a journalist and author with more than 30 years' experience of reporting on education. She has worked for all the national broadsheet newspaper groups and for 15 years was a reporter on BBC Radio 4's *File on 4* programme. She has written six previous books.

'This is a powerful, thoughtful book that goes beyond treating symptoms, towards looking at the root causes of poor wellbeing. We are shown that leaders who build teams that are trusted offer teachers high levels of agency, enabling workload to be viewed as meaningful and purposeful. Strategies are offered that are aimed at supporting leaders to develop a culture of collective endeavour. This is a compelling resource for leaders everywhere - highly recommended for practical audit resources alongside case studies that offer evidence about what truly makes a difference.'

Dame Alison Peacock, *Chief Executive of the Chartered College of Teaching*

'The book thoughtfully examines how leaders can create an engaging and vibrant school climate and culture, building an environment where teachers and all staff thrive. The research is clear, where staff report a positive climate, this underpins a virtuous cycle, impacting student learning, relationships and a sense of belonging. While much of the policy and frameworks referenced are from the UK, the practical strategies and steps are equally applicable in the US. This is a timely and must have resource for district leaders, principals, and those aspiring to these roles.'

Dr Clayton M. Wilcox, *Vice President and Ambassador for Community Relations, the Compass Group, CEO and founder of Thoughts2Lead, and former superintendent.*

What Makes Teachers Unhappy, and What Can You Do About It?

Building a Culture of Staff Wellbeing

Mark Solomons
Fran Abrams

Routledge
Taylor & Francis Group

LONDON AND NEW YORK

Cover image: © Getty Images

First published 2024
by Routledge
4 Park Square, Milton Park, Abingdon, Oxon OX14 4RN

and by Routledge
605 Third Avenue, New York, NY 10158

Routledge is an imprint of the Taylor & Francis Group, an informa business

British Library Cataloguing-in-Publication Data
A catalogue record for this book is available from the British Library

ISBN: 978-1-032-32589-7 (hbk)
ISBN: 978-1-032-32590-3 (pbk)
ISBN: 978-1-003-31576-6 (ebk)

DOI: 10.4324/9781003315766

Typeset in Melior
by codeMantra

Contents

Section 1: Mapping the issues

Section 2: Leading for wellbeing

Section 3: Getting and keeping a happy workforce

Section 4: School culture

Section 5: Overseeing change

Section 6: Rethinking education for wellbeing

List of illustrations

The case studies

The following school leaders have shared their experiences with us, and we meet them at relevant points throughout the book:

Mark Eager, Principal, Brixham College

Brixham College is an 11–18 comprehensive school in Devon with 1100 pupils. Mark Eager became principal in 2009. Previously a foundation school administered by Torbay Council, the college was converted to academy status on 1 January 2012, but continues to coordinate with Torbay Council for admissions. The college used to run 'donut Fridays' for staff, but when a survey was undertaken, the results on staff wellbeing and job satisfaction were poor. The results enabled the leadership team to devise a longer-term strategy which helped to improve recruitment, retention and wellbeing.

John Maher, Headteacher, Ashfield School

Ashfield School in Nottinghamshire is the largest single-site secondary school in England, with 360 staff including 185 teachers and 150 support staff, and 2700 students. John Maher has taught in 5 schools over a 30-year career as an English teacher, head of department and senior leader. He was appointed as headteacher at Ashfield School in 2017 and set about establishing a clear and fresh strategic direction for this large and vibrant school. He is proud of the positive culture and caring ethos of the school.

David Bignell, Former Primary School Principal and Mindfulness Expert

David Bignell has worked in primary education for 33 years: 8 as a classroom teacher, 5 as a deputy headteacher and 20 as a headteacher in 4 different schools. Since 2015, he has worked closely with the Mindfulness in Schools Project and has trained with colleagues from the Centre for Mindfulness Research and Practice at Bangor University and the Oxford Mindfulness Centre to deliver the Frantic World course to adults.

Debbie Duggan, Director of Operational Resources at The Two Counties Trust

Before joining the Two Counties Trust in 2017, Debbie Duggan was Vice Principal for Organisational Development at Central College, Nottingham, where she led areas including human resources and as Ofsted nominee led the college from Requires Improvement to Good. She has worked in education for more than 20 years and at Two Counties has led a process of measuring and tracking staff wellbeing. The Two Counties Trust is a family of nine secondary schools in Derbyshire and Nottinghamshire.

Ben Solly, Principal of Uppingham Community College, Rutland

Ben Solly began his career as a PE teacher at The Coseley School, a Specialist Sports College in the Black Country, and later became Assistant Vice Principal at Long Field Academy in Melton Mowbray. His first headship was at Lutterworth College, and he moved to Uppingham, an 11–16 school with 900 students, in 2017. He has worked to create a system of distributed leadership and to remove bureaucratic barriers which might impede teachers' ability to do their jobs well.

Sinéad Ormston, Assistant Headteacher, The Skinners' School, Tunbridge Wells

Sinéad Ormston joined the Skinners' School, an 11–18 boys' grammar in Kent, in 2010 as a science teacher. She later became Key Stage 3 Science Co-Ordinator and Head of Year before taking on her current role in 2016. She has led an initiative to identify and address issues relating to staff wellbeing.

Anne-Louise Payne

Anne-Louise Payne is Executive Principal at the Howard Partnership Trust in Surrey and led the transformation and rebuilding of the Three Rivers Academy, a large comprehensive school in Surrey. The school was built using wellbeing design principles drawn up by Scott Brownrigg and the Learning Crowd.

Authors

Mark Solomons, MBA, is a former operating board member of Sainsbury's Bank who has subsequently had more than 12 years' experience of leadership and culture development in the United Kingdom and International schools' market. He co-authored *Building Resilience; Seven steps to a Highly Successful Life* and has been a school governor and trustee for more than 20 years. In 2018, he founded Welbee, a multi-award winning venture capital-backed tech start-up supporting schools to measure and systematically improve the wellbeing of staff.

Fran Abrams is a journalist and author with more than 30 years' experience of reporting on education. She has worked for all the national broadsheet newspaper groups as well spending 15 years as a reporter on BBC Radio 4's *File on 4* programme. She is a trustee of the Education Media Centre, a charity devoted to raising the profile of good evidence about what works in education. She has previously written six factual books, four of them on education.

Authors' note

If there has ever been a right time for a book about staff wellbeing in schools, it is now. In the wake of Covid-19, the English Government pledged to put the mental health of those working in education at the heart of policy. Its new Education Staff Wellbeing Charter pledges to 'design in' wellbeing, to support efforts to drive down unnecessary workload and to measure levels of anxiety, happiness, worthwhileness, life satisfaction and job satisfaction across the teaching profession. In the United States, the Biden administration is providing US$190bn of post-Covid emergency relief funding and further money to support mental health.

This book's aim is to help schools to put their houses in order, to deliver evidence-backed benefits for staff and students and to help make sure they will not be found lacking as inspectors begin to assess staff wellbeing.

Even before Covid added to staff workload, education was facing a staffing crisis fuelled by stress and mental ill-health, and the crisis has only made things worse: a third of new teachers leave within five years, and more than 8 out of 10 staff report symptoms of stress. As a result, pupil outcomes are lower than they should be.

This book is a practical guide for educational leaders on improving workplace and mental wellbeing among the workforce: we hope it will become an essential tool for all schools.

We come to this project from very different directions: Mark works at the chalk face running Welbee, a company which helps schools, colleges, multi-academy trusts and school districts to measure and to address wellbeing issues among their staff, so he sees at close quarters just how critical they are to success.

Fran is a journalist and author with more than 30 years' experience of reporting on education and other areas in the UK national media, and she believes schools need to have the best possible evidence base if their efforts are to be successful.

We hope we have synthesised those two perspectives to create a book which will feel real and will be packed with both evidence and practical tips for those in education leadership positions, in the United Kingdom – where we're based – and around the globe. Mark works particularly closely with school districts in the United States and has tried to ensure their needs are covered here too.

A brief note: we want this book to be written accessibly and sometimes that has meant using shorthand terms. When we say 'schools,' we may also mean colleges, trusts and districts. When we say 'teachers' that doesn't mean we've forgotten that the majority of staff in schools aren't actually teachers. We hope much of the information in this book will apply to non-teaching staff and other members of the wider community, too – we have addressed their needs in Chapters 10 and 14. While this is mostly a book about the workforce – there are lots of good books about pupil wellbeing – we have tried to cover their needs, too, and have particularly focused in Chapter 13 on making staff wellbeing work for students. While some of the specific policy sections focus on the United Kingdom, all of the practical sections are relevant wherever you are.

Introduction

JOHN MAHER, HEADTEACHER, ASHFIELD SCHOOL

I have never consciously thought that I must make staff feel valued – it's more that every action we have taken collectively has worked to that end. When I took on the role, I thought I've got one chance to make a real difference, to make an impact: I just decided almost subconsciously what school I wanted. I was going to embody that school. I was going to explain directly to staff that behaviours lead to culture change. From day one we have asked staff to do the positive and visible things that can be sustained over long periods of time and trust that they will lead to sustained improvement; we're not weighing the pig every five minutes.

I suppose I've learned from a successful class how you mould a successful school. And you don't teach a successful class if they are fearful or anxious. You've got to create a safe environment where risks can be taken, where you're in it together, the sky's the limit and you're constantly revisiting and explaining – it is hard and repetitive work, to be honest, but I thought, well, if that doesn't work, that's all I've got. And it has worked so far, but you can never be complacent.

There is a reason why you picked up this book. Something about the cover maybe sparked your interest? Or maybe you read a review that made you think you needed to know more? One thing is clear so far: it's a book about teacher wellbeing and about how school, college, district or multi-academy trust (MAT) leaders can help to improve it.

It won't come as a surprise that there are books about teacher wellbeing: this isn't the first, and it won't be the last. After all, it's a topic which is talked about a lot. News headlines on the subject tend to be little short of apocalyptic. Here are a couple of recent ones – picked at random from the many hundreds on offer via a simple internet search.

Teacher wellbeing is 'on a knife edge' after the stress of the pandemic, the London Evening Standard reports. This is based on a survey by the TES, a news

DOI: 10.4324/9781003315766-1

organisation for education professionals, which surveyed almost 3000 UK teachers on how they felt about their work. Two-thirds told the TES their workload was not manageable, compared to 36 per cent in the rest of the world; and 38 per cent felt confident in their roles in 2022, compared to 79 per cent the previous year. The UK Government has highlighted the costs of this – its teacher recruitment strategy says that for some small providers, the price of recruitment is now a significant part of the budget.[1]

Across the Atlantic, similar stories can be found. Newsweek reports,[2] based on a survey of teachers by the National Education Association (NEA), that 55 per cent of teachers may soon leave the field, citing Covid burnout.

The problem isn't unique to any country, and it isn't caused by Covid – though, of course, there have been self-evident stresses upon those in education who have found themselves on the front line fighting multiple fires on a daily basis. The NEA President, Becky Pringle, told Newsweek the problem of teacher retention, now particularly acute among black and Hispanic teachers in the United States, was a by-product of decades of disinvestment. Teachers from the poorest backgrounds suffered most, she suggested.

Pringle's solutions – based on the teacher survey – were paying teachers more, hiring more teachers, providing additional counsellors, psychologists and mental health services for students, hiring more support staff, cutting paperwork and reducing testing. (All of which, you may well be thinking, aren't really in the gift of the average school leader, as they either cost money or are the result of regulatory requirements. But we will return to that via the practical steps all leaders in education can take without breaking the budget or the rules.)

A scan of the news headlines suggests high levels of teacher stress, and a crisis in teacher retention, are particular and recent problems. They aren't. The narrative has changed over the years, but the basic message – that large numbers of teachers are leaving because of the strains of the job – remains the same.

Back in 1990, for instance, the Daily Mirror ran a special 'Shock Issue' on the crisis caused by teachers leaving in droves.[3] Back then, low pay and pupil violence formed a larger part of the narrative, but the messages were similar: "Of course I miss the children, my colleagues and the stimulus of classroom contact. But not the migraines, meetings dragging into the evening, and poring over balance sheets wondering how I will make ends meet," a former head teacher who had 'quit to peel the spuds' told the paper.

As you have picked up this book, you probably already know the problems well. Probably you work in education, or you have a strong connection with it as a governor or as a parent. Probably you're looking not so much for the detail of the issue as for practical, workable solutions.

This is a book which aims to provide those solutions in a format which demonstrates the possible, even for the hardest-pressed schools. It will take a look at the policy context and at the history, but it will focus at every stage on what those on the ground can actually do: now, today, in the next few months and over the next few years. Its aim will be to provide the starting point for a journey which could lead to real, cultural change within schools and colleges, from the first tentative steps, if they haven't already been taken, to more major school-level initiatives.

Many of those who wish to use the insights in this book will already be some way down that road, of course. And the hope is that its format will facilitate a certain amount of cherry-picking, with clear signposting, via section and chapter headings, to enable readers to skip to the parts relevant to them.

The aim is to inform, but also to entertain: most readers will be giving up hard-earned 'leisure' time, so we will keep the tone light as far as possible. But the aim is to delve deep into the best evidence on the subject in order to extract those parts which are useful to professionals who want to make their working environments safer, happier, more stable places to be. In short, we hope this book will be useful, interesting, inspiring and powerful. We hope it will prove to be a tool which can change lives.

So, what is 'Wellbeing'?

There are many answers to this question, of course. But for the purposes of this book, the definition will be focused on the employer's perspective. It will look at wellbeing from an angle which will point clearly towards pathways which will help professionals to navigate this environment. Our definition will focus on:

- How staff feel (personally and socially).

- How they evaluate their life satisfaction rather than just their moment-to-moment happiness.

- How they develop and become fulfilled – training, continuing professional development and career aspirations are vital.

- How they function physically, emotionally, mentally and spiritually: the power of positive psychology.

- The degree to which they experience positive effects as being greater than negative effects.[4]

The last two points on this list are clearly linked to resilience, and to a focus on building protective factors (positives) while mitigating risk factors (negatives).

In order to improve staff wellbeing in the workplace, the biggest focus should be on the things staff see as being caused by work and therefore potentially influenced by workplace interventions. The UK Health and Safety Executive has a set of management standards setting out six key areas of work design that, if not properly managed, are associated with poor health, lower productivity and increased accident and sickness absence rates.[5] The six management standards – adapted here to fit our remit – are:

1. **Demands** (includes workload, working hours, deadlines, behaviour and anything that adds to the demands you face).

2. **Control** (the say staff have over what they do and how they work).

3. **Support** (from districts, MATs, schools and colleges, but particularly from line managers, senior leaders and colleagues).

4. **Relationships** (how well positive behaviours are encouraged and any inappropriate behaviours dealt with effectively and quickly).

5. **Role** (staff know what is expected of them and how their work fits with that of their department and the aims of the school, MAT and/or district).

6. **Change** (and how it is managed).

Yet it isn't simply workload, lack of autonomy, relationships or change that are the biggest issues. The biggest issue is how these are managed within each setting.

So what we are really talking about in much of this book is leadership: the biggest single cause of poor staff wellbeing is line managers. This isn't to apportion blame: they are a product of their knowledge and experience, their role models and the training and development they receive. One day you're a teacher or support staff member, the next you're leading a team, often with no or little training. And you often have to continue to do more than 80 per cent of your previous job. It's no wonder line managers can have such a negative impact. They learn the hard way through trial and error and are sometimes simply unaware of how their behaviours affect others.

Professor Sir Cary Cooper, a leading UK expert on organisational wellbeing and President of the Chartered Institute of Personnel and Development, believes too many line managers simply do not have the necessary social and soft skills to lead. But the good news is these skills are all learnable.[6]

By creating an environment that supports staff development and encourages staff to make decisions, take responsibility and learn from mistakes, rather than being judged from them, it's possible to improve staff wellbeing and deliver significant benefits to school leaders and students. In short, it's vital that wellbeing is built into the culture of organisations from top to bottom if real and lasting change is to take place.

Taking a step back

There tends to be – if you follow the media and the pronouncements of the teacher unions – a sense of permanent crisis in education. Things, it seems, are always getting worse. So where are we really, in the third decade of the 21st century? *Have things got worse?* How does teachers' sense of wellbeing really compare with that of workers in other fields, and was it always thus? If there are stresses – and there certainly are – what are the specific factors, now, that are likely to be causing them? Are they external, or internal? Which can largely be disregarded here, either because they aren't usually as important as they seem, or because they can't readily be changed by the actions of leaders in schools, colleges, MATs or districts? Which of them can't be changed, but can be mitigated?

First, let us take a long view. How has teachers' sense of wellbeing changed over time? Is it really getting worse, and if so, why?

Surprisingly, given the level of interest in the topic, there isn't a great deal of evidence on the trends in teacher wellbeing. Recently a group of academics from the UCL Institute of Education in London[7] carried out an analysis of three large-scale, long-running government surveys to assess whether there had been changes over time.

On the face of it, their findings looked grim. Over a 20-year period, the proportion of teachers reporting lasting issues with their mental health had risen very significantly, from less than one per cent to five per cent by 2018. At the same time, there had been an accompanying rise in the percentage of education professionals who were taking prescribed antidepressant medication.

But conversely, the evidence also showed the proportion of education professionals with high scores on a standard assessment scale, administered by health professionals, had remained stable over time. And furthermore, when the researchers compared teachers' mental health with that of other professionals, such as accountants, nurses and human resource managers, they found a similar upward trend to the one they had found for teachers.

The researchers concluded more people, in all walks of life, were now reporting mental health conditions and health professionals were also more likely to diagnose them than previously. This could be seen in a positive light: the reduction of stigma around mental health had enabled it to gain better recognition, leading to more of those in need receiving treatment.

What is unique about the current situation is the level of openness on offer around teacher wellbeing: it's being talked about, a lot. For the first time, in many cases, teachers are feeling able to express how long hours and high levels of scrutiny make them feel. And for school leaders, that presents a huge opportunity.

Working hours

This isn't to say, of course, that there aren't specific stress factors which are exacerbating a teacher retention crisis. Researchers have also looked at some of these factors more closely and have reached some surprising – and useful – conclusions.

One key question is the hours teachers work. There's been a great deal of comment on this, and the assumption has been that policy changes over the years have placed education professionals under increasing stress.

To what extent is this true? A key source of information on teachers' professional lives is the OECD's Teaching and Learning International Survey (TALIS)[8] which every five years asks teachers and school leaders about their working conditions and learning environments. It covers about 260,000 teachers in 15,000 schools across 48 countries and economies and is much quoted by academics and policymakers.

What can it tell us about whether teachers' working hours have got longer? After analysing the survey's 2018 results, the United Kingdom's Education Policy Institute took a rather gloomy line.[9]

> Teachers in England work longer hours than their counterparts across the OECD and do so largely because of the time they spend on planning, marking, writing assessments, and doing other administrative tasks. We found that the long hours hindered their ability to complete professional development and that these problems are particularly acute among novice teachers.

In England, teacher workload and the pressures of complying with accountability measures have been a key theme in this debate ever since the 1988 Education Reform Act introduced a raft of measures which included performance tables, publicly available inspection reports and market exposure through increased parental choice. Similar reforms have sparked parallel debates around the world.

Researchers at the UCL Institute of Education in London analysed the 2018 TALIS findings on teacher workload alongside three other datasets[10] and came up with a new conclusion. Working hours during term time *were* high, they found: a quarter of teachers regularly worked more than 60 hours per week, 4 out of 10 usually worked in the evening and about 1 in 10 at the weekend.

However, they did not find evidence that average working hours had increased. Teachers had always worked long hours, they said. In the previous 20 years, there had been no notable change in the total hours worked by teachers, and in the past 15, there had been no change in weekend or evening working.

In the United States, an analysis using the American Time Use Survey[11] compared the working hours of teachers with those of other college graduates and found that when reduced hours over the Summer were factored in, they actually worked very slightly less.

The wrong kind of work?

So it isn't teachers' hours, *per se*, which cause them to feel stressed: that isn't a new problem. Maybe, then, the question relates not just to the time spent, but to *how* the time is spent? Again, the UCL researchers had some insights.[12]

They analysed the TALIS data to look at teacher stress in relation to how much time was spent on a variety of specific tasks: lesson planning and preparation, teamwork, marking, student counselling, management, administration, professional development, parent liaison and extracurricular activities.

Their findings were very clear: for every hour spent on less enjoyable parts of the job – specifically lesson planning and marking – teachers' stress increased significantly. So extra hours spent on teaching, working with colleagues or on extracurricular activities were fine; extra hours spent on certain kinds of paperwork were not.

There were good kinds of work, then, and less good kinds. The researchers turned their attention to a key factor in the debate around teacher stress: to what extent were government accountability measures to blame? Two of the UCL team looked again at the TALIS data with this in mind.

Using evidence from more than 100,000 teachers in 40 countries, they asked if using student performance data to judge teachers – increasingly common across the globe – affected teacher stress. They found there was a modest but positive correlation between these measures and levels of stress among both teachers and head teachers.

Looking within schools, they found little evidence that the management practices of headteachers differed when they reported feeling stressed about accountability, or that they transmitted these feelings onto their staff. But there was strong evidence of what they called "emotional contagion" within schools: teachers were notably more likely to feel stressed by accountability if their colleagues felt the same way.

So teacher accountability measures are not a 'one-way street.' They can lead to higher standards, but they can also lead to stress which can rob the profession of valuable talent and skill.

The researchers reached a conclusion which will form a key thread in this book: whole-school approaches to reducing stress can be particularly effective. In some schools, more than others, there is an atmosphere in which staff feel particularly anxious about facing scrutiny, and where school leaders need to intervene to change that. The use of student data in teacher appraisals is not a problem in itself, but the atmosphere around it within the school can become one.

...But how do teachers actually *feel?*

It's all very well to say teaching has always been hard work; that the hours have always been long and that while it's a deeply rewarding job, it's a tough one. It's easy, too, to say that everyone's more likely to report stress these days, and that structural factors such as increased amounts of regulation and accountability are to blame.

What does that actually feel like, day to day, on the ground? How does it affect teachers' perceptions of their working lives? And more crucially, what can be done about it?

We know quite a lot about this. Every year the Education Support charity carries out a survey of teacher wellbeing with the YouGov polling organisation: the last one, at time of writing, was carried out in the Summer of 2022[13] and covered the views of some 3000 education staff.

It contained bad news: 7 out of 10 staff and 8 out of 10 senior leaders in schools said they felt stressed, 6 out of 10 leaders went into work when unwell, and 4 out of 10 teachers felt their organisation's culture had a negative effect on their wellbeing.

Overall, the numbers feeling stressed had risen by three per cent since the previous year, and had been well over 60 per cent for the past six years. Signs of depression and anxiety were also above the levels reported by the general population. And for the first time 'lack of resources' was one of the top five reasons staff considered leaving the profession, particularly in primary schools.

There were long-term health implications to this, the charity said. The current context of financial and staffing challenges, government and policy instability and pressure from inspections made the creation of positive, productive and psychologically safe cultures incredibly challenging.

No wonder, then, that Education Support was reporting half of classroom teachers and 6 in 10 senior leaders were thinking of quitting: official figures suggest a third will leave within five years of qualifying. Workload was cited as the main reason, along with relationships between staff and senior leadership.

The charity concluded the best way for schools and colleges to improve the mental health of their workforce was for managers to work with staff to reduce workload.

Elsewhere, too, there has been growing concern about the effect of wellbeing on both the retention of teachers and on recruitment. Back in 2018, the English Department for Education published a report on teacher retention[14]: the word 'wellbeing' didn't feature. While the report did focus on improving support for teachers, it put the issue at least partly down to poor messaging: "Considerations would be how the message to senior leaders and teachers can be strengthened to dispel the myths around inspection and the commitment to reduce workload," it said. Beyond that, key measures would need to be on workload, progression, flexibility and professional recognition, it said.

Note the change of tone, then, in a briefing paper by the House of Commons Library in 2021.[15] The report contained the news that for the first time in a decade, due to economic uncertainty around Covid, teacher training targets had largely been met. But this was not likely to be sustained, it said.

The report went on to detail a range of measures put in place in the intervening years to support teacher recruitment and retention. There were two key planks of the government's strategy:

- An Early Career Framework for teachers, which would fund an increase in non-contact time.

- A Wellbeing Charter[16] to help create a positive, supportive culture in schools.

The charter, published in 2021, changed the focus of policy on teacher retention, putting wellbeing at its heart. The key outcomes for schools, it said, should be that staff understood their wellbeing was taken seriously; that open conversations should take place in all schools about wellbeing and mental health; that all schools should have a staff wellbeing strategy and that all schools should work to create a wellbeing-focused culture.

THE IMPACT OF POOR STAFF WELLBEING: MARK SOLOMONS

In late 2018, I founded Welbee with a clear aim: to help school leaders develop the right skills, tools and support to manage staff and as a result, to improve their wellbeing. I wanted to help give staff a bigger voice and to make staff wellbeing a central part of school life.

Welbee has continued to grow and to help more and more schools understand how to make the biggest impact for their staff. In 2021, we conducted our first national staff wellbeing survey, covering the English regions and home countries.[17]

During March and April 2021, we invited nearly 165,000 staff to share their views and experiences via an email direct to their inboxes. Nearly 8000 responded, including teachers, support staff and leaders, and their insights helped us to build a picture of the issues schools faced.

We used the Health and Safety Executive's Management Standards to measure what was happening, so we could effectively compare scores across geographies, sectors and phases and with cross sector organisations. They allowed us to measure workplace wellbeing and how well leaders were managing the risks of workplace stress.

Were they building a culture where staff were likely to thrive and do their best work? We felt putting staff first in this way should underpin pupil outcomes and contribute significantly to Covid catch-up. Rather than increasing the number of lessons through extended hours and shorter breaks, this would provide schools with a long-term solution.

Looking at the results, I was heartened by a renewed focus on improving the wellbeing of staff in schools and of the commitment of so many leaders to maintain a focus on this, alongside everything else they were being asked to deliver.

Prior to the pandemic, there were already significant attraction, retention, absence and mental health challenges in schools: missed recruitment targets, too many new teachers leaving within five years and more than one-third of staff reporting some kind of mental ill-health, to mention a few key areas.

There were a number of key findings:

- Respondents to our survey scored comparatively higher than those across other sectors in three of the six management standards: they were in the top 20 per cent for role; knowing what was expected and how their work fitted into the aims of their organisation. In terms of support from colleagues, our respondents were in the top 30 per cent when asked about peers, and in the top 50 per cent when asked about their managers. They scored highly – in the top 30 per cent again – on relationships.

They felt they were consulted about change, and how it would work out in practice. These all relate to people and suggest there is a strong base on which to build a wellbeing culture.

- School and college staff scored comparatively lower than those across other sectors in two of the six management standards: they were in the bottom 20 per cent when it came to having control over their working lives, and also felt they had few opportunities to question leaders about how and when change was made. Workload and flexibility were two key challenges to be addressed.

- Staff working in SEN schools recorded the highest scores of any school type across the management standards: they were the top-scoring school type in five standards and were very close to the top in the sixth. We felt this was surprising given the additional demands staff face in these schools but concluded greater one-to-one support and a sense of purpose from supporting vulnerable students could be a reason for this.

- Staff in Local Authority maintained secondary schools recorded the lowest scores across all of the management standards and those in academy secondary schools were not far behind. Higher demands from colleagues, focus on more regular student testing and challenges for leaders in communicating with larger numbers were among the reasons for this.

- There was little difference between the scores of staff in the same phases of academies and Local Authority maintained schools. This supported our belief that staff wellbeing is largely about school culture, driven by leaders, rather than school type. We felt our results suggested there were opportunities for staff development and economies of scale which were not being taken by all academies.

- Independent schools generally scored similarly to state primary and secondary schools. Independent school staff scored comparatively highest in control, suggesting they had a little more flexibility, while they scored lowest of all school types for change. Differences were not significant in most standards, again supporting the view that wellbeing is about the culture leaders create.

- There were differences between regions, though further work is needed to understand the significance of this. The North East scored lower in most standards and for all job roles. Staff in Northern Ireland, particularly support staff, had high scores.

- Across all but one of the management standards support staff had the highest scores, followed by teaching staff, middle leaders then senior leaders, though senior leaders had the second highest score for change. Support staff were less likely to be in the classroom and therefore might have had greater freedom to plan, operate and meet deadlines.

- Senior leaders had the lowest scores in the majority of cases, though this was not supported by surveys we had run directly with schools. Middle leaders had the second lowest scores, and in our school surveys, they were usually the ones needing most attention. They were caught between the senior team and staff, and with limited time available, particularly if they were teaching. It was clear leader wellbeing needed focus.

These were the five questions with the highest comparative scores – all in the top 20 per cent when compared with other sectors.

1. If work gets difficult, my colleagues will help me (peer support).

2. I receive the respect at work I deserve from my colleagues (peer support).

3. I am clear what my duties and responsibilities are (role).

4. I am given supportive feedback on the work I do (manager support).

5. Staff are always consulted about changes at work (change).

And these were the questions with the lowest comparative scores – in the bottom 20 per cent when compared to those across other sectors.

1. My working time can be flexible (control).

2. My line manager encourages me at work (manager support).

3. I am unable to take sufficient breaks (demands).

4. I have to work very intensively (demands).

5. I have a say in my own work speed (control).

One thing stands out: such scores are not determined by the type of school, college or MAT. It is the leadership of them that matters most. The behaviours of leaders, how they communicate, and the support processes established, such as appraisals and one-to-ones, make the biggest difference. It is all about the culture.

There really has never been a better time for leaders to focus on their own well-being and that of those they lead. It is time schools properly put staff first. This is the only sustainable way of achieving the pupil outcomes we need, and the catch-up that is still going on after the pandemic.

Many leaders and staff members were exhausted at the end of the 2021 school year, given the additional efforts everyone put in, on top of what was already a high workload. Since March 2020, they had done a fantastic job continuing to educate and support young people and many were feeling, with justification, their work had not had the recognition it deserved from government and the wider public.

And before Covid, we were already at a crossroads:

- Teacher shortages with demand outstripping supply in some locations and subjects.

- The challenges of retention, with teachers and other staff leaving (retirement and Covid-related impact is predicted to accelerate this).

- Rising mental ill-health and stress being the biggest cause of long-term absence.

I know from the work I do with schools that it is important to include all staff.

How do we best improve school climate and staff wellbeing in schools?

Here are two things schools do to foster a sense of wellbeing among staff:

- There are cakes on the table when staff are asked to attend that after school meeting. Or perhaps it's free fruit in the staffroom, or breakfast when there's an early morning start.

- Staff are offered the opportunity to take part in activities, for example a wellbeing day or even a wellbeing week. It might be yoga, other exercise, team building or some form of training on self-care.

If your school or college already has the right climate and staff wellbeing foundations in place, and supports staff throughout the year, these will add to what you are already doing. They are just not the place to start or to focus on first.

If staff do not feel supported or valued, do not have good relationships with their line managers or do not enjoy their work, then after they have eaten their cake, practiced yoga or participated in a wellbeing day, what has changed?

Climate and staff wellbeing is all about the culture that leaders create. It is like building a house. It is about putting down the right foundations. This means establishing effective behaviours and having the right supporting processes in place, so staff always feel valued and supported.

I see many organisations spending time on building the middle and top floors first. They provide cakes, fruit, yoga and wellbeing days as their solution. It is understandable – it's much easier treating symptoms and providing sticking plaster solutions than addressing the real causes. It may give a short-term adrenaline shot, a boost, yet we need long-term solutions.

While it is important to provide additional support for those that need it, firm foundations need to be in place first.

Over the course of the school year, we have Teacher Day, Stress Awareness Week and World Wellbeing Week. The purpose of these is to raise awareness, yet they add to the feeling that these are not part of everyday life – as they should be.

Awareness of stress, wellbeing and appreciating teachers and other school staff should be for every working day.

Before looking at problems and solutions, let's ask the questions, why improve staff wellbeing?

The costs of poor climate and poor staff wellbeing can be significant, and it is important to monitor staff wellbeing and target resources to areas known to be problematic.

Other benefits of improving staff wellbeing, in addition to raising student outcomes include:

- Reducing staff absence and the need for cover, and therefore ensuring continuity of teaching.

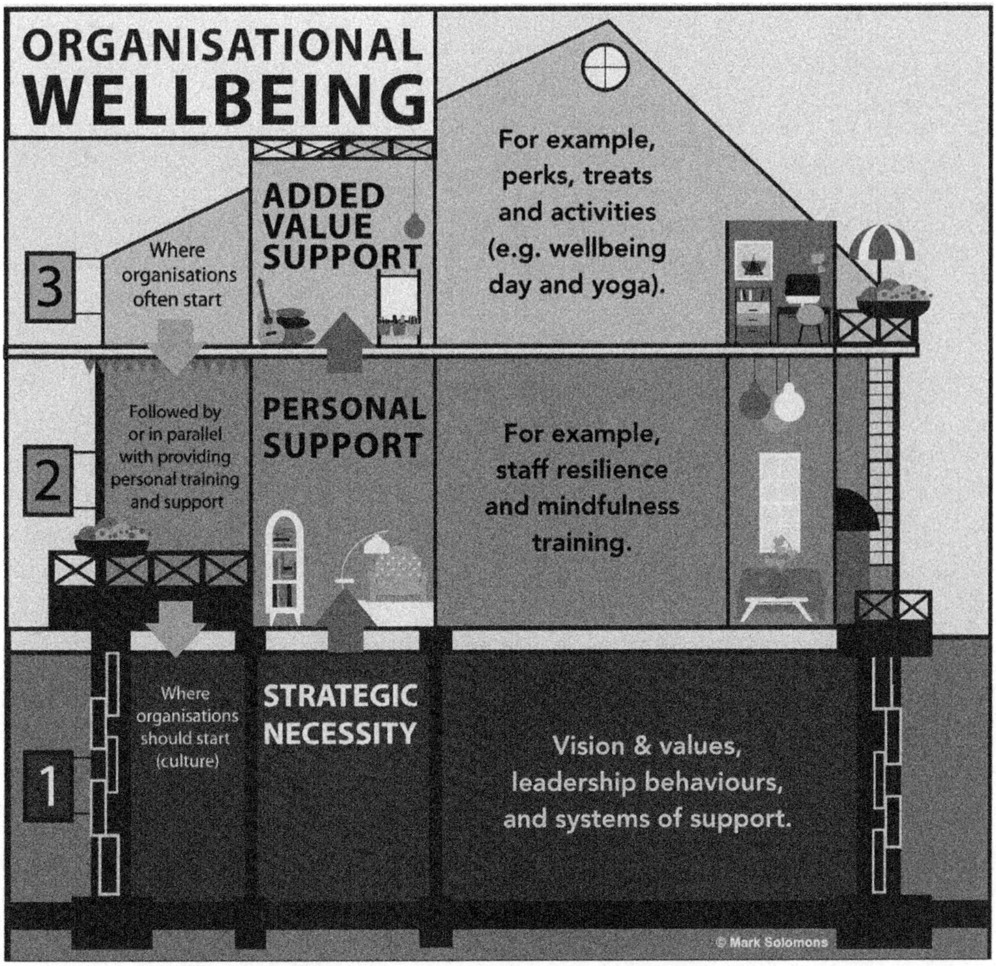

Illustration 1.1 House of organisational wellbeing

● Improving staff attraction and retention and reducing the need for recruitment, training and development.

● Reducing management time spent on those other unproductive tasks we just don't need, such as staff friction, poor performance or grievances.

If you want to improve climate and culture for staff, where should you start?

You need to know where you are now, if you are to make the right plans and track progress. Know your numbers.

Start with existing school data, and use existing systems and information where possible – you don't want to add significant (or any) workload. Hopefully you are already collecting this in some form and data to consider includes:

- Staff sickness and absence rates.

- Staff turnover.

- How often your support schemes or counselling provision or occupational health is used.

- Information on staff grievances, disputes or instances of poor behaviour.

- School performance trends.

In all of these, you should consider both the current situation and how this might compare to the national position, where known, or what you might expect it to be, as well as changes you can see over time.

In addition, you can seek staff feedback through group discussions, conversations and through targeting specific situations. These include return-to-work interviews, welfare discussions, exit interviews, regular check-ins and one-to-ones. These will all give you clues to the likely wellbeing of your staff, the climate in which they are working and possible solutions.

To add to this, you should use a staff survey, like the one we used for our National Survey Report. Whether you are going to do it yourself or it is being run by a third party, there are some key points to think about.

- The survey should have an evidence base and make sure it has benchmarks so you can see your comparative performance. It is probable that in some areas a score of 4 out of 5 will leave you with significant headroom for growth, while a score in the low 3s in another area could be in the top decile of schools and waste time and effort if you focus on it.

- Use the same questions and repeat. There is a tendency for some leaders to change questions to suit external or internal experiences. While you might add a few new ones, avoid wholesale changes, otherwise you cannot track changes.

- Use a survey that measures working conditions and climate.

- Think about how you will achieve a high participation rate. Make sure the survey is anonymous and that you explain why you are doing it and what is in it for staff members. That is about how you will act on their feedback. Ideally give staff time to take it at work – it sends the right message about the importance you place on their wellbeing.

- Finally, think about how you will share results with staff and engage with them in solutions. It cannot be about you solving everything.

The results from such a survey will allow you to focus on those things that will improve your foundations and will be embedded in your culture, so staff wellbeing is simply part of what happens every day.

So, what has the biggest impact on staff wellbeing and school climate?

All the usual things about workload, having a greater say in what you do and opportunities for progression and development are important, but perhaps most important of all is how these are led and managed in school.

Schools and colleges will always be busy environments and workload will always be too high. Leaders have to help themselves and others understand this; there is no light at the end of the workload tunnel. There is simply too much to do, and staff have to become comfortable with that. They have to know how to prioritise, to undertake the most important work and to accept it's OK to go home with work outstanding and pick it up in the morning.

That doesn't mean we should not be taking steps to drive out unnecessary work which has little impact on student, staff or school outcomes. Again, leaders and leadership are the key ingredient.

> The thing that is causing people to get ill at work and adversely affect their quality of working life is line managers who are not socially and interpersonally skilled. They don't have the soft skills that are needed.[18]

These are the words of Professor Sir Cary Cooper, one of the UK's leading experts on workplace wellbeing.

Tackling this before adding wellness programmes and perks; making sure wellbeing is part of your school culture is the solution.

It is what cakes and yoga cannot deliver: the long-term consistent performance and culture that is needed. Put this at the centre of your house foundations and it will stand for a long-time.

Yet we know how challenging this is within schools and for leaders. On first appointment and throughout middle leadership structures, many leaders have to continue to do their previous jobs, often continuing to teach in the classroom. With such limited time, how do they spend enough time checking in with staff, coaching others or developing as leaders?

Often, potential leaders are not given the opportunity to develop much-needed skills before appointment and receive limited support after. When it does happen, it's usually squashed into short and rushed twilight or inset sessions. Even when training takes place, it is often limited when it comes to what's needed effectively and consistently to lead people. It doesn't provide sufficient focus on those missing soft skills mentioned by Professor Cooper.

This is often not the fault of leaders: the current system is broken. We need change if we are to improve the wellbeing of staff more easily. While we need to campaign for increased resources, capacity and training, it is down to school leaders to act.

This book is about giving leaders the tools and resources they need to support the wellbeing of those they line manage. A useful place to start is the leadership competencies drawn up for the Health and Safety Executive.[19] Their aim is that leaders who demonstrate them will engage their teams and create an environment where more people thrive. Staff will copy and take greater ownership of their own wellbeing.

The behaviours within these competencies include, among many others:

- Doing what you say you will.

- Not talking about people behind their back.

- Not taking feedback as criticism.

- Being consistent in your behaviours and moods.

- Praising more than you criticise.

Asking leaders to self-assess against these competencies is the easy bit. Supporting them to choose to adapt and change behaviour is much harder. People have deep and long-held beliefs and need to understand why they should change, as well as regular and deliberate reflection and practice to develop new habits.

Senior leaders have to be role models for others to copy, and as line managers they have to coach their middle leaders. Without this, people will very quickly return to their default position.

Introducing this across your school, college or MAT is a great step, and a cornerstone on which to build a people strategy that will reduce absences and costs and improve retention and results. We look at these competencies in more detail in Chapter 6.

Yet simply sharing these competencies does not address the fact there is not enough capacity or time available for leaders. Time is the one thing over which none of us has control – unless we happen to have a time turner like Hermione in Harry Potter, there is no simple answer for this.

What we can control is what we focus on; setting our priorities and deciding what is most important. The good news is that making these changes does not add work. It just means doing things differently.

If you choose to put staff first and focus on culture, wellbeing simply becomes part of what happens every day. The more effectively you do this, the less you will need to talk about it and make specific plans. By all means add cake, yoga and other self-care activities but make sure they are not the first or only things you do.

Build those strong foundations, and systemise how you go about improving them. Measure, set your goals and plans, implement, follow up, embed, track and finally repeat. Make this simply a part of what you do.

And the benefits of building a strong wellbeing culture?

The benefits are manifest, of course – but we're not just talking here about fostering happiness for its own sake. Well-supported staff are much better placed to ensure pupils' wellbeing is supported, too. And with a whole-school culture of wellbeing, there's plenty of evidence that academic outcomes will improve. Look after your staff and they will look after your students, and that will give you the best chance of satisfying your other stakeholders.

So, let's take a look at the evidence. There has been limited research into school staff wellbeing and its impact on outcomes. The only major report[20] was written in 2007 by Birkbeck College, University of London, in partnership with Worklife Support, and highlighted the following:

- Staff wellbeing had a statistically significant impact on the SAT results of English primary schools.

- Teacher enjoyment was linked with a higher value-added measure for primary pupil performance.

- Increases in staff wellbeing were linked to an increased performance in 5+ GCSEs A to C.

- Higher staff wellbeing also led to improved value-added progress through key stages 2–4.

While staff wellbeing wasn't the only factor involved in improving results, the evidence for improving it was seen as significant and the researchers were excited because they saw it as being more easily influenced than many other actions schools were taking to improve student outcomes.

Education research is limited, but the role self-reported staff wellbeing plays in improving results is supported through other research, in business and more significantly in the health service.

A 2014 report for the Department of Business Innovation and Skills[21] found that staff wellbeing showed a strong and positive link with improved workplace performance for both profitability and labour productivity, as well as the quality of outputs and services.

It also showed a strong link between wellbeing and job satisfaction, including aspects such as training, skills development opportunities, how much autonomy staff had in their role, and how much scope they had to use their own initiative and influence decisions.

Dame Carol Black's 2008 review of the health of Britain's working-age population[22] found considerable evidence that health and wellbeing programmes produced economic benefits across all sectors and all sizes of business: in other words, that good health is good business. She also concluded that the benefits of wellbeing went beyond the quality of life of staff and extended to increasing an organisation's productivity and profitability.

Far more research has been carried out within the health sector, where staff wellbeing has consistently been shown to be linked with patient care, welfare and mortality.

Among the highlights from findings are:

- Evidence of a causal link between staff wellbeing and performance outcomes.

- A relationship between staff wellbeing and staff reported patient care, patient reported patient care and hospital mortality rates.

- Staff wellbeing is shown to be a driver of patient care performance. Seeking to systematically enhance staff wellbeing is not only important in its own right but also for the quality of patient experiences.

- Local climate is important, even for high-performing staff in demanding jobs.

- It is important to monitor employee wellbeing and target resources to areas known to be problematic.

- Management practices are significantly linked to NHS staff health and wellbeing.

- Staff wellbeing is linked to multiple outcomes, including staff absenteeism, turnover, agency spend (e.g., supply staff), patient satisfaction, infection rates and mortality rates.

- The associated financial costs of these can be significant.

So, if you're faced with a stay in an NHS hospital, it is well worth checking out how staff report their wellbeing. Put simply, the better staff report their own wellbeing, the greater your chance of survival. Lower wellbeing leads to more deaths.

While the outcomes are not quite as stark in education, we can transfer many of these findings and apply them to the school setting. This adds even further to the evidence for improving staff wellbeing and delivering better outcomes.

Chapter 1: Key points

- Wellbeing is how staff feel, personally and socially: how they evaluate their life satisfaction, how they can develop and become fulfilled; how they function physically, mentally, emotionally and spiritually; their sense of positivity about their working lives.

- The key factors in achieving good levels of wellbeing can be viewed through the Health and Safety Executive's Management Standards. These are: Demands, Control, Support, Relationships, Role and Change.

- National teacher wellbeing surveys consistently show poor results, with many respondents reporting overwork, burnout and a desire to leave the profession. UK teachers work some of the longest hours in the OECD.

● Research shows the situation is more stable than the headlines suggest: more teachers are reporting mental health problems, but so are professionals in other walks of life. Similarly, teachers work long hours and are often working at weekends and in evenings, but this has always been the case.

● Stress is linked less to the hours teachers work than to *how* they spend their working hours: extra hours spent on teaching, working with colleagues or extra-curricular activities are generally OK; extra hours spent on paperwork, lesson planning and marking are stressful.

● Accountability is a factor in causing stress, and therefore in policy terms, it has drawbacks as well as benefits. Teachers are more likely to be stressed by accountability measures such as inspections and appraisals if their colleagues feel the same way. Whole-school approaches are vital in effecting change.

● A Welbee staff survey revealed teachers scored higher than other professions in terms of Role, Support and Relationships. They scored comparatively lower in terms of Demands, Control and Change. Staff in special schools scored higher than in other types but there was little difference between Local Authority, academy and independent schools – staff wellbeing is mostly about culture, driven by leaders. Support staff had the highest scores, followed by teaching staff, middle leaders and then senior leaders with the lowest.

● The benefits of building a strong wellbeing culture can include better staff recruitment and retention, better staff performance, higher student outcomes and improved financial performance.

● Leadership is crucial: do what you say, be open, be consistent, praise more than you criticise and ideally deliver feedback directly in a one-to-one situation.

● The first step in effecting whole-school change should be gathering data – first through what's available in school, such as staff turnover and absence, and then using an effective staff survey.

Notes

1 Department for Education (2019). Teacher recruitment and retention. [online] Available at: https://assets.publishing.service.gov.uk/government/uploads/system/uploads/attachment_data/file/786856/DFE_Teacher_Retention_Strategy_Report.pdf [Accessed 2 January 2023].

2 Mordowanec, N. (2022). *55 per cent of educators may soon leave field, citing COVID burnout: Poll.* [online] Newsweek. Available at: https://www.newsweek.com/55-per cent-educators-may-soon-leave-field-citing-covid-burnout-poll-1677761 [Accessed 14 December 2022].

3 Cunningham, P. (1992). Teachers' Professional Image and the Press 1950–1990. *History of Education*, 21(1), pp.37–56. doi:10.1080/0046760920210103.

4 Welbee (2020). *What Is Staff Wellbeing & How Can You Improve It?* [online] Welbee. Available at: https://welbee.co.uk/learning-centre/what-is-staff-wellbeing/ [Accessed 14 December 2022].

5 Her Majesty's Stationery Office (2007). *Managing the causes of work-related stress: A step-by-step approach using the management standards.* [online] Great Britain: HMSO. Available at: https://www.hse.gov.uk/pubns/wbk01.htm.

6 CIPD (2018). *Health and well-being at work.* [online] Available at: https://www.cipd.co.uk/Images/health-and-well-being-at-work_tcm18-40863.pdf.

7 Jerrim, J., Sims, S., Taylor, H. and Allen, R. (2020). How Does the Mental Health and Wellbeing of Teachers Compare to Other Professions? Evidence from eleven survey datasets. *Review of Education.* doi:10.1002/rev3.3228.

8 OECD (2020). *TALIS 2018 Results (Volume II). TALIS.* OECD. doi:10.1787/19cf08df-en

9 Education Policy Institute (2019). *What the latest TALIS results mean for England's teacher recruitment crisis.* [online] Education Policy Institute. Available at: https://epi.org.uk/publications-and-research/talis-teacher-recruitment/ [Accessed 14 December 2022].

10 Allen, R., Benhenda, A., Jerrim, J. and Sims, S. (2019). *New evidence on teachers' working hours in England. An empirical analysis of four datasets.* [online] Available at: https://johnjerrim.files.wordpress.com/2019/09/working_paper_teacher_hours.pdf.

11 Startz, D. (2019). *Do teachers work long hours?* [online] Brookings. Available at: https://www.brookings.edu/blog/brown-center-chalkboard/2019/06/12/do-teachers-work-long-hours/.

12 Jerrim, J. and Sims, S. (2021). School Accountability and Teacher Stress: International Evidence from the OECD TALIS Study. *Educational Assessment, Evaluation and Accountability.* [online] doi:10.1007/s11092-021-09360-0.

13 Education Support (2022). *Wellbeing index 2022.* [online] Education Support. Available at: https://www.educationsupport.org.uk/media/zoga2r13/teacher-wellbeing-index-2022.pdf [Accessed 14 December 2022].

14 Cooper Gibson Research (2018). *Factors affecting teacher retention: Qualitative investigation.* [online] Available at: https://assets.publishing.service.gov.uk/government/uploads/system/uploads/attachment_data/file/686947/Factors_affecting_teacher_retention_-_qualitative_investigation.pdf.

15 Long, R. and Danechi, S. (2019). *Teacher recruitment and retention in England.* [online] Parliament.uk. Available at: https://researchbriefings.files.parliament.uk/documents/CBP-7222/CBP-7222.pdf [Accessed 14 December 2022].

16 Department for Education (2021). *Education staff wellbeing charter.* [online] gov.uk. Available at: https://www.gov.uk/guidance/education-staff-wellbeing-charter.

17 Welbee Ltd (2021). *National school staff wellbeing survey summary report.* [online] schools.welbee.co.uk. Available at: https://schools.welbee.co.uk/national-staff-survey-report-download [Accessed 14 December 2022].

18 Chartered Management Institute (2016). *How 'socially Unskilled' managers are denting productivity.* [online] CMI. Available at: https://www.managers.org.uk/knowledge-and-insights/article/how-socially-unskilled-managers-are-denting-productivity [Accessed 14 December 2022].

19 HSE (2008). *Executive health and safety management competencies for preventing and reducing stress at work identifying and developing the management behaviours necessary to implement the HSE management standards: Phase two.* [online] Available at: https://www.hse.gov.uk/research/rrpdf/rr633.pdf.

20 Dewberry, C. and Briner, R. (2007). *Staff wellbeing is key to school success – full report | PDF | job satisfaction | correlation and dependence.* [online] Scribd. Available at:

https://www.scribd.com/document/34205400/Staff-wellbeing-is-key-to-school-success-Full-Report [Accessed 14 December 2022].

21 Bryson, A., Forth, J. and Stokes, L. (2014). *Does worker wellbeing affect workplace performance?* [online] Available at: https://assets.publishing.service.gov.uk/government/uploads/system/uploads/attachment_data/file/366637/bis-14-1120-does-worker-wellbeing-affect-workplace-performance-final.pdf.

22 Hulshof, C.T.J. (2009). Working for a Healthier Tomorrow. *Occupational and Environmental Medicine*, [online] 66(1), pp.1–2. doi:10.1136/oem.2008.040899.

SECTION I
Mapping the issues

2 Knowing your numbers

How will you know if staff wellbeing is a problem in your school; or if you know there's a problem, how will you highlight its causes and possible remedies? Where are the particular pressure points for you, and how can you begin to formulate a plan for improvement? In this chapter, we set out a course of action which will help your school leadership team to work through the issues, so you have a full picture before you start. This chapter has three sections:

● The major causes of stress in the workplace.

● Using existing data to identify stress within your institution.

● Running a staff survey to gather information.

DOI: 10.4324/9781003315766-3

Major causes of stress in the workplace

Here we return to the management standards created by the Health and Safety Executive, which were discussed in Chapter 1. It will help if you and your senior team use these as a focal point for your discussions and investigations: becoming familiar with them will help you to plan and manage these operations in a way that builds wellbeing and resilience rather than reducing it.

To recap, the six standards – and therefore the risks you need to manage – are:

● **Demands** faced by staff, including workload, work patterns, working environment and the things that create demands, such as student behaviour.

● **Control** – how much say people have over what they do at work, and over how they do it.

● The **support** staff receive: are leaders and colleagues encouraging; do they have access to good resources?

● **Relationships** at work (the extent to which positive working practices and behaviours are encouraged and problems dealt with quickly and effectively).

● **Roles** (whether expectations are clearly understood and how well individuals' roles and functions fit with the aims of the school).

● **Change** (how it's managed and how it's communicated).

We are all likely to experience stress when we perceive a risk that sits in one of these areas and is greater than our ability to cope with it. There are many examples in schools that can cause staff members to feel this way, particularly during the busiest times. We will explore some of these throughout the rest of this section.

Demands

If staff are to be productive, happy and successful, then they have to be able to cope with the demands of the job. This includes being able successfully to manage workload, work patterns and the environment.

Schools and colleges are busy places, and demands are often increased through staff absence and sickness, planning for parents' evenings and other events, extracurricular activities and taking on additional work or responsibility without having the necessary knowledge or skills. Other factors which can lead to extra demands include dealing with parents, training and supporting new staff members, poor student behaviour and disruptions, the requirement to attend meetings and systems change.

It isn't possible to remove these features from the school landscape, of course, but through a better understanding of the pressures they create, it's possible to manage them better. A key part of that is the recognition that not everyone is the same: some people will find parts of the job more challenging than others, and staff will react in different ways to the situations that arise in their working lives. If there's recognition and acceptance of this within the school, action can be taken to manage this better when it happens.

Control

People who feel they have some say about the way they carry out your work are likely to feel more in control, and more resilient in the face of adversity. But it isn't always possible to have control, particularly when there is a need to respond to student demands and other factors, such as:

- The demands of a timetable which is set by others.
- A curriculum which is largely set externally and over which junior staff in particular have only limited choices.
- Staff absence or student behaviour which adds to the demands of the job and reduces choice over what is done.
- Interruptions, and being asked to solve other people's problems.
- External influences such as Government initiatives and inspections.
- The demands of the leadership team on staff to work in particular ways.

Those who continually challenge or try to change things that sit outside their circle of control are bound to experience increased stress, and impact on their enjoyment and performance.

Support

A key source of stress, and a key factor in relieving it, is information: do staff know what they need to know in order to do their jobs effectively and to enjoy them? They also need to know that where necessary, support is available:

- Through knowing what is expected from marking: in some cases the fear of getting it wrong may lead to people doing too much.
- Through knowing where to find documents and planning tools.
- Through systems and other school processes.

The role of colleagues is crucial, of course, and staff need to know they have this support (and what to do if they feel it is lacking):

- Proactively offered by line managers and other members of school leadership, who have the necessary soft skills to deliver it.

- From peers and other colleagues.

- In dealing with parents, particularly where issues raised cannot be easily or quickly resolved.

- In dealing with issues in their team, or with student behaviour.

The absence of one or more of these can be a major source of stress.

Relationships

Relationships are key to creating an effective and enjoyable working environment and in the provision of support, and it's worth thinking about how your school promotes the positive working practices that foster them. If a school doesn't do this, or doesn't take sufficient steps to deal with unacceptable behaviour, for example instances of real or perceived harassment or bullying, relationships will become strained. Staff need to know they have a trusted line manager or colleague they can speak to if a relationship becomes difficult or if they feel they have been subjected to behaviour which is inappropriate or causes stress.

Signs that there may be a problem in this area include:

- Increases in -or a high level of -sickness and absence.

- A high level of turnover and/or inexperience in the school.

- Staff grievances or disputes being raised.

- People regularly turning up late for meetings, events or places they should be, or letting colleagues down.

Role

How well your staff understand their role and what is expected of them can help reduce workplace stress and build resilience. This also includes understanding how what they do fits with the objectives of their team and the vision of the school. This can also help make sure staff perform effectively.

Here are some examples that may cause people to struggle in this area:

- They are new and still learning and do not find it easy to ask questions.

- They have multiple roles, for example, teaching, form tutor, and head of year or department.

- They have recently undergone significant changes at work.

- They receive conflicting messages or directions from one or more leaders.

Change

How change is managed and communicated will affect staff in dealing with any challenge or adversity. The unknown, uncertainty, fear of failure and worry about what others think, make change in an organisation difficult to cope with. When change is taking place, you and your staff need to know:

- How it will impact on them and their workload.

- If it might mean they need to take on new responsibilities or even change roles.

- Any changes to structures or ways of working that affect them.

- The timetable for change.

- That they will be involved in decision-making where possible, or at least consulted in decisions that affect them.

Leaders also need to consider the effect it might have on the emotions of staff members, particularly if change is being imposed and they have little control.

It may not always be possible to keep everyone fully informed, and some change may be outside the school's control. Change is stressful, and it is natural for those undergoing change to feel pressure. But if everyone recognises they have choices, and if a culture exists where staff can take change in their stride, there are huge benefits to be gained. In order to manage change well, school leaders need to be clear about the behaviours that build a thriving culture and to model them every day and consistently – and they need to eliminate those that don't.

Using existing data to identify stressors

The starting point for measuring staff wellbeing is to look at existing school data. This will include:

- Teacher retention levels, and details of why they leave.

- Staff absence rates, reasons and patterns.

- The number of grievances and disputes.

- Staff and student behaviour.

- Observation and feedback on staff performance and relationships (how they work together).

This and other data provide clues.

Teacher retention levels vary between schools, and often for good reasons. Some schools may do well at recruiting young, newly qualified teachers, for instance, but may tend to lose them at the next stage as they move to areas where they can afford a house to start a family. Some staff turnover is a good thing, and schools where no one leaves or arrives may find they have other types of issues.

Nonetheless, a good look at the recruitment and retention data for your school may well prove a useful starting point on a journey to improved staff wellbeing. If you're seeing a lot of staff leave to find promotion in other schools, that may be a good sign – your school has a good reputation and you should be able to attract good new staff. There may be steps you could take through succession and talent plans to help better manage staff looking for promotion – we'll talk about this more in Chapter 7. But if you identify a pattern of people simply leaving to go to another school at a similar level, or joining the large cohort who leave the profession each year, then these are signs that all may not be well.

Understanding why staff leave is really important in becoming an employer of choice. Holding effective staff exit interviews is a big part of this and listening to and acting on their feedback will make a real difference: how people are led and managed is often a key factor in a staff member's decision to leave.

An exit interview

Exit interviews are vital tools in identifying issues that need to be addressed, and it's important that they should be carried out by an appropriate person. This needs to be someone with enough experience and confidence to ask the right questions, and someone who is trusted by other staff members. It shouldn't be the headteacher or principal, and it shouldn't be the leaver's immediate line manager.

The role of the interviewer is to create a positive experience: the interviewee must feel this person has their best interests in mind. It's important to create an atmosphere which encourages candid feedback without any fear of repercussions.

Treat them well, listen and show them you value their opinion. These questions will help you understand what steps you can take to better meet staff expectations and help to create a place where more people want to work.

Why are you leaving?

If it's for a new role:

■ What prompted you to start looking for a new job?

■ What ultimately led you to accept the new position?

General questions

■ Why are you leaving? You may know from the resignation letter and this is an opportunity to explore and confirm details.

■ Do you have any concerns about the school?

■ If so, did you share your concerns with anyone at the school prior to deciding to leave?

■ What could have been done for you to remain employed here?

Their experience in school

■ Did you feel you were equipped to do your job well? You can prompt with clarity of role, skills, development, available resources, support provided and the working environment.

■ How would you describe the culture of our school? Can you provide more information, such as specific examples?

■ If you could have changed anything about your job or the school, what would it be?

■ How satisfied were you with the way you were managed? What could we have done differently?

■ How well did managers recognise your contributions?

■ What did you like most and least about your job?

■ Did you have clear goals and objectives?

■ Did you receive constructive feedback to help you improve your performance?

Looking ahead

■ Would you consider coming back to work here in the future? What would need to change?

■ What would make our school a better place to work?

■ How likely are you to recommend a friend to apply for a position here? You can ask them to score 1–10 if a yes/no answer is proving difficult for them. Why?

■ How can our school improve training and development for staff?

■ Is there anything else you would add?

It is important to gather this information from every member of staff that leaves and you can also add a questionnaire to the process. However, nothing will give you the level of useful information that a skilled and trusted questioner will obtain.

The one challenge of an exit interview is that it is too late in preventing that particular staff member from leaving – while you should do them, there is a second interview you should also carry out that may just stop good staff members from leaving. It is called a stay interview.

The stay interview

Adding stay interviews can give you a competitive advantage and enable you to better understand what keeps people working in your school and identify and address issues ahead of them leaving.

It's a short interview to learn why staff will stay with you and to understand any circumstances that might cause them to leave. It should be conducted as part of your standard operation, rather than an ad-hoc reaction to events.

Unlike an exit interview, when you ask why people are leaving, this focuses on what is likely to make sure they stay.

The questions used differ significantly from those asked in an exit interview. It should be conducted by someone with enough experience and confidence to ask the right questions and where possible, unlike exit interviews, this could be their immediate line manager, though this may not always be possible due to their experience and skills.

The role of the interviewer is to make the experience positive and the person must feel they have their best interests in mind (and this should be the intent of the interviewer). They have to make them feel comfortable and encourage them to give candid feedback without repercussions and demonstrate how important their feedback is.

The object is to check in with staff and learn more about how they're feeling about their work, their future, the school, and wider organisation where appropriate, such as a MAT. Finding out the reasons people stay in a role will provide invaluable insights which, when aggregated, can be used to create a better employee experience and help make sure you are an employer of choice.

The interview

The tone of the conversation should be informal and focused on the staff member's feelings and needs. You are asking for and receiving feedback, rather than delivering it. Concentrate on gathering information, rather than responding to feedback or justifying why events have happened.

You can create a standard set of questions and use these consistently and review and adapt them as needed. However, interviewers should ask follow-up questions to find out any further details behind answers given.

Interviews should feel like a conversation and not an interrogation and should also be seen by the line manager as an opportunity to find out what they can do more of and less of and how they can best support the staff member being interviewed. Feedback from stay interviews should be aggregated and those staff providing information should be updated on actions taken as a result of the information they have given.

Below are questions that you can choose from and use.

Assessing a staff member's general outlook

- What do you look forward to when you come to work each day?
- What do you like most/least about working here?

- What keeps you working here?
- What might tempt you to leave?
- When was the last time you thought about leaving the school?
- What situation made you think of leaving?
- Would you recommend working here to your friends? You can use a 1–10 scale if this helps. Why (or why not)?

How staff members feel about their work

- What would you change about your job, if you could?
- What do you think about your objectives?
- How meaningful do you find your work?
- Do you have the right resources and support to do your best work?

Staff motivation

- What would make your work more satisfying?
- How do you like to be recognised? Is this happening for you here?
- What (motivates/demotivates) you?
- Are your work contributions valued? (If no, why not?)

How do they feel about their future

- What future do you see for yourself here?
- What strengths and talents of yours are we fully utilising/not utilising?
- What learning and development would you like?
- What do you think of the professional development you receive now?

How do they feel about their manager (which ideally is the interviewer)

- How can I better support you?
- What can I do more/less of?
- What advice would you give me?
- Thinking of the best manager you have worked with, what did you appreciate most about them?

Asking about the stay interview

- How did this interview/discussion make you feel?
- What question(s) would you have liked me to ask?
- What are we currently not doing, that you feel we should?

Stay interviews are not currently widely used, and yet they can deliver significant insights and conducting them regularly and consistently can make sure more staff, and particularly those with talent are retained within your school (and in the wider organisation where appropriate).

Staff absences are inevitable, but a deep dive into the patterns of absence is often instructive. The number one cause of long-term absence and number two cause of short-term absence – after minor illness – is now stress. If this is a common reason, if absence patterns involve a high number of staff, a high number of short absences, absences either side of the weekend, or reasons relating to mental and/or physical aches or minor causes, this can indicate action is needed to improve wellbeing.

The Return to Work Interview

Carrying out effective return-to-work interviews which staff members feel are supportive and in their best interests, rather than checking up on them, can play an important part. Though not a legal requirement, evidence from the Advisory, Conciliation and Arbitration Service (Acas) suggests this can deliver significant benefits, including a reduction in absence rates and improved retention. Acas is a non-departmental public body of the Department for Business, Energy and Industrial Strategy (BEIS).

Acas provides very helpful expert advice to both employers and employees.[1]

Fit for Work, a government initiative, suggests six key steps for a return-to-work interview. These are:

1. **Welcome them back.** Make their return to work a positive occasion – they may be feeling anxious, particularly if they have been off for some time. Put them at ease so you can have a more open and productive discussion – ask open questions about why they have been absent and give them plenty of time to explain as well as taking the opportunity to make sure they really are well enough to return.

2. **Update.** Make sure you update them about anything that has happened in their absence. This will make the employee feel included in the work environment and allow them to resume their normal duties effectively.

3. **Identify adjustments.** Find out if there are any adjustments which could be made to ease the staff member's transition back into the work environment. If the employee has a fit note from their GP, this would be a good time to discuss the particulars of that note. For example, if the employee has been deemed 'fit for some work,' you should find out what duties they can and cannot undertake.

4. **Make a plan.** Agree a plan where needed, for example, if adjustments are necessary. Create this with the staff member and set out how they will transition back to work. This may include a phased return or part-time work until the staff member has adjusted, or if certain activities are prohibited assigning them different duties.

5. **Record absence.** Record the staff member's absence and agree the details with them – ask them to confirm the recorded dates are correct, as this will prevent them disputing the dates should they appeal against an attendance warning later. If regular absenteeism is a problem for this staff member, make sure they are aware that continuing to miss work may result in further action.

6. **Open for questions.** To conclude the interview, the manager should ask the employee if they have any questions or comments. Give them the chance to express any concerns they have about returning to work.

Finally, grievances, disputes or other things that regularly take up management time are strong indications that action is needed, and you will have school policies to deal with these – it is important they are followed.

Further data you might consider will include the use of occupational health, counselling or your employee assistance scheme, where you have one (they should provide you with anonymised usage). Questions to ask might include: has there been an increase? How does your staff members' take-up of these services compare with others'?

Moving beyond existing data

WHERE ONE TRUST STARTED: DEBBIE DUGGAN, DIRECTOR OF OPERATIONAL RESOURCES AT TWO COUNTIES TRUST

When I started with the trust, I was presented with just a desk: I didn't even get a pen, I had to go shopping to get basic stationery. It was very early days for the trust, but my day one experience has always stuck with me as first impressions are so important when setting out who we are as an employer. I wanted some feedback on how content and valued people felt in their roles. Was this a place they saw their career developing, where they wanted to stay, where they felt motivated and happy?

The first employee survey I developed was on Survey Monkey, and I ran it myself: I'm never doing that again in my life – the analysis took days! We developed the questions ourselves; we didn't have any information around the HSE indicators – so only measured things that I felt seemed important and there were no benchmarks.

I was fortunate that one of our schools had used Welbee previously so I contacted them to see what they could do for the trust. The ability to tailor and customise to what we needed really worked well, and we were able to measure things at school level and MAT level, which was really useful because it meant we could cut information lots of different ways – by different dimensions, such as role, length of service and so we could get a sense of what really was going on in schools. The driver was very much about getting some information, some data, because we needed to know the actions that we needed to take as an employer to drive our human resources strategy.

> *When we looked at the Health and Safety Executive Management Standards for Demand and Control, we had two schools that were in the top decile. There was a follow-up conversation with all Headteachers around the table to see what we could learn from those schools. I'm sure some would have been a bit unhappy because of their school's score, they weren't greens, they were in the ambers and reds. So what were the two schools in the first decile doing that was different? Having that conversation around the table with all the Headteachers, we got to the point that actually it's about walking the walk and managing the interaction they have with their staff. It could be things about the individual or it could be quite structural:*
>
> *'So, John Maher, Headteacher at Ashfield School, given the feedback what is it that makes you connect so well with your staff, that another school can learn from? What are the steps you take?' One thing that came up from that school was staff wellbeing is a regular item on their senior leadership team (SLT) meeting every week: 'Who do we need to watch out for, who's struggling, who's got some personal issues, so people in the SLT can be aware of issues, look out for people and manage situations recognising that somebody might not be on top form this week, or somebody might need a little bit of extra support.*
>
> *As a result, we've asked all schools to make sure that wellbeing is on their SLT agenda. It sounds a really small thing, doesn't it, just putting wellbeing on your agenda every week? But actually, if you just talk about things, it shows it's important and it shows people that you care. It's all part and parcel of the culture we're able to build.*

The number of leavers, staff absence levels, grievances, student outcome trends and other data will have given you clues and it's important to review and use this to talk to staff, so that you can understand things from their perspective. A staff survey is another useful way of collecting feedback and measuring staff wellbeing. Done well, it will play a big part in identifying where the major challenges may be and in helping to inform your actions and plans.

There are a number of ways you might run a survey.

You might run your own, which is what many MATs, Schools and colleges do. While there is likely to be little cash outlay, unless you have dedicated resource and expertise, this can be very time consuming to set up, run and analyse. The biggest danger is likely to be a lack of clarity about exactly what is being measured and without benchmarks, it's likely there will be uncertainty about the reliability of the results.

You will need to find the questions you want to use and decide on how you will deliver these to staff – pen and paper or digitally through a platform like Survey-Monkey or Google forms. It is also likely that staff may not be open as they think that their feedback might be attributed to them.

When identifying questions or a survey, ensure it has a strong evidence base, ideally with proven psychometric qualities to demonstrate its validity, consistency and reliability. If interested in the new DfE's Education Staff Wellbeing Charter, you might also want to check if the measurement used is recognised within it, meeting commitment 11. Benchmarks will also make sure you can see the true comparative performance of your school against others.

STAFF WELLBEING SURVEY CHECKLIST

1. What date will you launch and close your survey?

2. What survey or questions will you use?

3. How will you deliver the survey to staff?

4. What will you do to ensure a high participation rate?

5. How and when will you engage with and brief staff?

6. How will results be collated and analysed?

7. Book time in to review results as a team, as close as possible to closing the survey.

8. Plan to involve your wellbeing team, council or committee (if you have one).

9. Plan when and how to feed back results to all staff.

10. Plan how you will respond to specific staff comments.

11. After feedback and engagement with all staff, finalise goals and actions.

12. Add actions to the school development plan.

13. Repeat the survey.

A longer version of this checklist is available online at: https://welbee.co.uk/learning-centre/everything-you-need-to-know-about-running-your-staff-wellbeing-survey/

Alternatively, you can ask a third party to help. This is likely to significantly reduce your workload, improve analysis and participation rates.

There are different kinds of surveys, with the three most popular being:

1. The Pulse Survey – this allows you to take a regular temperature check, and this can be very helpful for leaders who want to receive regular feedback. However, this idea can also be seductive for leaders, because to continually ask for feedback without staff seeing it being acted on presents a big challenge. School workload and processes mean in many cases that action takes time and as a result staff participation declines over time – they may even resent being continually asked. If you are able to take quick action, this could be a good option for you.

2. General Survey Platform – There are platforms available that allow you to select a range of evidence-built surveys – this can be useful if you want to ask different questions and have the time to work through results and create your own analysis and actions – they don't usually come with these. If you want to track progress, you do need to keep using the same survey.

3. Specific Survey Platform – This will use the same evidence-based survey each time you run it and so is ideal from measuring and tracking progress. In some cases, you will get more comprehensive reporting too, including suggested actions. As a result, you are likely to run these only once or twice a year. If you want to reduce workload and have guidance on where to act and who with, this may be the choice for you.

There are a small number of suppliers that also allow you to respond to open feedback and have anonymous two-way conversations – this can add significantly to staff engagement and you might want to ask if this is available.

So which survey might you use?

One that we like, because of its evidence base and independent evaluation is the UK Health and Safety Executive Indicator Tool, which is freely available to use. If you manage the survey internally, it's possible to add it to an online tool such as SurveyMonkey to make distribution and collection of results easier.

The HSE do offer a paid-for service and the survey is also used by Welbee, who have developed a comprehensive reporting system focused on schools and MATs, including benchmarks. The survey uses the HSE management standards framework to assess risks against known workplace stressors and against evidence on what creates a good working environment.

It has been designed to provide a broad indication of how well staff rate their leaders' and organisations' performance in managing the risks associated with work-related stress and wellbeing. It is also recognised by the DfE Education Staff Wellbeing Charter and the management standards align well with the Ofsted Leadership and Management Judgement, for those inspected by them.

Mental health outcomes questions

The HSE tool includes questions from a brief mental health screening tool – it is important that organisations understand not only where the stress risks lie, but also where the experience of stress exists. Not everyone responds in the same way to stressors – so some of your staff may have competing demands at work and still cope well with that, for instance. There are different stressors in different institutions, too – some will find friction within teams is a major issue for health and wellbeing, for instance, whereas others may not.

A stress risk assessment can enable you to assess where the risks lie, so that your interventions will have maximum impact once you've decided on them. It's also important to prioritise, and by understanding where the greatest pressure points lie in your institution, you should be able to do that.

Getting a good participation rate

In order to measure staff wellbeing effectively and in a way which provides an-swers, it may be important also to consider how you will get buy-in from staff, and a high participation rate. You must commit to sharing the results, at least at a summary level, irrespective of what they tell you. It will be difficult to share disappointing results, and schools may struggle to find the time. But if they aren't shared, staff will assume there is something to hide – and that will prove coun-terproductive. Staff will be less likely to engage in the next phase, or in future surveys. That is likely to lead to a further deterioration in staff wellbeing and performance.

As a crude rule of thumb for a survey, a response rate of over 50 per cent could be considered adequate; over 60 per cent desirable, over 70 per cent good and more than 80 per cent very good. With a response rate of less than 50 per cent, the data should be considered as indicative only, and treated with caution.

There are several things you can do to encourage a good response rate before you start your survey. Not least is that staff should feel it is important, that their views matter and that they will be listened to and acted on. Steps you can take include:

● Publicising the survey; including supportive comments from senior manage-ment and staff or union representatives where appropriate, and encouraging people to take part before it is distributed.

● Explaining the purpose of the survey to all staff: why should they take part, and what's in it for them? How and when they will be receiving a link to the survey; how and when they will get feedback on results; and what actions will be taken to address findings?

● Promising anonymity of responses. This will encourage staff to give frank and honest feedback. A formal statement of anonymity at the beginning of the survey is the best way to do this, and you should reinforce this when writing to and talking with staff.

● Ensuring line managers understand that the process is important and that they will encourage staff to take time to complete the survey.

● Giving people enough time to complete the survey and ideally allowing them to complete it in work time, rather than expecting them to complete it in their own time. We know this provides much better response rates.

● Continuing to publicise the survey throughout the process.

● Providing a contact person or persons for staff questions and support.

You will also want to support this through meetings, briefings and asking line managers to encourage their team members to take part.

Before launching your survey

It is important to plot the survey process. Plan when and how findings will be fed back to staff and how you will engage with them in agreeing actions moving forward. Don't wait until you have the results as you may end up feeding back too late and in a piecemeal way.

An effective plan that you stick to will help to ensure improving staff wellbeing is delivered coherently and becomes part of what you do each day, rather than a series of random activities that address symptoms rather than causes.

It also makes it more likely that staff will continue to engage in solutions and participate in future surveys.

EXAMPLE MESSAGE TO STAFF ABOUT A WELLBEING SURVEY

You will have your own words and context, but some of this wording may help:

Dear *[Colleague/Name]*,

[School Name] is committed to protecting your health, safety and welfare and that of all staff and we acknowledge the importance of wellbeing and tackling the causes of stress in our workplace.

We would like your support in undertaking a survey, which is designed to find out how you feel about various aspects of your working conditions. We are asking you and your colleagues to do this to be sure that we are doing all we can to make this the best place for you to work. The survey is anonymous and the questions asked do not allow for any individual to be identified.

You will receive an invitation, with a link to allow you to take the survey online. Please complete it as soon as you can *(or enter details of when you are making time for them to take it at work)* and before *(enter date)*. When the survey responses have been collated, summary results will be shared with you and we will reach agreement on appropriate action.

Please take the time to complete the survey. It will provide an indication of how well we are performing and of where there may be opportunities for improvement. Don't rely on others to raise issues, as wellbeing and stress is subjective and can affect people in different ways.

Your results

If your school is running its own survey, this is likely to be the hardest part. Collating the feedback into aggregate results will take time, though with the right tool this should be relatively straightforward.

Analysing what the results mean is likely to be the most challenging and time-consuming element of running your own survey and needs care.

Most surveys are likely to use a Likert scale, where possible responses may typically be on a 1–5 or 1–10 scale (ranging from strongly agree to strongly disagree or from always to never. Where benchmarks are not available this can make it difficult to interpret the scores as they may not be created equal. For example, in the HSE Indicator Tool, scores for Support, Role and Relationships are likely to be significantly higher than those for Demands and Control. So scoring 4 in one area may not be a particularly good score, whereas 3 in another area could be comparatively far higher.

You will also need to work out what the feedback is telling you, and what specific actions you should take. It's important to do this alongside your staff, rather than doing it to them. The school leadership team has a disproportionate influence on the wellbeing of your staff. Start by sharing and celebrating success – you can ask staff for further insights into the scores and you can work with them to identify which actions are likely to have the greatest impact for them and for your school.

Setting goals and creating your plan

You will want to identify and recognise progress and so you should set specific goals. This will give you a focus for engagement and action. Work out how you will deliver these goals and make them part of your school development or improvement plan. You can then report on progress, just as you do on other activities and without adding further workload.

Finally, celebrate successes and authentically and effectively remind people of the changes and improvements that have been made. Be explicit: staff are busy and have short memories, and part of your role is to make sure they understand and share the journey with you.

Repeat and systemise this process, rather than taking random action. Build on your foundations, taking and tracking action each time.

Chapter 2: Key points

- Start by looking at existing data: teacher retention levels (and why staff leave), absence rates, grievances and disputes, staff and student behaviour, feedback on performance and relationships.

- Effective exit interviews are a good way to identify key reasons why staff members leave, though they come too late to stop someone from leaving.

- Stay interviews are a way to identify what you might do to ensure staff members stay – focus first on asking questions of the staff members you value most.

- Use return-to-work interviews to support staff with absences and to better understand causes and whether there are trends that can be addressed.

● Move beyond data and use a staff survey to seek further feedback – while you can do this yourself, there are benefits from using a third party – increased participation, better analysis, even recommended actions – and reduced workload.

● Use an evidence-built survey and choose what will work for you – pulse, question set and annual survey with comprehensive reporting are all available.

● The HSE's Indicator Tool is recommended, as this assesses risks against known stress factors to find out what is going well and where to focus energy and effort for improvement.

● Communicate, communicate, communicate. Let staff members know why you want their feedback and how important it is to you. Encourage participation and share results with staff and other key stakeholders.

● Celebrate successes along with recognising those areas that require focus and action.

● Set clear goals and a plan of how to deliver them. Focus on foundations first – behaviours of leaders and processes that support them, so wellbeing is simply part of the culture.

Note

1 Acas (n.d.). *Returning to work after absence | Acas*. [Online] www.acas.org.uk. Available at: https://www.acas.org.uk/absence-from-work/returning-to-work-after-absence.

3 Having a clear plan

You've measured your current staff wellbeing by reviewing your data and running a survey. What next? If you don't want these results to end up languishing at the back of a cupboard, it's vital to have a very clear idea of the way forward.

What *shouldn't* you do, at this stage? One thing is absolutely to be avoided: don't organise a wellbeing day, activity or event.

These kinds of one-off actions can be useful, and in the future you may well want to have a wellbeing event, but this isn't the right moment. A wellbeing day might well tackle the symptoms, but it won't get to the causes. So it won't do much for staff members who are not engaged or feeling valued because nothing changes.

You and your school are setting out on a journey, and that crucial first step has to be the right one and about building your foundations. The key is to set clear goals – your aim now should be to embed staff wellbeing in your institution, so it becomes simply a part of everyday life.

DOI: 10.4324/9781003315766-4

Step one: share your results

Staff, and other key stakeholders such as governors, need to feel they have some ownership – it won't work if it's just another thing that's being done *to* them. So share your results in a transparent way before you do anything else. That way, the people who are meant to benefit from this will feel involved and can have a say in creating plans and solutions.

It's not always easy to do this and in particular to involve everyone. Staff meetings often already have full agendas and some support staff, such as teaching and learning support assistants, are not always in school when these are held. Yet finding a way to make sure all staff included in feedback is important – after all, they were invited to take the survey.

This is why planning when you will give feedback, as both a senior team and to all staff, should be planned as part of your survey set-up. It is one of the 13 steps referred to in the previous chapter and that you should set out before starting.

Where it isn't easy to get staff together or it takes time to do it, you should at least prepare and share a short summary of results quickly – celebrate what is going well and headline those areas where attention and focus for improvement may be needed.

Whether sharing over email or in person, consider how you will deliver the information. Some schools do this by using a PowerPoint of results, or you might prepare a document with headlines. However, you choose to do this, the information should be clear and complete. There's no point in glossing over the difficult bits; that will only create more issues down the line.

Everyone needs to be involved. You should ask staff to take responsibility for their own wellbeing, and to support colleagues too. And ask them for their suggestions – what one or two things would have the greatest impact on the wellbeing of staff. Make it clear that this isn't just a task for the senior leadership team.

Failure to share results will suggest to staff that there may be something to hide, which will reduce trust and participation in future surveys.

Step two: set your goals

Before moving to action and after meeting with staff and agreeing on areas for focus, you should set clear goals, ahead of planning specific action. Your stated goals should be clear and specific, and they should fit with your school vision and values. If they don't, you will need to change them and ensure they are aligned with the goals you set and actions you will take. While this can be a painful part of the process, it will also be instructive: when you put wellbeing at the forefront of your vision you may well throw into relief the root causes of the issues you are facing.

Many leaders move to action without setting goals first – this is a mistake. Without goals you will never agree what success looks like, will not be able to share this with your wider team, and fail to track whether you have arrived at the point at which you are aiming.

Illustration 3.1 Goal achievement starts with a first step

Nothing is insurmountable, though. Just prioritise a small number of steps to start with – wherever you want to get to, you will always start with a first step and keeping these small means you can generate quick wins and build momentum. It is always better to under promise and over deliver.

A first step might be to focus on how the senior and middle leadership teams behave. If they can act as strong role models, it will bring faster results.

Add the goals you set and associated actions into your school improvement or development plan, so that they become part of business as usual and are monitored and reviewed regularly. Examples of very quick wins include making sure there is regular and authentic staff recognition – as a goal this might be for all senior leaders to catch one staff member doing something right each day. This should be done in the moment, and not simply through shout-outs at meetings. This should already be something staff are good at with students.

Just making sure people are asked 'how are you' – and making sure they know their answer will be listened to, will have a significant impact.

Here are some further examples of goals schools have set as part of their planning process:

- Setting specific working hours, including aspirations for limiting the amount of work staff do at home – need to be role modelled by the senior team.

- Agreeing email protocols. This can include when to email (and when to use another means of communication), format, use of the copy function and the times at which emails should not be sent so as not to invade 'home time.' This doesn't stop people from doing the work at times convenient to them – setting times for doing things can also cause anxiety and impact on mental health. This is about becoming disciplined about what emails you send and when. You can set a time or leave the mail in drafts until it is appropriate for it to arrive in colleagues' inboxes.

However, if you are not careful, this simply means staff members end up with a flood of emails between 7.30 and 8.00 a.m. on a Monday. It may therefore be more appropriate to allow staff to send emails outside their usual hours, if that works best for them and if everyone agrees. Emails should be annotated appropriately so that a response is not expected outside usual hours.

- Numbers of meetings to be held, and rules for ensuring meetings are effective. For example, meetings should start and finish on time, everyone should be prepared properly, the items under discussion should be limited to what's strictly necessary, and attendees should be limited to those who really need to be there.

- Setting a limit for time spent on marking and on planning, or sharing how it is created, including steps to help staff stick to it.

- Reducing the regularity of data and reporting requirements.

- Agreeing team rules for courtesy and behaviour, and ensuring they are implemented.

- Adopting specific rules on behaviour for senior leaders, and supporting them through coaching, praising and holding them to account.

- Having a clear vision and values for student (and staff) behaviour and ensuring responsibility is taken at all levels to ensure this is delivered.

- Setting specific targets for the number of staff leaving and/or for staff absences.

- Choosing specific scores from the survey and setting targets for improvements when the school runs another.

These are just some of the goals you might set – you should set your own, of course. But do make sure the outcomes are measurable. The usual 'SMART' tips apply: Specific, Measurable, Achievable (with stretch), Relevant and Timescale. This will make it easier to track and share the progress that is being made in improving staff wellbeing.

You should also agree who will lead and have responsibility for managing each goal. Identify supporters, champions and potential blockers as part of this step.

All this may sound simple – though let's face it, it probably won't be. You, your leadership colleagues and your staff are all very busy already, and this is going to add to your workload – at first. So there needs to be a strong hand to ensure action happens as planned.

Here are some tips that will help you to succeed, and to refocus when things get tough:

- Make sure there is a clear and shared vision of what the intended outcomes look like in practice – and a sense of urgency about reaching them.

- Allocate specific responsibility for individual actions and allow them the right level of decision-making and authority for effective leadership.

- Set out a clear plan of communication and follow it. Too much communication is better than too little but think about how you can use the right mix of channels to reach all staff.

- Maintain momentum and celebrate each win, even the small ones.

- Re-work the plan or reschedule actions if or when needed.

- Identify blockers early, involving them where possible and managing them closely to reduce possible negativity and prevent sabotage.

- Create champions, focusing first on early adopters and making sure effective support is given to those who are finding change difficult.

- Praise those staff who demonstrate the right behaviours while holding to account those who don't.

- Don't move on too early. This is usually the biggest mistake when outcomes are not met. Each action needs to be embedded before you move on to the next.

Finally… if you want to improve staff wellbeing, don't forget to continue to measure. You will need to track progress through regularly reviewing your school improvement or development plan. Reviewing where you are now, learning lessons, understanding what went well and what could have been even better will provide you with further insight.

And then, go right back to where you started. Once you have some results from your monitoring, go back and repeat the initial steps of this exercise. Interrogate your school data again. If you ran a survey, run it again.

The cycle is a continuous one which will enable you to build wellbeing and all its associated benefits into daily school life and culture. All this should become simply: "Just what we do round here."

Chapter 3: Key points

Once you have reviewed your school data and run a staff survey, you need a clear idea of what you want to do and what to focus on. Below are some tips for you to follow.

- Set clear goals with the aim of embedding wellbeing in everyday life so it is simply part of the culture.

- Share your results with all staff – everyone needs to buy into and feel ownership of actions and changes that are agreed. Include governors, trustees and other stakeholders.

- Don't take on too much – take small and agreed steps and communicate about them regularly. As well as looking forward, remind people what has been achieved.

- Start with the foundations, for example, vision and values, leadership behaviours and processes that support them.

- Identify responsibilities for making sure each action is delivered (remembering everyone has to take ownership for their part) and be clear how success will be measured.

- Keep monitoring until it becomes part of everyday culture and business as usual for all staff.

- Don't organise activities, such as a wellbeing day as a means of starting – these should only be considered where you have built firm foundations.

- Don't move on too quickly; it is important you follow up and embed actions before going forward.

- Add actions and track progress as part of your school development plan, so staff wellbeing is seen as part of your current processes. This also makes sure you do not add any unnecessary workload.

- Repeat reviewing data and your staff survey so you can effectively track progress and better understand the actions that work and deliver improvements.

4 Where to take action

MOMENTS OF TRUTH: MARK SOLOMONS

I remember looking for my first job. Fresh from university, desperate to get on with life and earn that first paycheque. There were many little things that affected my decision – if you look back at your own experience, you may remember them too – the school's reputation, word of mouth, the job advert, the recruitment process, your first day, the training and development you received and how you were treated.

Of course, 35 years ago things were a little different (though we don't yet know the long-term impact of the Covid pandemic) – higher unemployment, less choice and information wasn't easily available. Times have changed. It's a highly competitive labour market now, and your applicants may well already know about any issues you have with workload, budgets or mental health issues. Schools and MATs are now fighting to recruit and retain the best staff from a shrinking pool.

When your prospective staff members interact with your school and the people in it, they will still experience that 'moment of truth.' In other words, they will evaluate and will think: 'I want to be part of this,' or maybe, 'Where's the door?'

How these 'moments of truth' are handled will determine how well you are able to attract and keep staff. They'll also be reflected in your school's long-term results.

We'll return to the issue of recruiting and retaining staff in Chapter 7. At this point, having looked in depth at the issues your school faces and then begun planning for action, the key thing is to draw up your own plan for staff wellbeing. Your school is unique, of course, and you should by now know where you're strong and where there's hard work to be done. But have you considered all the angles? From the mass of data you now have, what are the important things to draw out?

Get this right and you will build staff engagement, improve loyalty, increase retention, reduce stress and raise student outcomes. Get it wrong… enough said.

Not always easy to do and while it's important to talk about staff wellbeing as a priority, behaviours and actions need to demonstrate that it is. So despite high workload, limited time and the many interruptions faced, this topic has to become part of the management infrastructure and discussed regularly. You have to carve out time for it and follow through on agreed actions – there can be no excuses.

Below are some questions you can ask yourself: use them to reflect on the analysis you've been carrying out and to help with your planning and action. Have you considered all the key angles? Is workload distributed and managed in a way which is likely to minimise stress and lead to better outcomes?

● Is the school calendar planned in the best way to support this, with deadlines spread, notice given and competing demands from multiple leaders or processes managed effectively?

● To what degree do staff feel involved in decisions affecting them?

● Do staff feel listened to and supported?

● What behaviours do they experience from all leaders, their line managers and colleagues?

● Do leaders understand the impact of their behaviours? We consider leaders' behaviours in Chapter 6.

- Are interactions between staff and line managers well managed and supportive?

- How well do leaders recognise and praise their team members and do they do so appropriately, for example, in the moment and not just through shout-outs or via email?

- Do staff clearly know what is expected of them and are they clear how this aligns with their department and school goals?

- How effective is communication within the school? Do the majority of staff feel they know what's going on?

These are great questions to start with. Feedback from school data, for example, from exit, stay and return to work interviews, and from your survey – where one has been used – will help guide answers. Where you have collected comments from staff or a third-party survey provides recommended actions based on your results, use these to support your discussions.

A wellbeing charter[1]

The Education Staff Wellbeing Charter was published in May 2021 by the English Department for Education (DfE), created with the support of schools, unions and mental health charities.

It suggests schools should declare their commitment to the wellbeing and mental health of everyone working in education, including temporary and support staff. State funded schools and colleges in England are invited to sign up to the charter – but its contents are relevant to all schools and colleges everywhere.

It also briefly sets out the commitment that the DfE and Ofsted will make in supporting staff wellbeing in schools – use these to hold them to account.

Should you sign up? Given current staff challenges and the likelihood that others are taking this step, is there any reason not to? However, to use the charter effectively means living up to the commitments set out. It is, however, important to realise this should be a journey. You do not have to try to do everything at once. Read on to see if this is something that will benefit your school and staff.

Below is a list of key points from the 11 school commitments set out in the charter – they will help you reflect on what you've learned about your own school and actions you might take. It asks schools to pledge to:

1. **Tackle mental health stigma** and promote an open and understanding culture. This means giving equal weight to mental and physical health, including in the management of staff absence; fulfilling the legal duty to control work-related stress; and supporting those whose roles are known to have significant emotional components, such as pastoral staff. This might include peer support, supervision, and/or counselling; as well as ensuring staff understand the benefits of pastoral support while recognising their own limits as non-specialists.

2. **Give staff support** to take responsibility for their own and other people's wellbeing. This includes providing training and easily accessible resources on mental health, financial and physical wellbeing.

3. **Provide managers with tools and resources** to support the wellbeing of those they line manage. This does **not** mean asking managers to provide support for which they have no professional training.

4. **Establish a clear communications policy**. This means providing clear guidance to both internal and external members of the school community – including parents and governors – on when it is and isn't reasonable to expect staff to respond to queries.

5. **Give staff a voice** in decision-making – this may include engagement with key stakeholders such as trade unions. In particular, schools should draw on the experience of those who have experienced mental health issues and/or discrimination, ensuring they are able to share confidently and safely.

6. **Drive down unnecessary workload** and make use of available tools such as the Workload Reduction Toolkit for schools.[2]

7. **Champion flexible working and diversity**, not only recognising employees' legal right to request flexible working but also acknowledging that for some staff working flexibly can be a key means of protecting and enhancing personal wellbeing. Schools should promote diversity – eliminating discrimination and advancing equality of opportunity.

8. **Create a good behaviour culture**: All staff and pupils should have a shared understanding of how good behaviour is encouraged and rewarded, and the sanctions for pupils who misbehave. Schools should foster calm, safe and disciplined environments which allow teachers to teach and pupils to learn.

9. **Enable staff to progress** in their careers and support them in pursuing professional development without adversely impacting their own or other people's workload.

10. **Have a strategy for protecting leader wellbeing** and mental health. Those with strategic decision-making responsibility, including governors or trustees, should collaborate to develop this. It should include access to confidential counselling and/or coaching.

11. **Measure staff wellbeing** using recognised tools and metrics and be transparent about the results. This includes monitoring trends over time and responding to changes. Parents, trade unions and others should be asked to agree an approach to organisational accountability on these commitments, giving due consideration to workload.

That is a lot to cover: so where might you start?

There are three that stand out as starting points and are likely to have an impact across other commitments.

1. The first is what we covered in Chapter 2: Know Your Numbers. Commitment 11 asks you to measure and track the wellbeing of staff. If you do not effectively establish your starting point and benchmark this, how confident can you be that the right action will be taken. If you do not then track progress and see the impact of action taken, how will you know what works and what to do next.

What gets measured gets done is often a truism, and you wouldn't dream of entering students into their exams and hoping for the best. You track their progress and offer up the best support you can – should staff wellbeing be any different.

2. The second is commitment 10 – protecting the wellbeing of leaders. If leaders are not operating effectively, unwell or looking after themselves, how can they possibly support others? You know this and it is regularly talked about – having an effective life balance, role modelling for others and demonstrating effective behaviours.

3. Giving managers the tools and resources to support others – commitment 3. Focusing on leaders and ensuring they understand the impact they have and are equipped to effectively lead is the only way to reduce firefighting. Ensuring every newly appointed leader is part of the solution, rather than adding to the problem, is so important, alongside developing those who have been in the role for some time.

By focusing on the above three commitments, first we will also make inroads into others, for example 1, 4, 5 and 6. Improving leadership and talking about the support needed is going to help with creating a more open culture, improving communication, enabling staff voice and reducing workload.

While commitment 2, giving staff support to take responsibility is important and the next one to focus on, doing this before ensuring leaders have the tools needed, is simply going to ensure that fires continue to break out and are being constantly fought. This does not mean that you should not provide an employee assistance scheme or counselling, as these are much needed by some staff and will ideally already be in place.

Focusing action on the three commitments listed first is preventative medicine and will help create your culture as one where more people thrive.

The English Department for Education used evidence from What Works Wellbeing,[3] an independent centre whose mission is to develop and share robust and accessible wellbeing evidence to improve decision-making. The centre sets out five areas which need to be considered in creating a culture of wellbeing:

- Health: including mental and physical health. In education, there is often a focus on stress caused by excessive workload and lack of recovery time. When pupils and students have highly complex emotional needs, this can also impact the health of those who support them.

- Security: this includes working conditions, safety, bullying and harassment and financial security. Equality and diversity are also important here, especially if members of staff have protected characteristics that make them vulnerable to discrimination.

- Environment: This covers the physical environment; the organisational environment, such as systems for flexible working; and the policy environment, both internal and external – this includes public perception of the teaching profession.

- Relationships: the degree of support and respect an individual has from immediate colleagues, line managers and leadership. This can also include relationships with parents.

- Purpose: high-quality job design should mean staff have the right type of work for them, a sense of 'belonging' which includes shared organisational goals and vision, the opportunity to develop and demonstrate competence and to progress, and an appropriate degree of autonomy.

These fit well with the Health and Safety Executive's (HSE) management standards, and they also share a range of tools and resources which can help, particularly in building a case for change, if one is needed. For example, there is a calculator which helps estimate the cost of ill health and the likely return from a renewed focus and action on wellbeing.[4]

The HSE also provides an action plan template which could help you keep track during the next phase.[5] This provides a route map from where you are now to where you want to be. If we take the six management standards we covered in Chapter 2, the areas for work are:

- **Demands** faced by staff.

- **Control over** what staff do at work.

- The **support** staff receive.

- **Relationships** at work.

- **Roles** and expectations.

- **Change** and how it's managed.

Each of these standards can then be applied, according to the information you've gathered, under the following headings:

- Desired state

- Current state

- Practical solutions

- Who will take the work forward?

- When?

- How will staff receive feedback?

- Action completed?

Under each of the six standards you may wish to consider the quick wins you may be able to make, along with plans for the medium and longer term.

A worked-through example from the HSE tool kit might look like is shown on the following page.

More resources:

The Thriving Places Index identifies the local conditions for wellbeing and measures whether those conditions are being delivered fairly and sustainably. Created by the Centre for Thriving Places, it's designed to give a balanced and easily read 'dashboard' of information on the different elements that support places to thrive. It cuts across different policy areas and is structured to provide a holistic way of approaching different priorities.

https://www.centreforthrivingplaces.org/about-measurement-policy/thriving-places-index/

You may also want to visit some or all of these websites:

The Education Support charity provides a range of resources for schools and for individuals: https://www.educationsupport.org.uk/resources/

Mentally Healthy Schools brings together quality-assured mental health resources, information and advice for schools and further education settings in England, Northern Ireland, Scotland and Wales. https://www.mentallyhealthyschools.org.uk/

Anna Freud National Centre for Children and Families offers practical guidance about what school staff and senior leaders can do to support their own and their colleagues' wellbeing: https://www.annafreud.org/schools-and-colleges/resources/supporting-staff-wellbeing-in-schools/

Mental Health at work has a range of resources which are useful though not education-specific: https://www.mentalhealthatwork.org.uk/?s=resources+for+schools

The Headspace Science Blog aims to help students build healthy habits, and offers free access to primary and secondary teachers and supporting staff in the United States, the United Kingdom, Canada and Australia.

https://www.headspace.com/educators

Welbee offer a free Staff Wellbeing Toolkit for leaders and all staff: https://toolkit.welbee.co.uk

Area	Desired state	Current state	Practical solutions	Who will take it forward	When	How will staff receive feedback	Action completed
Workload	The organisation provides employees with adequate and achievable demands in relation to the agreed hours of work.	Workloads are not planned as effectively as they might be and include multiple requests and deadlines.	Review the school calendar and current spread of deadlines to ensure these are coordinated throughout the year.	Line managers to lead for their department and agree with senior managers.	Initial meeting to agree plan on DD/MM/YYYY.	Via monthly update meetings and through the staff bulletins.	

The Local Government Association is a useful source of guidance and official documents for England: https://www.local.gov.uk/our-support/workforce-and-hr-support/education-and-young-people;

Chapter 4: Key points

Questions to ask regularly:

- Is workload distributed and managed effectively to prevent and reduce stress?

- Do staff feel sufficiently involved, listened to and supported?

- Are leaders and colleagues treating each other with respect and compassion? Are interactions well managed and supported?

- Do leaders understand the impact of their behaviours, both positively and negatively?

For English state schools, the DfE has introduced the Education Staff Wellbeing Charter – reviewing this may also be useful for those from other countries and other sectors. Should you sign up to it, if you are in England or follow its lead, if you aren't.

This means agreeing to the following 11 commitments, though you do not have to tackle everything at once. Numbers 3, 10 and 11 are the place to start.

1. Tackle mental health stigma.

2. Give staff support.

3. Provide managers with the right tools and resources.

4. Establish a clear communications policy.

5. Give staff a voice.

6. Drive down unnecessary workload.

7. Champion flexible working and diversity.

8. Create a good behaviour culture.

9. Support staff to progress.

10. Have a strategy for protecting leader wellbeing.

11. Measure staff wellbeing regularly?

Notes

1 Department for Education (2021). *Education staff wellbeing charter.* [online] gov.uk. Available at: https://www.gov.uk/guidance/education-staff-wellbeing-charter [Accessed 14 December 2022].
2 HSE (2021). *Talking toolkit.* [online] *Health and safety executive.* Available at: https://www.hse.gov.uk/stress/assets/docs/stress-talking-toolkit.pdf [Accessed 14 December 2022].
3 What Works Wellbeing (2017). *Evidence gap: Five ways to wellbeing.* [online] What Works Wellbeing. Available at: https://whatworkswellbeing.org/blog/evidence-gap-five-ways-to-wellbeing/#:~:text=The%20Five%20Ways%20to%20Wellbeing [Accessed 14 December 2022].
4 Department for Education (2021). *Education staff wellbeing charter.* [online] gov.uk. Available at: https://www.gov.uk/guidance/education-staff-wellbeing-charter [Accessed 14 December 2022]. https://www.hse.gov.uk/stress/standards/downloads.htm
5 HSE (2017). *Work related stress – Tools and templates.* [online] Hse.gov.uk. Available at: https://www.hse.gov.uk/stress/standards/downloads.htm.

SECTION 2
Leading for wellbeing

5 Being the change

JOHN MAHER, HEADTEACHER, ASHFIELD SCHOOL

This job is constantly whirling around in your head; you can never quite switch off from it. I do think there's a massive difference between the deputy and the head of a school. I don't like the kind of hero head nonsense but it is a lonely job. If something goes wrong, it's your head on the chopping block – years ago a head's job was fairly safe, but not now. One day you may be asked to leave with your belongings in a box and you're never seen again.

I'm not worried about that, in a sense, but I do think I probably don't consider my own well-being as much as I do the rest of the staff. I'm not silly and I try not to work too much at home but I'm here early. I've learned that I work best in the mornings so, although there are many late evenings in the calendar, on most days by five o'clock in the afternoon I'm exhausted and I go home. I don't think the job is great for relationships and your life in general. So, I don't suppose I've got any answers, other than that I'm paid a lot of money, I didn't have to do the job, I've chosen to do it and I don't have to do it for ever. While I am doing it I want to do it the best I can so that when I'm retired, I can sit there and think it was worth it.

DOI: 10.4324/9781003315766-7

> Often a sign that a head is struggling is when they disappear, they start staying in their office, asking others to do staff meetings. Staff are very astute – for example, some staff will occasionally say, 'I could tell you had something on your mind last week,' and I didn't think I'd shown it. If I'm getting stressed I go for a walk around the school and find things that are the reason why I do this. Often it's an administrative problem, staffing issue or financial headache, or it's a complaint from a parent that can't be easily resolved. My insecurity is being 'found out' – impostor syndrome. I think heads have their own way of coping, but I think most would say they try very hard not to pass their anxieties or feelings on to the staff because that affects everyone, and you are paid to carry that burden and protect staff from having to carry it.
>
> I sometimes worry about heads who've got jobs too early in their career: had I been a head teacher in my early 40s I don't think I would have been very good at it. And I think it would have affected me a lot more, because It's a long old time to wait for retirement. It's hard, draining work. And you're only as good as your last day and your last decision if you are to keep everyone's trust and commitment to the cause. So, you have got to get a lot more than 90 per cent of your decisions right. And sometimes you can be tempted to make them on the hoof – one thing I've learned is never to make a decision in the corridor. A member of staff stops me with a request and I say, 'email me and I'll have a think about it.'
>
> Heads have as a shelf life, at least of effectiveness: I don't know, for five to eight years I'd say you can have real impact. After that you are in danger of losing the effectiveness of your methods and messages. I suppose what drives me is the fear that one day I'll come in and I'll realise standards have slipped and I have let it happen. That would be the time to leave.

We've already discussed some of the pressures faced by leaders in education: their roles have become increasingly complex in the last decade. They manage day-to-day crises, minor and major, while sustaining their institution and its people, scanning the horizon for future issues and keeping abreast of strategic planning. It's a daily juggling act, and it's not surprising it can be hard to switch off. If you aren't managing your own wellbeing, you aren't managing the wellbeing of your staff or your school.

There's plenty of research on the topic: in the United States, Penn State University has been a leading voice on the issue.[1] Its research highlights the impact the wellbeing of principals has both on staff and on students: school leaders, it finds, play a crucial role in creating healthy, caring schools. It's easy to feel guilty about making time for yourself when others seem to need so much from you.

By looking after yourself, you're likely to increase your effectiveness, work smarter and provide others with the role models and leadership they need to do the same. There is a way in which your school can become not just healthier but also more efficient and more successful. By learning to regulate your own emotions and behaviour, increasing your social awareness, cultivating healthy relationships and improving your decision-making skills, you can begin to create a culture where everyone wins.

The researchers produced a flow chart showing how good leadership can create wide-ranging benefits:

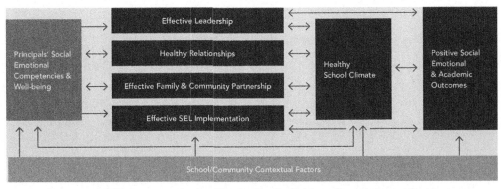

Illustration 5.1 The pro-social school leader. Credit: Mahfouz, Greenberg and Rodriguez, Penn State University

As you read through the book, you'll find more tips on how to achieve this, particularly in Chapter 11.

Taking a long, hard look at yourself

How well are you able to manage the many everyday challenges? Do you find it difficult to navigate or recover from difficult situations, or do you not feel particularly resilient? Perhaps you feel you are in a state of prolonged and chronic stress. Any or all of these may mean you experience symptoms which – if they continue – might indicate you need to take action.

So what is the first step on the road to a healthier and better school, not to mention an improved work-life balance? First, be honest with yourself about the effect that your working practices can have on you. In the past year, have you thought any of the following?

"I'm feeling tired a lot of the time"
"I have no willpower to say no to eating unhelpfully, particularly on really busy, stressful days."
"It's too busy to take lunch or breaks – I need to keep working to get everything done."
"I have a lot going on in and out of work. I'm struggling to balance everything and have no time for myself."
"I haven't got the time to exercise."
"I keep making silly mistakes. I just can't seem to concentrate properly."

When you are tired, hungry or thirsty, you may find it far more difficult to manage busy periods and to take decisions.

Here are some signs that stress may be excessively affecting you:
You:

– Find it hard to sleep.

– Change your eating habits.

– Smoke or drink more.

– Avoid colleagues, friends and family.

– Overreact to problems.

Emotionally you:

– Become more irritable or angry.

– Have greater mood swings.

– Are more anxious.

– Feel numb.

– Feel disappointed with yourself.

– Are more tearful or aggressive.

– Feel less motivated or committed.

– Feel drained and listless.

Physical symptoms you experience include:

– Tiredness.

– Indigestion and nausea headaches.

– Changes in bowel habits.

– Aching or painful muscles, back or neck pain.

– Palpitations.

Mentally you:

– Are more indecisive.

– Find it hard to concentrate.

– Suffer loss of memory.

– Feel more confused than usual.

– Have feelings of inadequacy or low self-esteem.

All these can indicate stress and lowered resilience, but they can also indicate other conditions. If you are concerned, you should seek guidance from your GP. And if you are worried about a colleague, you might suggest they do the same.

Being aware of and addressing symptoms that affect you is important if you want to enjoy work and support others. Another cause of stress and anxiety is how we think and there are traps you should be aware of and avoid.

Thinking traps

Cognitive science has shown we have a strong bias when processing information.[2] We tend to use existing information that supports our beliefs, and we filter out information that doesn't. We regularly draw conclusions with less information than we need, particularly when we're under stress. This leads to 'thinking traps' – mental shortcuts we take to help us make sense of things, but which can be unhelpful and stressful. We need accurate and flexible thinking to deal effectively with stress and adversity and to avoid these traps. Understanding these concepts can help you to de-stress, and to help your staff to do so too.

Common thinking traps include:

- **Jumping to conclusions** – before reaching conclusions make sure you have facts to support you.

- **Personalising** – assuming blame for problems and situations for which you are not primarily responsible, leading to a loss of self-worth, feelings of sadness or guilt. If you do make a mistake, learn from it and use the experience to improve future performance.

- **Externalising** – blaming others for situations for which they are not primarily responsible: this can cause anger and relationship problems. Even if someone else has made a mistake, they are unlikely to have done so deliberately. Learn to forgive, and coach them on what they could do differently.

- **Mind-reading** – assuming we know what others are thinking without checking, or expecting them to know what we are thinking without telling them. For example, we walk into a room and it goes quiet, so we think people are talking about us. This involves assumptions about blame and is at the heart of relationship breakdowns and trust issues.

- **Emotional reasoning** – making a false conclusion about an experience based on how we feel, rather than on the facts. So we may feel relieved after a performance management conversation and as a result assume that because we talked about a problem it was resolved, when it wasn't. This can lead to incorrect expectations about what we or others should do. It can lead to feelings of inadequacy, and to labelling or stereotyping of others.

- **Overgeneralising** – making sweeping judgements about people or situations, often based on single experiences. This can lead to harsh and judgemental views of ourselves or others.

- **Magnifying/minimising** – over-emphasising and/or shrinking the importance of aspects of a situation. This can lead to self-deception, or to feeling overwhelmed.

- **Catastrophising** – assuming something bad will happen or exaggerating bad situations. This is linked to other negative traps such as magnifying and overgeneralising. For example, if we don't get the promotion we applied for, we begin to feel this is because the line manager doesn't like us. And that means we'll never get promoted. And that means we'll be stuck at the bottom of the pay scale. And that means we'll never get to own a home. And that means we'll always have to live with our parents... and so on.

Learn to manage your thinking, no matter the number or scale of the challenges you face. The first step in doing this is to raise your awareness of these traps and how they manifest. Then when you do face adversity or are feeling inadequate or under duress, you can use the thinking traps as a checklist. Check against each one and think about how you can choose to think differently – easier said than done with embedded behaviours. Recognise you have choice and practice taking a different path.

The embodiment of excellence

Aristotle is often quoted thus: "*We are what we repeatedly do. Excellence, therefore, is not an act but a habit.*" Actually there is no evidence to suggest he ever said this, but he might have: he did believe excellence requires time, experience and custom. Forming good habits and sticking to them, or returning to them repeatedly, is key to building personal and institutional cultures.

Illustration 5.2 Building good habits

Changing behaviours and habits is not easy, particularly in the context of life in a busy school. You may feel you can't control what you do, when you can take a break or the size of your workload. But you do have choices. There are small steps you can take which will help: you have the same 24 hours in a day as everyone else and you have the ability to plan effectively.

You can respond to pressures in a way that puts you in control and allows you to take the steps you want, for example to:

- **Take regular exercise:** schedule at least 20 minutes each day to take a brisk walk or run that gets you out of breath. You need your physical health to boost energy and deal better with busy periods.

- **Eat regularly:** Try eating little and often to keep your blood sugar level balanced and don't skip breakfast or lunch – you need to refuel.

- **Get enough sleep:** most people need 7–8 hours, work out your ideal amount and stick to it.

- **Stay hydrated**: it's really important to keep drinking throughout the day – the average needed is usually at least 2 litres and can be significantly more depending on your height, weight and physical activity.

- **Take time out**: take time during the day to do something you enjoy, alone or with others – this will help you to be more productive.

- **Form effective habits:** easier said than done. You have a limited amount of will power but effective habits help you make decisions despite this: take regular breaks, focus on the things you *can* control, see mistakes as learning opportunities, prioritise your work and regularly check in with your team.

Leading your staff to better wellbeing: how resilient is your team?

Resilience is about our ability to adapt and bounce back when things don't go as planned. Resilient people don't dwell on failures; they acknowledge the situation, learn from their mistakes and challenges, and then move forward.

It is challenged each day by the pressure and stress we all face, and it is important to note the difference between the two.

Pressure can be positive and a motivating factor and is often essential in helping you to carry out your job, particularly when something needs to be done quickly. It can help you to work at your best, achieve your goals and perform better.

Stress occurs when this pressure becomes excessive and it is a natural reaction which is also called the fight or flight response. It is not an illness but a state. Acute stress can occur when faced with a challenging situation, such as a job interview or exam, and is natural. It is when this state remains and becomes chronic that mental and physical illness can develop.

The diagram and table below will help you identify how your performance level is impacted when pressure increases and you move through the stages. They will help you to build an understanding of how you and your colleagues are experiencing pressure and stress. You can use the diagram to plot where you feel you and they are currently. You could share it in a team briefing or in one-to-ones and ask others where they would say they are on the curve. It's a useful tool for identifying what support everyone needs to keep them in the optimal performance area.

The table provides some information for each of the stages and what you might do when you are in each one.

From boredom to crisis

	The impact	Top tips
Boredom	While workload may be heavy, you or colleagues may be doing things that you don't want to. A lack of interest in achieving deadlines and targets can leave team members feeling undervalued, with little sense of purpose. They may appear unenthusiastic, slow and lethargic because they aren't engaged.	• Talk to your team members and ask what they can do to change their situation and how they feel. • Agree SMART objectives and targets and clearly communicate and regularly check in on progress. • You should address this early
Comfort	Team members are mainly doing what they know how to do and are presented with no great challenge. For some, this can be a good place but it also means there is probably little risk being taken or innovation shown. Others may find it unstimulating without enough stretch.	• Team members who are coasting in the comfort zone may be ready for promotion. If there are no vacancies, offer them some additional responsibilities, tasks or challenges. • Ask what would provide greater stretch or fulfilment and agree on actions they will take. • Do address this before they slip backwards or become frustrated.

(Continued)

(*Continued*)

Stretch	Team members are generally working at pace – they have a heavy workload, may also be learning something new or pushing themselves to perform and be more productive. Some enjoy the challenge but others may start to feel uncomfortable and need to include recuperation and recovery time.	• Keep an eye on anyone in this zone who might be showing signs of strain and ask how they might remove some pressure or find some recovery time. • Stretch those team members who appear to be thriving with additional responsibilities and invite them to contribute ideas for their own and the school's development. • Remember that people need recovery and a sustained period in stretch can lead to strain.
Strain	The line between stretch and strain can be a fine one and can be influenced by both the length of time in stretch and the nature and pace of the challenges faced. There are some dangers to spending too long in 'stretch.' An increasing number of challenges may mean that team members feel less able to cope which could lead to a state of stress.	• If you notice one of your team feeling strain, speak with them immediately and agree any tasks they can let go or how they might address the situation. • Discuss the signs of strain and stress with your team so they can identify them. Act quickly to prevent this from getting out of control and moving to crisis. • Provide support through discussing coping strategies and encourage team members to take time out at lunch and break. Switching tasks, doing something you/they enjoy, and drinking and eating can all help.
Crisis	This is the tipping point for wellbeing and resilience, where a team member may sense a lack of control and feel exhausted. This can lead to burnout, negative attitudes, sickness and absence and if not addressed, mental ill-health.	• Encourage the team member to focus on wellbeing and find the right support and keep talking. • Have an open and honest conversation and reassure your team member that you will support them. • Agree to take responsibilities away so the individual can recover and regain a sense of control.

Manage yourself and your staff will follow your lead

It's important to stay calm and to manage your thinking. Otherwise worry can take over, you catastrophise and become overwhelmed during challenging or stressful times. So, start by thinking regularly about your own current state – how are you thinking, feeling and behaving? Being self-aware is so important. Focus on things that are within your control and dismiss those that are not. Some people find it helpful to write their worries down in two lists, one for the controllable and one for those things they cannot control.

Try asking these questions:

- What action can I take?

- Who can lead on this or support me?

- What needs to be done?

Communicate, communicate, communicate

Whether things are going well or whether you're facing challenging times, staff need to understand what is going on. Facts are neutral, so share them and make sure staff have the information they need to do their job. If there are good lines of communication in calm times, this will pay off on the days when you have difficult messages to convey. Use a range of channels to ensure information is delivered consistently and confidently. With all the free technology available, this can feel relatively easy, though this can lead to complacency and needs to be managed well. Through personal contact, and using other leaders and colleagues, you can ensure everyone feels connected.

Make decisions

Indecision leads to uncertainty, confusion, apprehension, anxiety and other emotions that are unlikely to be helpful in leading a school, particularly in challenging times. It also lowers trust.

If it turns out you made the wrong decision, that's OK – the best leaders are adaptable and are able to be honest when circumstances change or when new information comes to light. Don't spread yourself too thin – focus on the most important decisions first. Think through what will have the biggest impact for you and your school. This includes making sure your staff remain engaged and have the resources to look after their own wellbeing.

School leadership in a crisis: be a role model

When crises arise, try to use considered language and avoid exaggeration or inflammatory words. Be realistic about what can be achieved and don't try to accomplish too much.

Too often leaders ask others to do what they say and not what they do. Make sure you are not one of them. Stay self-aware and consciously reflect on this each day – that is the best way to keep on track.

Focus on the outcomes and make sure you have clarity about what you need to achieve. Set clear expectations – staff will find long-term objectives less engaging; it is just the way people think when under significant challenge. Create short-term goals and keep them simple. Explain why they are important and the part that each person has to play in meeting them. Thank staff for what they are doing – make sure this is authentic and specific. Ensure you deliver short-term wins and build momentum.

Encourage staff to share their successes, both personal and team, and praise those who make good progress or deliver anything noteworthy each day.

Being a role model also means following the actions, policies and processes you or other leaders in your school have set. Do this well and others will copy. Don't do it and you will find it much harder to lead your way through difficult times.

Managing yourself

Effectively leading on all the things shared immediately above starts with managing yourself and the rest of this chapter shares practical suggestions on how you can do this.

The biggest pressure you face often comes from a lack – or perceived lack – of time to get everything done. We often think of this as time management. But no one can manage time (unless you have a time-turner like Hermione in Harry Potter, or a Tardis like Doctor Who.) It's all about managing yourself and developing your personal effectiveness.

Stress beliefs

Do you think that how you think about stress is important? Do you believe it is good or bad? Researchers from the University of Wisconsin[3] studied nearly 29,000 people and showed that those who believed stress affected their health had a 43 per cent increased risk of premature death. This could be bad news for those working in education. However, they also discovered that those working in high-stress environments who believed stress was helpful in driving action had no increased risk of early death. They had the lowest risk of all – less than those working in low-stress environments.

Working in a school and accepting stress can have a positive effect in helping you to take action can be a good place to be. Your beliefs and habits and how you manage things now are a consequence of your past. How you manage in future and whether your beliefs and habits change are up to you.

So how can you recover and manage your stress? There are a wide range of actions, including:

- Exercise of all kinds, including sport, yoga and pilates.

- Reading, hobbies and doing something creative.

- Spending time with family, friends and positive people.

- Mindfulness and breathing activities.

- Music and dance.

- Owning a pet.

- Cooking, housework and DIY.

- Good nutrition.

- Good sleeping routine.

It's not an exhaustive list and of course people do also use things to cope that might include alcohol, caffeine and other stimulants. In moderation, these are fine, though they may not be beyond an initial short period and can cause longer-term problems and dependencies.

Managing your stressors

Start by identifying your own main stressors and prioritise them so you know your biggest one. This might be a specific aspect of workload, a leader or working with a colleague.

Once identified, you can learn to better manage them. One model you can follow was developed by the Mayo Clinic – the four As of stress relief. These are:

1. Avoid the stressor – remove it from your life.

2. Alter the stressor – change the thing that is causing the stress.

3. Adapt to the stressor – change how you respond to the stress.

4. Accept the stressor – so it no longer affects you.

Let's look at each in turn.

Avoid the stressor

What might you do to avoid or remove stressors from your life? Examples might include:

- Learn how to say "no" – know your limits and stick to them. While in peak times there is more to do, be aware of when you are approaching too much strain and explore what you can stop doing. Taking on more than you can handle may help in the short term but will ensure you are not able to give your best over longer periods.

- Take control of your environment – if there are specific jobs that you find more challenging, then you might be able to change them with other members of the team or change the way you do them.

- Avoid hot-button topics – if you repeatedly argue about the same subject or with the same people, stop bringing it up or excuse yourself when it's the topic of discussion.

- Prioritise – remove things from your daily to-do list by being clear about what is really important and learn to plan more effectively.

- Avoid distractions and interruptions – you can plan 'availability time' rather than always having to be available to make sure you can get important non-classroom tasks done.

- Avoid working excessive hours.

Alter the stressor

If you can't avoid your stressors or a stressful situation, try to alter it. Examples include:

- Figure out what you can do to change things, so the problem doesn't present itself in the future. Often, this involves changing the way you communicate and operate in your daily life. What can you do to change your stressors? Examples include:

- Express your feelings instead of bottling them up – if something or someone is bothering you, communicate your concerns in an open and respectful way.

- Be willing to compromise – if you ask someone to change their behaviour, be willing to do the same.

- Be more assertive – don't take a backseat in your own life. Deal with problems head on, doing your best to anticipate and prevent them.

- Plan ahead – poor personal management, preparation and planning can make you less resilient in the face of challenges. When you're stretched too thin and running behind, it's much harder to stay calm and focused.

Adapt to the stressor

If you can't alter the stressor, you might be able to change yourself or how you respond to it. You can adapt to pressure and stressful situations and regain your sense of control by changing your expectations and attitude.

What might you do to adapt to your stressors? Examples include:

- Reframe problems – rather than fuming about being given a different job, see it as an opportunity for more responsibility, variety or to recharge.

- Look at the big picture – how important will it be to you in the long term? Will it matter in a month? A year? If the answer is no, focus your time and energy elsewhere.

- Adjust your standards – perfectionism is a major source of avoidable stress. Usually "good enough" is good enough.

- Focus on the positive – reflect on all the things you appreciate in your life, including your own positive qualities and help keep things in perspective.

Accept the stressor

Accept some sources of pressure and stress are unavoidable. You can't prevent or change stressors such as people calling in sick, parents calling in with a complaint or some last-minute changes. In such cases, the best way to cope is to simply accept things as they are. Examples include:

- Focusing on the things you can control – recognise when you worry about things you can't control and choose how to react to them.

- Looking for the upside – when facing major challenges, try to look at them as opportunities for personal growth. If decisions you make contribute to stressful situations, reflect on them and learn from your mistakes.

- Sharing your feelings – talk to a trusted friend or make an appointment with a specialist. This can be cathartic, even if you can't alter the stressful situation.

- Learning to forgive – accept the fact that we live in an imperfect world and that people make mistakes and that often what you perceive isn't the intent of the other person/people involved. Learn to let go of anger and resentment and move on. It only hurts you in the long run.

- Being grateful for what you have.

- Showing kindness to others.

Of course, there are other things you can do to manage stress and improve your wellbeing – we have covered much of this already in this chapter:

- Take a break and/or switch tasks

- Do more of what you enjoy

- Take exercise

● Have the right friends, supporters and network

● Try and keep your sense of humour

To manage this effectively means being self-aware, reflecting on what you do and practicing good habits.

How much of what you do every day is done consciously and how much is on autopilot? Much of what we do is automatic, from breathing and other bodily functions to habits we have developed. Sometimes this can even be when we are in dangerous situations: for example if you drive, have you ever found yourself further along your route and wondered how you got there? You probably do similar things most days when you get up, get ready and arrive at work.

Being in the present and aware of what is happening allows you to take action and make changes. It allows you to respond rather than react. Without a high level of self-awareness, you cannot make any changes that might improve home and work life. You need an awareness of where you are now (your habits, achievements, behaviours, and more).

Then to decide where you want to be and what needs to change, in order for you to get there. It is also important to know why you want to change and to have a powerful reason for it. Finally, you will need to work out what and how you will make the change or take action to get to where you want to be. Start by setting one goal or objective for improvement.

Be very specific on any change you want to make – taking on too much or not having clarity is likely to lead to a lack of success. Set out clearly what you will do and translate this into daily actions. You will often see people with a vision and objective, but their daily actions are not aligned with it – to be successful, everything has to be in the same direction and consistently delivered. There are things you can do to help:

● Keep a diary or take notes to record when things go well or don't go as planned – get used to carrying a notebook or use your notes on your phone or other technique.

● Book in regular reflection time and use triggers to maintain this and other actions – if you are going to work on yourself, then you have to reflect regularly on how you are doing and give it some attention. What gets measured (or focused on) gets done. You can book a short weekly slot – a meeting with yourself. Book it in your calendar so it reminds you or have some other way to trigger it (phone alarm, Post-it note on the car steering wheel – anything that reminds you to do it). Work through your diary or examples of what you have done well and where you still want to improve. Think about opportunities coming up when you can try again. Keep repeating until what you are working on becomes a habit and then move to your next action.

● During reflection time, some people find it helpful to give themselves a score. Ask yourself, compared to where you want to be (10), where are you now. So, if you are a six, ask what do I need to do to be a seven? And keep working and scoring each week until you achieve what you want.

● Enlist a supporter or network – publicly declaring what you want to achieve, asking a trusted friend or mentor to help, working with others on a similar change, are all likely to increase your accountability and make it easier (and more fun) to achieve your goal.

● Practice, practice, practice – the biggest challenge is often expectations of immediate change or success. Depending on what you are looking to do, this can be hard and may be undoing years of current practice. Expect it to take time for change to happen and become natural and a long time before you become a master. Behaviour change is not difficult, but the commitment to make a change is, and being resolute in regular practice is too.

● Repeat – once something has become a habit, move on to the next thing and repeat the process (though it is useful to continue a little beyond being successful and also looking back and ensuring previous changes remain embedded).

Emotional intelligence

This is a very brief look at emotional intelligence, popularised by Daniel Goleman, and there are many books on the subject, including Goleman's first book of the same name – Emotional Intelligence.[4]

As we have already said, change starts with self-awareness, a key part of emotional intelligence. It is also emotional intelligence that determines the ability to build effective relationships as a leader. You can see more in the diagram below.

Illustration 5.3 Emotional intelligence – how change starts with self-awareness

It shows how all change starts in the top left box: without awareness, proactive self-managed change is not possible. The next stage, bottom left, is to take action and responsibility to self-manage and regulate. Top right is the need for awareness of others – both the impact they have on you and the impact you have on them. Bottom right is the need to take action to manage how you interact with others and build effective relationships.

All four quadrants are important in managing your emotions and in being a highly effective leader and colleague. How might you use this quadrant in raising and managing your awareness and in taking action for change, both for yourself and in how you interact with others?

Your inner voice

Self-talk can have a big effect on you, as it is the voice you hear the most. You can be your own biggest cheerleader or biggest critic. Which are you? What feedback do you currently give yourself, about you and your abilities?

Do you have a positive or negative self-image? Do you use language about yourself like, 'I always do my best, I will try, I am happy, I'm good enough, I can…,' or 'I am not good enough, I can't, I don't want to, I am scared….' Much of this happens without us thinking consciously about it.

When talking to leaders and others working in schools, I am often struck by the way they focus on what hasn't been achieved and on the inevitable mistakes which have been made. Yet they achieve so much every day and do not celebrate enough of the great work that has been completed. Does this describe you or those you work with, or do you have a good balance that includes focusing on things done well?

If the former, you might reflect at the end of each day and ask yourself or make a list of what you achieved or did well. Or to keep it simple you might just ask yourself to think of three things you have done well each day. To do this and to change behaviour is likely to need a trigger – this might be to do it at the same time each day, stick a Post-it note somewhere to remind you (car steering wheel or desk), set a digital alert, calendar or other reminder.

Schools are busy places

You will never get everything done so quit trying. You don't need to be told that schools are very busy places. Workload is high across the sector and there will always be too much to do, even though steps are likely to have been taken to remove work that does not have an impact.

There is little light at the end of the workload tunnel, so we need to get comfortable working in the tunnel. We all have the same time available, and some people seem to be able to manage what they have to do more effectively than others. What steps might help you to work more effectively?

Multi-tasking

One answer might be to multi-task – this rarely works. You are likely to end up doing two tasks badly. If we split our focus, we are likely to take longer and deliver work of a lower quality. Imagine marking books while watching television… better to mark and then watch television.

We live in the age of distraction. We are bombarded with emails, bad news, social media, constant interruptions, multiple demands from different people and much more. All this distracts us from the work we need to do and encourages us to try to deliver multiple tasks.

The most effective way of dealing with this is to chunk work and deliver it in batches. Below are some tips and rules you can apply to your workload:

- Do the most critical and important things first and before anything has the chance to sabotage your day. It also means that no matter what happens for the rest of the day, you will have achieved something. This means not doing your emails before completing your most important task (or maybe more than one) each day. If you are focused and ready to work and open your emails, what happens? Your focused energy becomes scattered and if there is anything disappointing, upsetting or that makes you angry, your emotional energy is also affected. Both of these things can affect your wellbeing, reduce your energy and make it less likely you will get your work done.

- When you do your emails, find time to do them together, rather than jumping in an out (doing them in batches as this will improve your productivity, rather than sharing them with other tasks). Consider setting up rules for common emails, so they go straight to a folder, if they do not need action. E-mail that can be dealt with quickly, do them. If you need further information or if it is a larger job, plan when you will do this and file the email until it is time to action it.

Only send emails when needed, do not copy people in and highlight the subject line if action is needed. People will copy you and you will reduce overall traffic. Finally use your out of office to tell staff, parents and others, when you will respond to emails. Companies tell you when they will respond and set reasonable expectations (unless it is an emergency you should not have to reply the same day). Let people know in your out of office message that if it is an emergency, they will need to call you or the school.

- Remember you control your work and not the other way round – all of us could work to midnight each day. Set your working hours and do the work you can do within them and then pick up anything not done on the next day. Otherwise, the day will expand to fit the work!

- Block time and avoid interruptions – if you have important things to do, then you have to block time to do them. Do not simply invite people to walk in and interrupt you. The average interruption adds significant time to any task and so having a few each day will make a big difference to your productivity.

Plan when you will be available and let staff know and be ready for this and not involved in any complex or significant tasks. You can also plan your visibility around school. The rest of the time be 'selfish' to make sure the most important things get done and in the most effective way.

- Use the Pareto principle – this helps you identify your most important tasks because it suggests that only a small part of what you do is responsible for a significant part of your results. It's named after Vilfredo Pareto, an Italian economist who investigated why a large number of his peas came from a small number of pods. It has been developed by others – for example by Dr Joseph Duran, who coined the term 'the vital few' – those few things that if done well, deliver the majority of outcomes.[5]

This has also become known as the 80/20 rule. About 80% of results come from 20% of the inputs. We could argue about whether this should be 80/20 or 70/30, or if it might vary in different circumstances, but the principle that a smaller number of actions delivers larger outputs is well known. What are the vital few tasks that you need to deliver at any time (which part of your workload is vitally important). These are the only ones to focus on.

- You will have seen models of prioritisation. We are going to take a look at one of them. These are just ways to raise your awareness and help you think about the steps you might take to effectively manage your work. You are likely to already take steps and so this may simply help as a reminder or you may have a different process or system.

This is one variation of a process first attributed to General Dwight D Eisenhower[6] and is a way to think about your work. Can you think of some tasks you do each day that fit within each category and some that you do that you can move categories? Use the model to support you – it may help in identifying the 'vital few' we mentioned above.

- Another way of thinking about workload is to consider the impact it has. Is it:

  ○ Low effort, high impact – do immediately.

  ○ High effort, high impact – evaluate and plan (is it worth it?).

  ○ Low effort, low impact – not a priority.

  ○ High effort, low impact – ditch it.

Also think about if you add any new work, either personally, for the team or school, then adopt a one in, one out policy.

- Many of you will use a 'to do' list. You could add to this a 'to don't' list. As with the prioritisation model, be ruthless and remove work that is not likely to make an impact.

- Only focus on those things you can control – anything else is a waste of your time and energy. It is sometimes easier said than done being aware of this. Asking the question, "can I do anything about this?" is a good starting point. In addition to awareness, preparation, regular reflection and practice will all help.

- Dealing with interruptions – an important area that adds significantly to demands. A typical interruption will add significant time to a task that is being undertaken. It interrupts flow, breaks concentration and you don't need many to affect your day! Think about interruptions you are regularly faced with – are they usually the same person or people and are the interruptions valid? What are some steps you might take to better manage them?

The first step is to plan when you can be available to others and to communicate this, as well as planning your visibility. This is more effective than allowing people to interrupt, other than in an emergency. It means when you meet, you can give them your full attention, rather than flicking between them and the task you are undertaking.

If someone does interrupt then know your options – listen now, book a time for later, coach others to find their own solutions (don't take on their problems or fix them) and don't be a perfectionist.

We talk a lot about work/life balance: a better term is 'life balance.' We all have the same 24 hours to get everything done – work, eat, sleep, spend time with family or friends, do things we enjoy and everything else we want to fit in. We all know people who do this well and this may include you.

For those of us looking for improvements, what matters is our behaviours each day and our awareness of them. It is about what we allow to happen and whether we choose to make the changes needed. It is about our thinking, the clarity of our goals, our discipline, preparation, reflection and practise.

Choice

Perhaps the most important word to consider is choice. While it may not always feel like it, we all have choices in what we do and how we respond to situations. We can choose whether and when we work additional hours or if we want to use some of the practical steps set out in this chapter to be more effective or to help manage stress.

No one is pretending this is easy or that there aren't staff members (and students) who need significant support to deal with mental health and other workplace challenges. Yet recognising that there is choice can be empowering.

What action will you choose to take?

Chapter 5: Key points

● **Principal wellbeing**. If you aren't managing your own wellbeing, you aren't managing the wellbeing of others in your school. The wellbeing of principals has a clear impact on both staff and students. School leaders play a crucial role in creating healthy and caring schools.

● **Take a rain check**. Are you overstressed? Are you getting enough sleep, food, drink, exercise? Are you smoking or drinking more than previously, avoiding social contact, reacting angrily to small irritations? Are you tired all the time, experiencing repeated physical symptoms such as headaches, finding it hard to make decisions? Feeling inadequate, or suffering from memory loss? If so, stress may be affecting you. If you notice these signs, you may want to seek help – this might be from an employee assistance scheme, if your school has one, counselling, if available, or from your GP.

● **Avoid thinking traps**: Are you using unhelpful mental shortcuts to help you deal with problems? These may include jumping to conclusions, personalising, externalising, mind-reading, emotional reasoning, overgeneralising, magnifying or minimising problems, catastrophising. When you face adversity, check and avoid these traps. The 'ABC' method can help: A is adversity; B is your belief about the reason for it, C is the consequence you expect. If you can find a more positive narrative about B, you can work towards more positive consequences.

● **Take time to reflect**: Do you tend to blame yourself, or others? Do you tend to think all problems are permanent or all-encompassing whereas maybe they are transient?

● **Be the change you want to see**: Exercise, eat and drink regularly, take time out, try to form effective thinking habits.

● **Focus on your team**: Imagine their state of mind as an arc which runs from boredom to comfort, then to stretch, then to strain, then to crisis. Boredom will leave them unengaged; crisis will tip them over into burnout. Try to help them to get to stretch, but no further.

● **Stay calm**, make decisions, communicate well, be a good role model.

● **Manage yourself** – understand that pressure and stress are normal and your beliefs about it matter. Working in a high-stress role and knowing how to manage stress give the lowest risk of early death.

● **Learn how to manage your stressors** – the Mayo model of Avoid, Alter, Adapt and Accept is a framework you can use to make good choices.

● **Having a high level of self-awareness** allows you to make good decisions and it is also at the heart of emotional intelligence. Without this, it is impossible to make changes.

- **Your inner voice** is either your greatest cheer leader or biggest critic. Focus on what you have achieved and done well, not what you still have to do and mistakes you have made.

- **Don't multi-task**, chunk work, such as emails, and do your most important task or tasks first each day.

- **Manage interruptions** and your availability so that you are able to give people your full focus and deliver your most important work.

- **Manage workload** to ensure the task you undertake delivers an impact for staff, pupils or the school community and when introducing new work, ensure something is removed.

Notes

1 Mahfouz, J., Greenberg, M. and Rodriguez, A. (2019). *Issue brief principals' social and emotional competence: A key factor for creating caring schools.* [online] Available at: https://www.prevention.psu.edu/uploads/files/PSU-Principals-Brief-103119.pdf [Accessed 14 December 2022].

2 Massachusetts Institute of Technology (2011). *Thinking traps: Functional fixedness, problem solving, and creativity | introduction to psychology | brain and cognitive sciences.* [online] MIT OpenCourseWare. Available at: https://ocw.mit.edu/courses/ 9-00sc-introduction-to-psychology-fall-2011/resources/thinking-traps-functional-fixedness-problem-solving-and-creativity-1/ [Accessed 14 December 2022].

3 Keller, A., Litzelman, K., Wisk, L. E., Maddox, T., Cheng, E. R., Creswell, P. D. and Witt, W. P. (2012). Does the Perception That Stress Affects Health Matter? The Association with Health and Mortality. *Health Psychology,* 31(5), pp.677–684. doi:10.1037/a0026743

4 Goleman, D. (2007). *Emotional Intelligence* (10th ed.). New York: Bantam Books.

5 Juran (2019). *Dr. Juran's history | Juran.* [online] Juran. Available at: https://www.juran.com/about-us/dr-jurans-history/.

6 Eisenhower (2011). *The Eisenhower Matrix: Introduction & 3-Minute Video Tutorial.* [online] Eisenhower. Available at: https://www.eisenhower.me/eisenhower-matrix/.

6 Becoming a competent leader

What do we know?

There has been some concern in recent years about the cohort of younger teachers who are now stepping up into management roles. They're getting younger, and the time they remain in the job is getting shorter. Could there be a link to workplace stress? And if so, what measures could you put in place to ensure the school leaders of the future are well supported on their journey?

In England, we know school leaders have been getting younger because Department for Education statistics tell us so[1]: Between 2010 and 2016, the median age of head teachers dropped from 51 to 48, while the median age for a school senior leader dropped from 44 to 42. And retention rates for those who step up to leadership roles aren't great: 4 out of 10 new middle leaders leave their roles within five years, and a fifth within a year. Among new head teachers, a fifth leave within five years in primary schools and a third in secondaries. Around one in ten heads last less than a year in their post.

DOI: 10.4324/9781003315766-8

So it's important that those who are promoted feel supported by their line managers, and that issues which might affect their wellbeing are addressed properly and in a timely way. It's also important that they learn to give the same support to those for whom they are line managers.

Professor Sir Cary Cooper, a leading UK expert on organisational wellbeing and former President of the Chartered Institute of Personnel and Development, believes too many line managers simply do not have the necessary social and soft skills to ensure staff wellbeing. Less than a third of senior leaders encourage a focus on mental wellbeing through their actions, and too few line managers are trained in supporting people with mental ill health, he says in his introduction to a recent report.[2] "Unless there is a substantial improvement in both these areas, it's hard to see how organisations will achieve the step change needed to improve people's wellbeing at work."

But the good news is these skills are all learnable.

Think about the stages of the employee life cycle. Each of them presents opportunities for you to show staff the benefits of working for your school or MAT, and for you to create a great employee experience:

1. Attraction – how prospective staff and other stakeholders view your school or MAT.

2. Recruitment – the process prospective staff go through in being considered for a job with you.

3. Onboarding – how welcome staff feel when they join you (this covers much more than the first day or your initial induction process and should start as soon as they are appointed).

4. Performance – how this is supported and managed.

5. Development – the time and focus given to staff CPD, career conversations and progression.

6. Retention – how you proactively retain good staff and identify those at risk.

7. Farewell – how staff feel when they leave and how well this is managed, irrespective of the reason they leave.

We'll come back to some of these areas in later chapters, but for now, let's focus on how staff are treated by leaders every day. There is little point in investing time and money in the seven areas above, if staff simply do not enjoy coming to work each day. This is a crucial part of building a culture in which everyone feels supported. Do those leading in your school or MAT have an awareness and understanding of the direct impact they have? Too often the answer is 'no.' One day you're a teacher, the next you're asked to lead a year group, key stage or department. Leaders remain subject or specialism experts when they need to become people experts.

Researchers at Goldsmiths, University of London have published extensively on how leaders can be helped to support staff wellbeing and reduce stress. They have come up with a list of specific 'leadership competencies' which should help you to assess where your school is, and to move things forward. Take a look at them in the table below and be honest. Can you think of times when you or your team have demonstrated the negative types of leadership listed here? How might you move towards the more positive approach suggested under each heading?

LEADERSHIP COMPETENCIES

Managing workload and resources

Positive...	Negative...
• Bringing in additional resources to handle workload • Aware of team members' ability when allocating tasks • Monitoring team workload • Refusing to take on additional work when the team is under pressure	• Delegating work unequally across the team • Creating unrealistic deadlines • Showing lack of awareness of how much pressure the team is under • Asking for tasks without checking workload first

Dealing with work problems

Positive...	Negative...
• Following through problems on behalf of employees • Developing action plans • Breaking problems down into manageable parts • Dealing rationally with problems	• Listening but not resolving problems • Being indecisive • Not taking issues and problems seriously • Assuming problems will sort themselves out • Not using consistent processes

Process planning and organisation

Positive...	Negative...
• Reviewing processes to see if work can be improved • Asking: 'could this be done better?' • Prioritising future workloads • Working proactively rather than reactively	• Sticking too rigidly to rules and procedures • Panicking about deadlines rather than planning

Empowerment

Positive...	Negative...
• Trusting employees to do their work • Giving employees responsibility • Steering employees in a direction rather than imposing direction	• Managing under a microscope • Extending so much authority employees feel a lack of direction • Imposing a culture of 'my way is the only way'

Participative approach

Positive...	Negative...
• Provides opportunity to air views • Provides regular team meetings • Knows when to consult employees and when to make a decision	• Not listening when an employee asks for help • Presenting a final solution rather than options • Making decisions without consultation

Development

Positive...	Negative...
• Encourages staff to go on training courses • Provides mentoring and coaching • Helps employees to develop within their roles	• Refuses requests for training • Does not provide upward mobility in the job • Does not allow employees to use their new training

Being accessible and visible

Positive...	Negative...
• Communicating that employees can talk to you at any time • Having an open door policy • Making time to talk to employees at their desks	• Being constantly at meetings or away from your desk • Saying 'Don't bother me now' • Not attending lunches or social events with employees

Health and safety

Positive...	Negative...
• Making sure everyone is safe • Structuring risk assessments • Ensuring all health and safety requirements are met	• Not taking health and safety seriously • Questioning the capability of an employee who has raised a safety issue

Feedback

Positive...	Negative...
• Praising good work • Acknowledging employees' efforts • Operating a no blame culture • Passing positive feedback about the team to senior management	• Not giving credit for hitting deadlines • Seeing feedback as only 'one way' • Giving feedback to employees that they are wrong just because their way of working is different

Managing conflict

Positive...	Negative...
• Listening objectively to both sides of a conflict • Supporting and investigating incidents of abuse • Dealing with conflict head on • Following up on conflicts after resolution	• Not addressing bullying • Trying to keep the peace rather than sorting out problems • Taking sides • Not taking employee complaints seriously

Expressing and managing own emotions

Positive...	Negative...
• Having a positive approach • Acting calmly when under pressure • Walking away when feeling unable to control emotion • Apologising for poor behaviour	• Passing on stress to employees • Acting aggressively • Losing temper with employees • Being unpredictable in mood

Acting with integrity

Positive...	Negative...
• Keeping employee issues private and confidential • Admitting mistakes • Treating all employees with same importance	• Speaking about employees behind their back • Making promises and not delivering • Making personal issues public

Friendly style	
Positive...	**Negative...**
• Willing to have a laugh and a joke • Socialising with team • Bringing in food and drinks for the team • Regularly having informal chats with employees	• Criticising people in front of colleagues • Pulling the team up for talking or laughing during working hours • Using a harsh tone of voice when asking for things

Communication	
Positive...	**Negative...**
• Keeps the team informed of what is happening in the organisation • Communicates clear goals and objectives • Explains exactly what is required	• Keeps people in the dark • Holds meetings 'behind closed doors' • Doesn't provide timely communication on organisational change

Taking responsibility	
Positive...	**Negative...**
• Leading 'from the front' • Stepping in to help out when needed • Communicating 'the buck stops with me' • Dealing with difficult situations on behalf of staff	• Saying 'It's not my problem' • Blaming the team if things go wrong • Walking away from problems

Knowledge of job	
Positive...	**Negative...**
• Able to put yourself in employees' shoes • Having enough expertise to give good advice • Knowing what employees are doing	• Doesn't have the necessary knowledge to do the job • Doesn't take time to learn about the employee's job

Empathy	
Positive...	**Negative...**
• Takes and interest in employees' personal lives • Aware of different personalities and styles of working within the team • Notices when a team member is behaving out of character	• Insensitive to people's personal issues • Refuses to believe someone is becoming stressed • Maintains distance from employees: 'Us and them'

Seeking advice	
Positive...	**Negative...**
• Seeks help from occupational health when necessary • Seeks advice from other managers with more experience • Uses HR when dealing with a problem	• n/a (there are no negative consequences from seeking advice)

This content is re-used with permission of the Health and Safety Executive under the terms of the Open Government Licence.

Source: Health and Safety Executive,[3] Goldsmiths[4]:

These were refined into a set of 12 competencies and the research showed that leaders demonstrating them prevented and reduced stress in those they led.

You might consider which of these fit with your school's values. When setting them did you consult with staff and together articulate what they meant in terms of everyday behaviours? This is the step that many leaders fail to take. They set the vision and come up with values, yet leave it to chance what different people think these might mean.

For example, if one of the values is respect, what would represent that this was being lived? Not simply leaving it to chance, but expressing for example this means people turn up to meetings on time, they start and finish on time, attendees are prepared, actions are agreed and deadlines are met, or where they are not, reasons are given in advance.

Ensuring specific behaviours are agreed for all school values means they can be reinforced through praise and people can be effectively and more easily held to account when they cut across them.

To help with this, we have turned the behaviours that deliver the 12 competencies into a set of statements that can be easily used by leaders to self-assess how well they meet them. That's because self-assessing against the competencies is the easy bit. Choosing to adapt and change your behaviour, and that of others in your team, is much harder. People have deep and long-held beliefs and need to understand why they should change, as well as regular and deliberate reflection and practice to develop new habits.

As a senior leader, you must be a role model that others can copy, and you will need to coach your middle leaders. Otherwise, everyone will quickly return to their old, default positions.

Introducing these behaviours to senior and middle leaders across your school would be a great first step: a cornerstone on which you can build your people strategy. You could discuss as a team how these behaviours are modelled within your school or MAT, and then agree on actions so they become part of your culture. The exercise should be the fastest way to improve the experience of your staff.

When working with schools, we often share these as 'flash cards' as this is a good way to facilitate discussion on each of them: you can prioritise which ones to work with first. A few example cards are shown below with a fuller list of statements below that.

I am someone who...
does what I say I will

welbee.co.uk

I am someone who...
never speaks about team members behind their back

welbee.co.uk

I am someone who...
acts calmly under pressure

welbee.co.uk

I am someone who...
**gives more positive
than negative feedback**

welbee.co.uk

I am someone who...
**asks for help
when needed**

welbee.co.uk

I am someone who...
**sees feedback as
challenge and criticism**

welbee.co.uk

Illustration 6.1–6.6 Competency behaviour flash cards 1–6

Self-assessment statements
I'm someone who...

- Is honest with people.

- Acts as a role model for staff and students.

- Acts consistently and whose moods are predictable.

- Doesn't pass on my worries and stress to others.

- Creates realistic deadlines for myself and my team.

- Allows my team a say in how they work.

- Allows my team to plan their own workload.

- Doesn't tend towards 'my way is the only way.'

- Has consideration for my team's work/life balance.

- Doesn't pass on my worries and stress to others.

- Prioritises future workload for myself and my team.

- When necessary, stops my team from adding more work.

- Sees projects and tasks through to delivery.

- Communicates job objectives clearly to my team.

- Encourages my team to review how they work.

- Deals calmly and rationally with problems.

- Is decisive when having to make decisions.

- Knows when to consult the team about a decision.

- Deals with problems as soon as they arise.

- Helps my team members to develop.

- Holds regular and effective team meetings.

- Encourages all team members to participate fully.

- Keeps my team informed about what is happening.

- Provides regular opportunities for team 1 to 1s.

- Delegates work effectively and equally.

- <u>Plans</u> to be available for my team members.

- Uses humour appropriately.

- Socialises with team members.

- Regularly asks team members "How are you?"

- Checks people are OK, rather than just assuming.

- Encourages individual input in discussions.

- Listens when a team member asks for help.

- Sees things from others' point of view.

- Takes an interest in team members; lives outside work.

- Deals quickly and objectively with staff conflicts.

- Identifies possible conflicts and acts to prevent them.

- Resolves conflicts rather than acting as the peace maker.

- Follows up on conflicts, even after they are resolved.

- Seeks advice from others, where needed.

- Can find help when acting outside my expertise.

- Finds help for those experiencing mental ill health.

- Supports staff through instances of abuse or bullying.

- Makes it clear I take responsibility when things go wrong.

Chapter 6: Key points

- School leaders are getting younger, and those who are newly promoted particularly need support: they tend not to stay long, and that's a waste of valuable resources. How do you support your teams?

- Think about whether your responses to the following issues are positive or negative. So positive responses would include following through, finding solutions, while a negative one might include making unrealistic demands or failing to make decisions.

  - ○ Workload

  - ○ Employee problems, managing conflict

  - ○ Planning

  - ○ Empowering staff and including them in decisions

  - ○ Facilitating staff development

  - ○ Being accessible

  - ○ Health and safety

  - ○ Giving feedback

○ Managing your own emotions

○ Having a friendly style, displaying empathy

○ Communicating well

○ Taking responsibility

○ Knowing your job – and knowing when you should seek advice

● Self-assess against the twelve competencies proven to prevent and reduce staff stress. Get the behaviours that underpin these right and watch staff members you lead flourish and do their best work

Notes

1 DfE School leadership in England 2010 to 2016: characteristics and trends April 2018: https://www.gov.uk/government/publications/school-leadership-2010-to-2016-characteristics-and-trends [Accessed 21 December 2022].

2 Health and Wellbeing at Work, CIPD May 2018: https://www.cipd.co.uk/Images/health-and-wellbeing-at-work_tcm18-40863.pdf

3 Donaldson-Feilder, E., Lewis, R. and Yarker, J. (2009). *Preventing stress, promoting positive manager behaviour.* [online] www.cipd.co.uk. Available at: https://www.cipd.co.uk/Images/preventing-stress_2009-promoting-positive-manager-behaviour_tcm18-16794.pdf [Accessed 21 December 2022].

4 Yarker, J. and Lewis, R. (2008). *Executive health and safety management competencies for preventing and reducing stress at work identifying and developing the management behaviours necessary to implement the HSE management standards: Phase two.* [online] Available at: https://www.hse.gov.uk/research/rrpdf/rr633.pdf. [Accessed 21 December 2022].

SECTION 3
Getting and keeping a happy workforce

7 Staff retention and recruitment

SINÉAD ORMSTON, ASSISTANT HEADTEACHER, THE SKINNERS' SCHOOL, TUNBRIDGE WELLS

When I was appointed, I did a bit of horizon scanning with the Deputy Head: workload issues were definitely becoming more apparent. Our initial hypothesis was a lot of teaching staff were not as resilient as they had been in the past; I think we got that wrong. It wasn't resilience; it was the extra pressure and stress of life as a teacher and of outside life in general.

I think there was a melting pot of people not being able to cope and it manifested itself with staff taking more days off when not exhibiting physical signs of illness. I wouldn't say we had high presenteeism, but some people would come in and someone would say 'You're not well, you need to go home.' And when people would call in sick, when they left

DOI: 10.4324/9781003315766-10

the voice message you could tell it wasn't a physical illness. So there was a feeling that we needed to talk about what was going on: the Skinners' community is very open and communicative, there's a lot of talk about teaching practice. We talk with the students about their wellbeing and their mental health; we were very good at looking after our students – we still are. But at that point we were not as good at looking after ourselves as staff, and not necessarily addressing the issue, if it was mental health and wellbeing related.

We formed a working group of staff to discuss what we felt the issues were. One issue raised was that we had an extra form of entry so there was more marking, more students to see. When we looked at the numbers staff weren't teaching any more classes than they had previously taught, but our class sizes had crept up.

Louise Aston, one of our governors, pointed me in the direction of the Mind Wellbeing Index, and we thought it would give us a benchmark, to identify if it's something other schools are facing: if it's the latter we can learn from each other, if not we have to do something about it. It was really a process of triangulation, MIND send you an employer assessment, a senior leadership questionnaire to complete and you send them your HR policies. They do an audit and a staff survey, and they triangulate those things to see where you sit and to give advice on the actions you can take to improve things. The awards are gold, silver, bronze and 'committed to action.' In the first year we were 'committed to action,' and our feedback was all around introducing flexible working, leadership and looking at modelling good mental health and wellbeing practices.

The suggestions around flexible working seemed really difficult to do, because our thought process was, 'you have to have somebody in front of the students all the time, you can't have 30 boys sitting there with no-one in front of them – how are we going to achieve this?' We felt it made sense to repeat on a two-yearly cycle, so it gave us a year to work with the recommendations. We felt we did a really good job with students and parent voice, but we didn't have anything in our results that told us whether we looked after our staff well enough.

But we also give people the days off they want, and we write our timetable around that. We have four full-time staff who want to be able to collect or drop off their children on a Monday or a Friday. Without exception if staff ask for leave, it's paid. So I can go to my child's nativity; we have a system where people support each other to go and do things.

All school leaders know the difficulties of recruiting and retaining the best teachers – in England it's been a major national issue for some years now.

The latest figures,[1] from 2021, revealed some good news. The overall number of teachers in England increased, fuelled partly by a rise in the state pension age which led to some staying on longer. Overall, the number of (full-time equivalent) teachers rose by 4400 in a year, and the number of teaching assistants rose by the same amount. Despite this, the number of teachers has not kept pace with pupil numbers since 2010 and more recently there have been signs that the numbers entering the profession will start to drop, with teacher recruitment targets missed by more than 40 per cent in 2022.[2]

But having the right workforce in your school isn't just about recruiting good staff – it's also about keeping them. And a third of teachers leave within five years of qualifying – so huge amounts of potential are being lost. The international picture is similar: an evidence review by Education Support looked at 42 studies carried out in the United Kingdom, Europe, the United States and Australia between 2011 and 2021 and found stress and burnout were strongly linked with teachers' job satisfaction as well as with their intention to leave the profession – the review looked at one major international study which showed a quarter of all teachers were seriously considering quitting.

Work-life balance is a major issue: an American study in this review included interviews with teachers about the demands of balancing family life and work: "My husband and I weren't doing well," said one. "We went to marriage counselling... everything just revolved around what I was doing in school," ... "Retirement was something that would have never crossed my mind, but the added stress of the evaluations is too much... I have a friend... she retired because teaching was just not enjoyable anymore."

Whatever the national picture is where you are, the retention of teachers will be a key issue in your school. It's a good indicator of the levels of staff wellbeing, and it's a major bonus you will reap if you can get things right.

In England, the government has tackled the issue with a new teacher recruitment and retention strategy, which was launched in 2019 by the then Education Secretary Damian Hinds. Its aim is to put support for teachers – particularly new teachers – at the heart of all schools[3]: this Early Career Framework comes with a funded two-year package of support, but the strategy is also supposed to be about changing school culture in a way that supports teacher wellbeing.

"People enter teaching motivated by the chance to change lives. I am determined that those who are called to this noble profession stay in it, where they will continue to inspire children for many years to come," Hinds said in his introduction to the strategy.

Much of the research and statistics are about teachers, their recruitment and retention. We should not forget support staff, as we are also seeing them leave in greater numbers and many schools are having greater difficulty in recruiting them.

Getting staff on board

Whenever your current or prospective staff members interact with your school and the people in it, they are being influenced in how they think. They evaluate and at some point they reach a conclusion: either they want to be a part of it, or they don't. We can think about these interactions as 'moments of truth.'

These are a big part of determining how well you attract and keep staff, so they are crucial to the long-term success of your school.

A significant number of such moments happen while staff interact with senior and middle leaders. Chapter 6 looked at how you can provide a great foundation for an effective and well-led school and to underpin your people strategy.

Now we will take a look at how you can manage the life cycle of each staff member, from that initial positive 'moment of truth' when they realise they like what they see in your school, to developing them, through to the day when you bid them farewell.

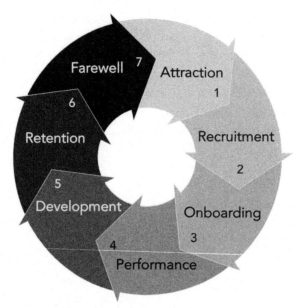

Illustration 7.1 Seven stages of the employee lifecycle – from attraction to farewell

Staff attraction

The very first step is employee attraction. This is all about generating interest in your school. It is more than simply sharing good news stories, as important as this is; I am sure you will tell the local paper what's going on and do your best to shout about what a great culture the school has.

But this initial attraction needs to be embedded as part of a comprehensive human resources strategy, and of course that involves much more than the odd press release. Even when you don't have vacancies, you should be identifying opportunities to get your message out to your ideal candidates and to give them reasons to engage with you.

Remember the best ambassadors you have are those already working with you: why would they tell anyone how great a place this is to work in, unless it really is? So you need to start with them. For instance, you might think about how well you manage professional development opportunities, flexible working and the offer of part-time roles for those who need them. Every time you do something to help a current member of staff manage their work-life balance better, you're creating an opportunity – hopefully when they run into teachers at other schools and they chat about their respective schools, and their respective heads' management styles, your staff member will have something good to say.

Use your staff to attract and recruit others – use them in videos, ask them to share why they love working in your school. Prospective staff would much prefer to hear from others like them.

Recruiting for your school (including teacher recruitment)

You are recruiting in a highly competitive market in which – depending on the position or subject – there may well be a national shortage of qualified candidates.

Management theory gives us a two-pronged means of looking at this: there are 'hygiene factors' or 'dissatisfiers' which can prove negative if you get them wrong, and there are 'motivators' which will be positive if you get them right. So the 'hygiene factors' in recruitment include the job description, person specification, application form and job advert. The materials produced by different schools often look similar, so are there ways you can make yours different? Perhaps by the questions you ask or by making the process simpler and easier – maybe ask them to make a short video about why they want the job, rather than having to fill in a big application form.

Job interviews and selection days are an opportunity to talk about your motivators: things like opportunities to develop and to achieve; the ways you recognise and reward good work. Ask yourself: "What would the best MAT or school in the world do?"

Be proud of your school and focus on attitude and cultural fit rather than just skills and experience. You should offer feedback to every candidate. Your time is tight and in demand, but taking time to deliver brief feedback will set you apart from other schools and MATs. There are relatively straightforward ways of doing this without adding time to the process. For example, ask the person who looks through the application forms to highlight, for all candidates, one positive thing that stands out, as well as the main reason they are not called for interview. You can then share this brief feedback by email, form or even via a short video (there are plenty of free ways of doing this, such as using Loom). Imagine the wow factor something like this would create.

The candidates in your recruitment exercise may apply again in future, and they probably will share their experience with others. Try to imagine how you can generate goodwill and even excitement, even for those who don't get the job.

Onboarding school staff

The term 'onboarding' is worth unpicking a bit. It isn't the same as induction. Onboarding is about helping staff to absorb and eventually to encapsulate the culture of the school. It isn't about their first hour, day or even week. It's the start of an ongoing process of support and challenge.

It begins on the day you appoint them, and it continues as you keep in touch from then until they start – how can you reinforce their belief that they have made the right decision to join you? Sharing key communications on people-related matters – development, benefits, access to resources and a line manager – can help them to feel they belong.

You may well be desperate to get your new teaching recruit or support staff member into their role on day one because they're in such high demand, but week one should include much more than that.

In that first week they should meet the CEO, principal or headteacher and other senior leaders; they should have lunch with a group of teachers; they should spend quality time with their department manager. They should have a personal plan to cover the coming months; regular one-to-one time; coaching; feedback; training; regular two-way reviews; a first career conversation and more.

It will make a big difference if on arrival the new recruit's line manager can tell them how much they have been looking forward to this, how valuable they will be and how big a difference their contribution will make. Ideally, the colleagues they will be working with should do this too. This will create a sense of belonging, which is so important to wellbeing.

Performance

Managing the performance of individual staff members is not just about delivering strong results. It is also a big part of staff wellbeing: when poor performance or behaviour is not tackled early, it can lead to resentment among others affected by it – and then those others may consciously or unconsciously suffer their own dips in performance.

Line managers often perceive dealing with staff issues as 'difficult.' But it will help if you can take out that word, and see it simply as a conversation. What you need is good preparation, the collection of evidence, the ability to ask questions, listening skills and a commitment to diarising and following up.

Make sure there is an ongoing dialogue and regular one-to-ones, rather than a single annual or bi-annual review. It takes time, particularly at the beginning, but it will save significant time in the long run.

Of course performance isn't just about managing people who need to improve, it is also about supporting others by using strengths and building on what is already strong performance.

Development

At an early stage of the employee lifecycle, think about the development opportunities you offer – do they fit with your staff members' interests and agendas as well as the school's? Going back to that management theory, development should be a motivator. If you are on their agenda, at least as much as your own, then they will see the benefits of being in your school and of staying there.

Development cannot simply be about short twilight sessions, 15-minute briefings, inset days and workshop merry-go-rounds. It is about career conversations, an agreed long- and short-term plan which is highly relevant to the individual.

Having a process to identify talent and then agreeing how to accelerate the development of those individuals, both for their benefit and for the school, is key. Providing opportunities to take on additional responsibility, to mix with other talented staff, to have a mentor, to take national qualifications or other training will all be part of the mix.

Staff retention

Each of the other five steps will strongly influence your chances of retaining great staff.

Identify and manage talented staff early, know what roles are at risk and have candidates ready and able to step into them. Build a succession plan for every level within your school.

You should also create alternative career paths. Keep in mind that not everyone is cut out to be a school leader. Strong classroom performers need to be rewarded without having to progress along a leadership path.

Big MATs are able to tackle this with cluster, regional and national roles, but if you're a single school or a smaller MAT, you may need to be creative. Flexible working and clear plans to retain those going on maternity leave need to be key parts of your strategy. If you are a MAT, you will want to consider ways of enabling staff to move between your schools more easily so that you can keep people within your family while allowing them to develop or to fit their working lives with their other commitments.

One way of managing this is using the nine-box grid.

Created by Mckinsey as long ago as 1970, the grid is designed to identify talent, to see how employees are performing and assess their potential. It became popular because it provided a more rounded way of assessing employees. It covers delivering objectives (track record), how they are delivered (behaviours), their likely stretch (can the employee perform at a higher level) and ambition (do they want to progress).

Assessing all four areas facilitates the plotting of employees against their performance and their potential. Depending on their score for each of these, they will be placed in one of nine boxes. You can see an example of this in the diagram below. This is taken from https://mypeoplestrategy.com,[4] and is a nine box grid process designed for the education sector.

Illustration 7.2 Nine-box grid, my people strategy

Where an employee is placed will suggest action that you might take to either manage performance, provide training or support, accelerate their development or a range of other interventions. As well as helping decide how best to lead each employee, the grid will provide a range of insights. These include quickly identifying those at risk of leaving, the likely impact of them leaving, their readiness for promotion, likely next and highest role and whether anyone is identified to replace them.

For multi-academy trusts and school groups in particular and larger schools, it is a great way of highlighting talent, opportunities and potential issues. For larger groups of schools that are geographically well located, it should minimise the likelihood of losing staff by managing placements and promotions between schools.

Other actions you might take will include the stay and exit interviews that were shared in Chapter 2.

Farewell

It's inevitable that some staff will move on. They may not be meeting expectations, despite being given support, and/or perhaps teaching really isn't for them. In this case, you can help them to depart in a prompt, professional and compassionate way, so that the way they tell others about it enhances your reputation and encourages others to work with you.

Maybe they're ready for promotion and you don't have an opportunity for them within the school or maybe there are others ahead of them in the 'queue.' In this case, you can proactively support them to find the role they want, even when it's external – though in the case of larger MATs and school groups, as mentioned above, internal opportunities ought to be found in most cases.

You may be disappointed to lose them but if they join another school and tell their new colleagues what a fantastic place they came from, that will build your reputation as an employer of choice and aid your recruitment. Maybe in the future, the right job *will* come up at the right time in your school, and then maybe they'll be back.

SINÉAD ORMSTON, ASSISTANT HEADTEACHER, THE SKINNERS' SCHOOL, TUNBRIDGE WELLS

One of the big features is we have 3.36 club on a Friday. School finishes at 3.35 and 3.36 is, 'come and have a sociable drink.' Lots of people will have one and go back to work, or they might finish their work and then go and see if anyone's in the pub. We try to set new staff a buddy who's not in their department, not their line manager. We have a school gym and staff have access, we have things like staff football, various groups of people who organise different staff events. Just after year 11 and 13 have left we do a staff wellbeing week, a whole host of activities as a kind of taster of things you could do on the school site during the day – art teachers do drawing courses, we've had jelly printing, a poetry group, a daily walk, a daily run. It's an opportunity to talk about our health and wellbeing and things we've come across during the year.

Certainly retention is better now. We still struggle with recruitment but I think that's a nationwide issue. But we have students who come to train and stay, we have teachers who left and who have reapplied for jobs because they know what we do: There's been a marked improvement.

Building effective activities on top of strong wellbeing foundations will help staff feel they belong.

Putting a people strategy together

School leaders are time-poor, and many schools are financially constrained. Delivering an effective and long-term people strategy isn't easy and is likely to need specialist HR support, as well as hard work. But if recruiting staff from a diminishing labour market and keeping more of them for longer is important to you – and it absolutely should be – then you have little choice. Start by prioritising every-day behaviours of leaders, as detailed in Chapter 6, and improve staff wellbeing so your school or MAT really *is* a great place to work. Then work through each of the other stages, prioritising and taking small and continuing steps.

Tackling this is not a time or financial cost, even though you will have to spend both. It is an investment with a significant return attached to it. Work out what this is likely to be in the form of future management time savings, impact on results and substantially lower staff costs.

Chapter 7: Key points

What's the word on the street about your school? Chances are you're recruiting from the local area – people talk to each other, so reputation is key. Think about every stage in the 'lifecycle' of an employee:

- **Attraction:** See above: give out good vibes in every way, and the job's done for you. Think about using staff videos on your website and in your attraction and recruitment.

- **Recruiting:** Think about what will differentiate you from others and how you can stand out. Think how the best school in the world would look to a candidate, and what steps that school would take to recruit them, for example always providing feedback.

- **Onboarding:** New recruits need to have support so they can understand the culture and what's expected, so they feel they belong. This starts from the day they are appointed and is much more than their first day. It is how they meet senior leaders, their line manager and colleagues and how they are managed and developed.

- **Performance:** Keep up a dialogue, don't wait for things to go wrong before engaging staff members – ensure this is an ongoing dialogue, as well as holding effective appraisals.

- **Development:** From day one, you should agree where this staff member is going in addition to discussing how they can support your school. What's their agenda; how can you help them meet it?

- **Retention:** This is not just about the rewards you can offer, although these are important. As well as delivering across the other six stages in the employee lifecycle, think about how you build wellbeing and other factors such as flexibility into the culture.

- **Farewell:** When someone moves on, make sure it's a positive experience: even when they move on through capability, how can you ensure this is dealt with effectively and with compassion? When people move on through promotion, this should be a partnership, in which you have supported their development. If you are part of a multi-academy trust or district, have a clear plan to manage careers and promotions. When people do leave unexpectedly, make sure you understand why – that's golden information. There's an exit interview template in the chapter. There is also a stay interview template – it is even better to ask questions about what will encourage staff members to stay with you.

- **Putting a people strategy together:** These stages, together with the everyday experiences of staff, form part of your people strategy. If effective, they will support the reputation of your school as one where staff choose to work and stay. In developing this, think long-term and don't crisis-manage.

Notes

1 Department for Education (2021). *School workforce in England: November 2021.* [online] gov.uk. Available at: https://www.gov.uk/government/statistics/school-workforce-in-england-november-2021.
2 My People Strategy (n.d.). *Making succession planning easier for schools and MATs.* [online] Available at: https://mypeoplestrategy.com/ [Accessed 14 December 2022].
3 DfE Recruitment and Retention Strategy (2019) https://www.gov.uk/government/publications/teacher-recruitment-and-retention-strategy
4 Walker, A. (2022). *DfE misses secondary teacher recruitment target by over 40%.* [online] schoolsweek.co.uk. Available at: https://schoolsweek.co.uk/dfe-misses-secondary-teacher-recruitment-target-by-over-40/ [Accessed 15 December 2022].

8 Making staff feel valued

"How can I find the time?"

BEN SOLLY, PRINCIPAL OF UPPINGHAM COMMUNITY COLLEGE, RUTLAND

My first headship was in a school in Lutterworth that at the time was heavily unionised, and staff were quite distrusting of senior leadership. And they certainly didn't trust me as someone coming in aged 33, so I had to fight this culture of distrust.

In Leicestershire one of the things they do for new heads is pair you up with the head of a good or outstanding school, and so I would go once a term for a coaching session. I hadn't really studied leadership, just got by on emotional intelligence and being reasonably proficient at my job. And he said to me, 'Look, if you're going to have longevity in your career, you've got to study those things. Because you can't implement them in your school with any authenticity, or sustainability if you don't understand them. So I threw myself into it.

I think distributed leadership was probably the first thing that I really looked at, largely because I knew I had a really vast school on my hands and I needed to create a model where there were really high expectations of the staff but people had ownership of it.

DOI: 10.4324/9781003315766-11

And that's evolved into this vision: I know that if I put the staff first, they will feel empowered and trusted. And if I get the right people on board and give them the conditions in which they can thrive, they will do an amazing job. Because the teachers, the support staff, have all got the conditions in which they can work brilliantly and continually strive to get better, and therefore the students get a great deal. And one of the most effective things I think I could do is remove all the **barriers, all the** *nonsense, all the bureaucracy that I think has always plagued teachers, to allow them to do their job to the best of their ability.*

Leaders at the school get the autonomy and the authority to make key decisions about their areas of responsibility. They can drive the strategy, they can make the key decisions, but they're accountable for delivering the outcomes. If you remove any one of those three elements it becomes problematic. If I don't give you the autonomy and the authority to drive it and if I micromanage you I cannot really hold you accountable. In one to ones with middle and senior leaders I would explicitly go through that AAA model, saying, you'll be trusted to do this. You're the expert, how can I tell the science department how to run their physics curriculum? For me to interfere with that would be absurd, really. You can make the decisions, you can drive the strategy.

But then I would say to people, the accountability is shared between the two of us because if it doesn't work I will hold myself accountable as much as you should hold yourself accountable, and then work out why it didn't work. That's empowering.

It probably took a year to earn trust from them. And I think one of the things I also learned was that there are some flaws with that model, because if you if you give that level of trust and autonomy to somebody who's not effective, or who's lazy, or deliberately disruptive, they might not do the work, or they do the work really badly, or they can use that freedom to be even more disruptive.

When I moved here it was different: the head had been in post 10 years and she had done a really good job but I think the school was ready for change, so I think they were quite enthusiastic about the younger person coming in with fresh ideas. And it wasn't my first headship.

People were deeply committed to school but really open and trusting. I think distributed leadership has enabled our middle and senior leaders to really own their areas of responsibility. I think it's helped drive an authentic but a self-sustaining leadership model across the school. Everything doesn't hinge on me, it hinges on all those other leaders who are taking the school vision and then delivering it in their discrete areas.

So the model we have here is the senior leaders are linked with a middle leader and we try to use that as a coaching relationship rather than as a line manager. The senior leader acts as facilitator so that the middle leader becomes a bit more autonomous, and that's how we tried to develop capacity across the school.

We employed an external leadership coach to work with senior leaders, and that was probably one of the most transformational things we've done. Its permeated throughout the organisation so people maybe have slightly less responsibility will get access to them as well. It really helps them become more effective practitioners.

As a leader, staying connected with your staff, acknowledging, listening and responding to them on a daily basis should be a core part of your work. It isn't an add-on; it's fundamental to ensuring you run not just a happy, healthy school but also a successful one.

You know this already, of course – why else would you be reading this book? But there are different levels, or rather maybe depths, of communication, support and nurturing to which you can aspire.

While it's right that staff need to take responsibility for their own performance and wellbeing, leaders have such an important part to play: give staff a bigger voice and they will be much more likely to thrive. This chapter will introduce some of the types of techniques you might wish to employ to help you facilitate staff voice and build on the individual leadership behaviours introduced in Chapter 6.

Keep the conversation going

The three major ways that staff have a direct voice, outside of performance reviews, are one-to-one discussions, wider meetings and staff surveys, in that order. And there is also representative participation, in which others including line manager, peers, colleagues and organisations such as unions speak for others: this is secondary to more direct approaches.

The Chartered Institute of Personnel and Development, the body which represents human resources professionals, publishes an annual Good Work Index Report[1] which is worth reading. It shares the significance of voice, and the impact it can have both on how staff feel valued and the likelihood of them giving greater discretionary effort.

For busy leaders in school, finding time for regular contact with staff can be hard. Even if you find time, your team members may not be available. So much of school life is timetabled and inflexible. Opening conversations that have the power to support wellbeing and bring about positive change is particularly difficult.

Improve teamwork

Building teamwork into everyday life is key to success it sits at the heart of how well leaders keep in touch and communicate with their immediate and wider teams.

Even when you make clear your availability and that you're listening, not every conversation you have will be an honest one. Often it's easier for staff to tell you what they think you want to hear, rather than what they really want to say. But if you can build a more open, resilient, positive and communicative culture in your school, you will reap rich rewards.

What does good teamwork look like? Read through this list from Spiegel and Torres'[2] *Manager's Official Guide to Teamworking* and ask yourself whether this happens in your institution:

Criteria for effective teamwork

Team members:

- Share a common identity.

- Share goals and objectives.

- Share success and failure.

- Work together and join in the work.

- Have rules that are followed by all members.

- Have a team leader.

- Make decisions as a team.

- Have a wide variety of backgrounds.

A team will have more opportunities to be successful if:

- It has detailed objectives to be achieved.

- It has an organisational culture that supports the concept of teamwork.

- There is sufficient time for training and to conduct debate and discussion.

- Its members have knowledge and diversification of problem-solving techniques.

Not everyone is a great team worker, of course. This list of likely weaknesses will help you to identify and to address possible deficits within your school's teams:[3]

- Lack of sensitivity towards diversified individual's characters.

- Less proficient communication.

- Lack of ability to lead.

- Inability to motivate.

- Inability to delegate wisely.

- Not calm when dealing with problems.

- Less skilled in leading a meeting or discussion.

- Unable to form creative plans.

- Finds it difficult to reach agreement with others.

Build psychological safety

In 2012, a group of Google employees decided to investigate what made for an effective team and what differentiated those that were successful from those that weren't. First, they reviewed academic research looking at how teams worked, before reviewing and collecting their own internal data.

From this, they scrutinised a wide number of factors, including:

- The degree to which team members socialised.

- Whether their educational backgrounds were similar.

- Did they have the same hobbies?

- Were they of a similar demographic?

- Were they all outgoing or were some more internal in focus?

- Was gender balance important?

These and other factors were considered as part of their people analytics. What they found was that none of these were important in determining a team's likely performance – they could find no patterns.

They called the project Aristotle and they spent over a year looking at behaviour and team norms. They identified the top five things that underpinned team high performance. These are shown below in a countdown from 5 to 1.[4]

5.	Does the work the team do matter and have impact
4.	Do team members feel their work is personally meaningful
3.	Are objectives, roles and plans clearly defined
2.	Can team members depend on one another
1.	Do team members have psychological safety

Illustration 8.1 Five key determinants of strong team performance: Amy Edmondson, Novartis Professor of Leadership and Management, Harvard Business School

For many working in schools, numbers 4 and 5 are why they entered the profession. 2 and 3 are delivered by the school leadership and by colleagues and are also underpinned by number 1 – psychological safety. This was the most important factor and a term popularised by Professor Amy Edmondson:[5] A belief that one will not be punished or humiliated for speaking up with ideas, questions, concerns or mistakes, and that the team is safe for interpersonal risk-taking.

In one study she worked on the hypothesis: "Do better hospital teams make fewer medication errors?" She used a standard team survey to assess effectiveness, and trained nurse investigators visited a number of teams in two hospitals every couple of days for six months.

The research set out the number of human medication errors per 1000 patients for each team. This data was cross-checked against the team effectiveness data and the findings showed the exact opposite of what was expected. Those scoring highest in effectiveness were showing the greatest number of errors, while those scoring lowest had the fewest number of errors. It appeared better teams were making more mistakes.

On further investigation, she asked: "What if the better teams had a climate of openness that allows them to report errors and even get to the bottom of why they occurred?" A research assistant followed up and found this is what was happening – rather than having the fewest mistakes, the lower scoring teams were simply concealing them. The team had no psychological safety, and a culture that looked to blame.

If you think about the high stakes accountability in schools, for example for results and inspection, creating a psychologically safe environment is important if you want to improve staff wellbeing and to reap the benefits this brings.

Amy Edmondson suggested three practical strategies:

● Frame the work as a learning problem, not an execution problem. Make it clear there is uncertainty ahead and enormous interdependence.

● Acknowledge your own fallibility – say simple things like: "I may miss something; I need to hear from you." This creates more safety for people speaking up.

● Model curiosity; ask a lot of questions. This creates a necessity for voice.

This is not a trade-off against accountability or expecting high performance. She saw these as two separate dimensions. You can still push hard but it is equally important to ensure people are not afraid of each other or mistakes.

These dimensions were put into the model below, showing the trade-off between accountability and psychological safety.

If your culture has neither, this is the apathy zone. If you lean too far towards psychological safety, you are creating a comfort zone. For instance, if we always pick young people up when they fall down, and if we fight their battles instead of helping them to fight their own, we aren't helping them in the long run.

But it's more worrying where there is high accountability and low psychological safety – the anxiety zone. Perhaps, this is at least in part why young people and those working in education are seeing greater mental health challenges. Exam results are seen as so important for life and yet we do not help young children to develop the life skills to manage the stress and strain they will face later.

This goes for leaders and staff, too – you're only ever as good as your last inspection and there's little tolerance of mistakes – this zone is also referred to as the blame zone.

The final zone is the high-performance zone, where we have high expectations and build a culture in which appropriate risk-taking is encouraged and mistakes are treated as learning opportunities – that's why this is also called the learning zone.

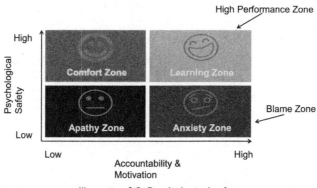

Illustration 8.2 Psychological safety

Embed coaching

In schools, there has been a tendency to associate coaching with remedial activity and a focus on poor performers. Yet in sport and business, it tends to be the elite and high performers who receive coaching. Coaching can and should be used with all members of your team in order to develop a culture of 'happy' high performance.

This isn't about becoming a coach: that isn't a leader's role. Rather it is about using coaching skills as a line manager and leader to improve personal and team effectiveness, staff engagement, motivation and of course, results.

What is coaching?

Coaching is a set of behaviours designed to raise awareness and develop responsibility in others by using effective questioning and listening skills.

Coaching bodies lack agreement on precise definitions, though there are generally agreed principles and characteristics which include:

● It's typically a non-directive development, helping others to find their own solutions, though leaders should share their own experiences at the appropriate time.

- It targets improvement and is often associated with high performers, high performance and results.

- It tends to focus on the development of specific skills and goals, and while usually associated with work, it should include personal attributes such as confidence or empathy as well as dealing with other life factors that affect performance.

- It forms the basis of a leadership style, and when delivered by an external coach, it will typically be for a short duration and a specific purpose.

- It has two key components: to raise awareness in the person being coached, for example: of the situation, opportunities or options, and to ask them to take personal responsibility for action.

- It is likely to cover both organisational and individual goals.

- It is a way of providing effective feedback.

- It will usually require a level of training and practice to achieve the necessary skills to be effective.

How does it differ from mentoring, which is far more widely used in schools?

Mentoring should involve the use of similar models and skills, such as questioning, listening, clarifying and feedback associated with coaching.

However, the term has tended to describe a relationship in which a more experienced colleague uses their greater knowledge and understanding of the job role, work or workplace to support the development of a more junior or inexperienced member of staff.

Mentoring relationships tend to be longer term than coaching arrangements. Traditionally, they are more directive, though to be more effective, mentors should use a coaching approach and provide learning opportunities for both parties.

When should you use coaching?

Coaching is often linked with performance improvement and the need to take remedial action. Yet coaching skills can be used in every situation – conversations, meetings, one-to-ones, with students and with parents. Coaching is a way of being and behaving that encourages participation and develops responsibility in others. It can take one minute and be just one question.

As a result, it builds capacity and saves significant time in the long run, though it will take time to develop and implement in the short term. This is one of the biggest barriers to its use.

Yet choose to adopt it, persevere and practise and the evidence shows you will get significant benefits in improved engagement, motivation, wellbeing, productivity, performance and results.

"Coaching is unlocking people's potential to maximise their own performance".
Sir John Whitmore, Author of 'Coaching for Performance'
and creator of the GROW coaching model.[6]

There are many ways you can adopt coaching in schools.

Some leaders might become experts through taking a coaching qualification through an external body, such as the Institute of Leadership and Management or the Chartered Management Institute, or through one of a number of external companies, some of whom specialise in education.

These leaders then pass on their skills and coordinate an approach to build coaching capacity across the school.

Alternatively there is online continuing professional development (CPD) available from a range of providers, for example the Welbee Toolkit provides an introduction to the skills needed and focuses on how line managers can use coaching in the workplace.[78]

Make praise part of every day

Recognition improves engagement and performance. Schools are often great at shout-outs, staff messages and saying well done and thank you by email. Yet they often miss out on giving praise in the moment. It is hard to do this when your staff are dispersed across your site or sites, particularly those in their respective classrooms; yet when it's done well, the impact can be significant – it's been suggested that if done consistently well it can deliver more than a pay rise.

Set a goal to catch people doing things right and ask all leaders to do the same. This means being in the present and spotting the brilliant things that happen each day. Imagine the impact if you and everyone in the senior leadership team caught three people every day... people copy each other, and it's contagious.

Here's what one head teacher had to say about trying this technique:

Walking around the school and talking to staff, it was so easy to focus on what hadn't been done that day, what had gone wrong, and the misbehaviour of pupils. It was also clear that we were all rushing, with our heads down, from one meeting or classroom to another.

I asked myself and others how many staff members we had praised that day. We are often good at this with pupils, but we noticed we weren't applying the same skills with team members and colleagues.

While we were doing all the usual shout-outs, I know that in the moment, well-delivered, regular, and authentic praise and recognition improves engagement and performance. Yet we were missing out on this when it came to our staff.

We set a shared goal for all our leaders to catch three staff members doing something right each day and sharing this with each other. It has proved to be infectious and had a big impact. In my view, it's the fastest way to build staff wellbeing into the school culture.

BEN SOLLY, PRINCIPAL OF UPPINGHAM COMMUNITY COLLEGE, RUTLAND

Through my coaching I've been introduced to the concept of invisible rewards, incentivizing and prioritising either the characteristics you want people to display and being really deliberate about when you praise people, and what you praise them for.

The basic premise, and this sounds really weird to start with, is to stop saying 'thank you' for things. Everyone's always saying 'thank you,' and that devalues the word. So stage one is if I want to praise somebody for demonstrating one of the school values in a meeting, I might say to them, 'I was really impressed with how you used honesty in that meeting and tell them what they said.' Using the phrase 'I was impressed with' or 'I am grateful for' allows me to praise and demonstrate gratitude, whilst preserving 'thank you' for when I really want it to have profound impact.

Stage two is making that a little bit more public. So if honesty is the attribute I want the whole organisation to really promote I might then praise this publicly. I might say it in the bulletin or I might raise it in a team meeting and ask the staff member to talk us through it. The third stage is to invite someone to a meeting, to use this opportunity to thank them sincerely, because what they have done is truly outstanding, or it has gone way above and beyond what is expected of them. This is the final tier and the only time I would genuinely use the phrase 'thank you.'

This has massive impact because I've upheld that authentic approach to praise.

Managing by walking around?

Managing by Walking Around (MBWA) as a way of keeping your ear to the ground, engaging with and praising individuals, is a well-recognised technique which originated from Hewlett Packard's David Packard in the 1940s and was popularised by best-selling author Tom Peters. Widely used in business and included in graduate and development programmes, it has helped many corporate businesses reinforce the behaviours they want to see. Maybe you're already using parts of this technique in your own school, though given the challenges of timetabling and lack of focus on leading people in leadership development within education, you are likely to be in a minority if you are.

MBWA involves senior managers in directly observing front line work, though it isn't simply the odd scheduled learning walk or observation. If it's your habit to regularly be out and about in your workplace, observing staff and students and learning about their routines and resources, identifying issues, taking suggestions and giving feedback and praise, this is possibly you.

It was also introduced to and used in hospitals, though the evidence for this type of technique within the health sector is very mixed. A randomised study by Harvard Business School[9] compared perceived results in a group of hospitals where MBWA was introduced, compared with those in hospitals where it wasn't. After 18 months, the nurses in the hospitals which implemented the programme actually felt the result had been negative, rather than positive.

The researchers concluded that putting senior managers on the front line was only helpful if it enabled active problem-solving. If the programme was to work well, it needed to prioritise easy-to-solve problems, and the managers involved had to be held to account for getting things fixed. They mentioned that better results had been obtained for the Japanese Kaizen method in which managers visit the factory floor to listen and deal with issues: This was likely to be because Kaizen 'Gemba Walks' involved managers being trained in structured techniques, and they used them to fix as many problems as possible within a given time period, they said.

Just walking about randomly, popping your head into classrooms and talking to support staff, is more likely to make staff anxious and won't do anything to foster a greater sense of wellbeing. But if it's clear your visits are unthreatening and designed simply to identify things that are going well, to praise people and to find easily fixable issues that might be causing daily headaches, then do go ahead. If you do this well, your staff will know you're there to support them and not to judge them.

To do it well means doing it with a clear purpose and plan.

How do leaders MBWA?

You may know much of what is written below and as this book is aimed at all leaders, this covers the basics.

First you need to overcome that feeling that you are too busy and plan for it. Carve out time and ring-fence this in the calendar and treat it as if it were a lesson and non-negotiable. The impact it will have means it should be a priority.

Think about key topics and things that might be going on and think through conversation starters you can use. Keep it simple and treat it as you would any casual conversation. Ask questions and be curious, but make sure you are not interrogating or being intrusive. You can ask them how they are, about work and what they have on and also what might be going on for them out of work.

After asking, remember to listen and follow up on what they say. While you can work out a range of questions before starting, don't try and think of what to say next while they are talking – it is OK to have a gap after they finish. When they see you are interested in what they are doing or have to say, they are likely to open up and be more receptive. This builds rapport.

You should also plan your route and the people you intend to speak with and ensure these change so you cover the full site or sites and all staff members over a time period. You don't want staff to say, 'here you come again,' as you take the same route or do the same thing. You can also use a spreadsheet or checklist to cover all staff and to check who you have checked in with over a week, month, half-term or term. Often people spend more time with those who work near them or whom they feel more comfortable talking with, and this provides a sense check to make sure your time is effectively spread.

One key part of MBWA is catching people doing the right thing. This should go beyond your planned MBWA and covers any time you are outside your place of work, whether that is an office, classroom or elsewhere. It means being present and in the moment, and not thinking about all the tasks that need doing while walking through the school.

Instead, just as teachers do in the classroom, be on the lookout for anything that you can praise. It has to be authentic and specific, yet so many great things happen every day in and across your school that finding them should not be difficult if you are looking for them. Doing this not only shows staff you value them; it reinforces the behaviours and actions you want to see.

For many leaders, it will require a change in behaviour, and in some cases, these have been embedded for some time. To support this approach across the school, you may need to provide support and training, even if it is simply creating time to talk about it and share experiences. As part of this, you can encourage leaders to set themselves a trigger at the end of each day to remind them that they were to catch someone doing something right – for example, a post-it note on the steering wheel; a calendar notice or alarm on the phone.

Build discussing MBWA and catching people doing things right into senior team meetings – every two or three weeks. Don't ask people to bring a list of who they have talked with or praised, as this will simply make it a chore and add stress. Instead create a psychologically safe place where they can talk about how they are finding it, including admitting difficulties. By continuing to share, you will help it become a leadership habit which others are likely to copy.

Include it as an objective in the appraisals of leaders and make how they deliver as important as what they deliver. As a senior team, make sure you are role models and that you coach other leaders on developing this important skill.

For many school leaders it will be new. Developing this as an organisational competency will give you a competitive advantage as part of your people strategy – it will develop skills, build your reputation, improve retention, reduce absences, lead to better financial performance and further raise student attainment.

While it will take time and practice for it to become a habit, it is a relatively simple and non-costly way of improving the wellbeing of staff, when compared to other options.

Difficult conversations

MBWA and giving praise are important, and they need to be matched by holding staff members to account on performance. If something is not up to expectations, feedback should be delivered professionally and with compassion.

Many leaders, particularly line managers new to the role, think of these as difficult conversations. What differentiates 'difficult' conversations from other conversations? Conversations can be 'difficult' for many reasons, including:

● The conversation may have the potential to make people anxious or to feel uncomfortable – for example, when you are discussing personal challenges or a distressing subject matter.

● The topic of conversation could be cutting across the personal preferences of the other person, for example, when you are changing ways of working.

● The stakes may be high, or the conversation's outcome could have significant consequences – for example, when discussing the need to improve performance, change behaviour or if it may result in capability or disciplinary action or involves the possibility of redundancy.

● The topic of the conversation may be one where opinions will vary, and people may have firmly held views – for example, conversations relating to pedagogy.

Difficult conversations often feature a degree of uncertainty regarding how the person you are speaking to may react. This may also mean that those carrying them out may feel a range of emotions. Think about a difficult conversation you have had – what emotions were you feeling before, during and after it? And what about the person on the other end?

Difficult conversations often take leaders out of their comfort zones, and you may be worried that they could turn into a confrontation or that they will not go as planned. This feeling of anxiety is a natural and understandable response to a situation with an uncertain outcome. A study by the Chartered Management Institute found that two-thirds of managers felt stressed or anxious if they knew a 'difficult' conversation was coming, and 11 per cent said they suffered from nightmares or poor sleep in the build-up.

Research by Acas[10] suggests this feeling of anxiety is often due to leaders not feeling they are in complete control of the conversation. If you recognise this, you may feel that you are not in control of:

- The facts – you feel you do not know the full facts or what the other person perceives the facts to be.

- Your emotions – you may worry that you won't be able to manage your emotions or that there is the potential for a heated exchange of views.

- How the other person will respond and their emotions – for example, you may be anxious that the other person may become upset or angry.

The level of support senior leaders give (or get) is important and you might be concerned about whether those you are accountable to will agree with your approach or the decisions you take.

You should prepare for a conversation, and where you perceive there may be difficulties you can anticipate all the different things that could happen and prepare a response to them before the conversation takes place.

By doing this, you will reduce the stress you will feel and will be able to think clearly.

TCUP, or Thinking Clearly Under Pressure, is a process introduced by Sir Clive Woodward to the England Rugby Team,[11] and he attributes it as a key reason why they were able to win the World Cup in 2003. He now shares this technique with organisations and individuals across the globe.

He organised regular short meetings with rules, such as the start and end time, the right people in the room, a clear agenda and an outcome needed.

He would pose specific scenarios, for example, the team are 16–12 points down with 4 minutes to go. Team members would come to the front and quickly answer what they would do.

Then they discussed as a team and no one left until they had an agreed answer – but they had to finish in the allotted time to replicate pressure.

Continually doing this, and covering more and more situations and scenarios about what the other team might do, meant that whenever they came across it in a match they knew what to do and were able to respond effectively rather than to react.

While you are more likely to be on your own or may be able to discuss things with one or a few colleagues, these principles work well for 'difficult' conversations.

Think ahead about all the different things that could happen and have a response ready. The following are some examples of possible scenarios.

What will you do if someone becomes upset and cries?

Always have a box of tissues with you and work out what you will say – "It's OK to be upset, let's just take a moment. Would you like a tissue?" In most cases, they will recover quickly and you can move on, though if they remain very upset, offer to reschedule.

What will you do if someone becomes angry or even aggressive?

If you feel this might occur (hopefully this is rare), you might invite someone to attend with you. If the staff member becomes angry during the conversation, you can give them the opportunity to vent, then ask for a break or offer them a coffee. Take action that allows them to calm down before proceeding. If you have strategies worked out in advance, it means you think clearly when there is pressure.

What will you do if they refuse to acknowledge there is an issue?

If someone refuses to acknowledge there is an issue after being given the opportunity to respond to questions, you should share the evidence – this needs to be specific and cannot be your opinion. Evidence is hard to dispute.

If they still will not accept there is a problem, you will need to go on and tell them what the expected resolution is, for example, the specific ways in which their performance will need to improve. You may also have to share what action will be needed to get there and by when. Ideally you will ask them to summarise and agree this. If they do not, the outcome you have set needs to be the expectation and a date for review will need to be set.

Now make a list of other scenarios you think may happen and that could cause you to feel anxious or under pressure.

Under each one, detail some steps you would take to address these.

Even with good preparation and thinking through these different scenarios, it is likely you will come across something you have not experienced before. See this as an opportunity and a good experience – you can now add it to the playbook for next time. You can also train yourself to give yourself time to think through a new experience.

Dealing with pressure is all about anticipating the future and the action to take, and ensuring that it is thought through.

Being clear how you can handle situations. Without TCUP, people freeze and choke or make poor decisions.

Finally, the other person also needs to have the opportunity to prepare, if the conversation relates to issues such as performance, behaviours or disciplinary matters. This may need an initial conversation to share the need for a full discussion and sharing of the issue.

They should also be given the opportunity to invite a colleague or other person to attend, including a union representative if appropriate.

It is very easy to lose focus during a 'difficult' conversation and come away without a clear action or outcome, which may make the situation worse.

Once information has been shared, you have asked effective questions and have listened to and responded to the other person's views and opinions, you must work together to create a positive outcome from the discussion. As part of your discussion, ask the staff member what outcomes are needed to address the issue/concern or prevent the situation from occurring again in the future.

Asking open questions will be helpful here – remember that both you and the person you are talking with may need to adjust previously held views or preconceived outcomes.

If the person you are meeting with can identify the next steps themselves, then they are more likely to own the performance improvement needed. However, there may be occasions where the staff member can't set out clear steps, so they may need your assistance or direction, but it's essential to get their agreement to them.

Once an agreement has been reached on the next steps, clarify what has been decided, who is responsible for what; and set a workable timescale for agreed actions or changes. Depending on the topic of the 'difficult' conversation, you may also want to set a timescale for review or set a date/time for a follow-up meeting.

Whether you have been able to elicit the next steps from the other person or have had to tell them what is needed, it is very important that you ask them to summarise what will happen next. This is more likely to mean they take ownership. You can do this by asking them questions such as:

- What is the outcome you need to deliver?

- What will you do to deliver this?

- When will you do it?

- When will we review progress?

This last question is also important as without effective follow-up and review, the situation may remain unchanged.

If your follow-up or first review does not demonstrate the changes expected, you should repeat the process until such time as changes are made or you need to escalate to the next step, for example, capability.

Where conversations relate to performance or other matters that could lead to a capability procedure or disciplinary action, it is important school policies are followed right from the start.

Where a review shows a successful outcome, you should continue to follow up for a period beyond this and make sure the changes are embedded. Too often leaders think a change has been made, stop discussions at the first sign of success, only to see the issue arise once again.

Distributed leadership

Distributed leadership is a model based on sharing responsibility and accountability as widely as possible. If you can get this right, it can make a real difference in terms of improved performance and staff wellbeing: in brief, it gives agency and control to far more people within your school. It takes pressure off the senior leadership team, and it builds esteem among middle leaders and even more junior staff.

As with MBWA, distributed leadership will only work if it's carefully planned and carried out. It isn't about 'letting a thousand flowers bloom.' It's about you, as a leader, creating opportunities for others to lead.

Our case study principal, Ben Solly,[12] describes this as 'leadership by expertise' rather than leadership by role or years of experience. To do this, you'll need to have a high level of trust, transparency and mutual respect within your teams.

As we covered earlier in the book, providing leadership capacity is one of the single biggest challenges to improving outcomes and staff wellbeing. The demands placed on leaders and staff and time they have to spend doing non-leadership work is significant. There are few work sectors where this happens – in most as you are promoted to leadership positions much of your previous role is removed, and it is accepted the majority of your time will be spent leading others.

Finding solutions to this and creating the capacity needed for training, coaching and for regular one-to-one conversations, and developing people expertise is the fastest way to greater success.

Management specialist and best-selling author Tom Peters said: "Great leaders do not create followers, they create more leaders." This links very closely with building your people strategy, identifying and developing talent and creating a culture where coaching skills are a significant part of a leader's armoury.

Helping leaders to find their own solutions and supporting them to develop the behaviours and competencies we covered in Chapter 6 can best be delivered through one-to-one coaching, as well as training that is followed up by it. Providing all staff with the necessary knowledge and skills and allowing them to practise will ensure that leadership is seen and decisions are taken at all levels.

Leadership is an act and not a position – so teachers leading and supporting teaching assistants and those working in support roles leading the processes they manage, reduces workload and ensures the school is performing at its best. It also reduces workplace stress and improves staff wellbeing as you will be better meeting the Health and Safety Executive's Management Standards.

There is a good evidence base for distributed leadership. Researchers from Toronto, for instance,[13] surveyed more than 2500 teachers and also looked at data on language and maths results in their schools over three years. They found collective leadership techniques could explain a major part of the variation they saw in student achievement.

Leaders at the school have the autonomy and the authority to make key decisions about their areas of responsibility. They can drive the strategy, they can make the key decisions, but they're accountable for delivering the outcomes. If you remove any one of those three elements, it becomes problematic.

Finally, build greater self-awareness by encouraging leaders to ask for honest feedback, so they learn about blind spots in their management style and take account of differing staff member perspectives, meaning they will be more effective and inclusive in dealing with their needs.

Remind school leaders they can model courage and show that being vulnerable or making mistakes is not a weakness. Sometimes our greatest growth comes from the things we don't get right.

Chapter 8: Key points

Good staff wellbeing is all about culture and climate. Putting staff first is the best way to ensure students achieve their best academic and all-round outcomes. Here are eight key techniques you may wish to consider:

- **Keep the conversation going**: ensure staff have a voice. Life is busy and school timetables are inflexible but if you can schedule in regular one-to-ones with key colleagues, wider meetings and surveys, you will reap rewards. Build this into the life of your school so that everyone takes part, with senior and middle leaders seeing their team members regularly.

- **Build in teamwork**: team members should share a sense of identity; common goals; successes and failures. They should work together and follow the same rules and should make decisions collectively. There should be rules which everyone buys into and team members should have a variety of skills and backgrounds. A team will have more opportunities to be successful if it has clear objectives and sufficient time and skill and is supported by the organisational culture.

- **Create psychological safety**: balance accountability with making sure people are not fearful of making mistakes, so they are able to deliver their best performance.

- **Embed coaching**: coaching is designed to raise awareness and develop responsibility in others by using effective questioning and listening skills. It's usually non-directive, target-specific goals that form the basis of a leadership style by raising awareness of both opportunities and responsibilities. It is different from mentoring, which tends to be a longer and more directive process.

- **Make praise part of every day**: set a goal to catch people doing the right things every day, and ask other leaders to do the same: it builds morale and your culture: it's contagious.

- **Manage by walking around**: don't just walk about randomly, popping your head into classrooms: it makes staff anxious. Instead have a clear purpose and plan and build this into your own and organisational routines.

- **Don't avoid difficult conversations**: identify when these conversations need to happen and prepare for them – use TCUP (Thinking Clearly Under Pressure) and you will be ready for any eventuality. This process can be used for all situations you might face – meaning you are more likely to make the right decisions and deliver an effective outcome.

- **Implement distributed leadership**: this is a model based on sharing responsibility and accountability as widely as possible and it can make a real difference. It takes pressure off the senior leadership team, and it builds esteem among middle managers and even more junior staff.

Notes

1 CIPD (2021). *Good work index | survey reports.* [online] CIPD. Available at: https://www.cipd.co.uk/knowledge/work/trends/goodwork#gref [Accessed 14 December 2022].

2 Spiegel, J. and Torres, C. (1994). *Manager's Official Guide to Teamworking.* Hoboken, NJ: Wiley.

3 Don, Y. and Raman, A. (2020). School management and leadership: Teamwork in schools. *Multidisciplinary Journal of Instruction*, 1(2), pp.14–36. https://journal.mdji.org/index.php/MDJI/article/view/8

4 Google (2011). *re: Work.* [online] Withgoogle.com. Available at: https://rework.withgoogle.com/print/guides/5721312655835136/.

5 Edmondson, A. (1999). Psychological safety and learning behavior in work teams. *Administrative Science Quarterly*, [online] 44(2), pp.350–383. doi:10.2307/2666999, Edmondson, A.C. (1996). Learning from mistakes is easier said than done: Group and organizational influences on the detection and correction of human error. *The Journal of Applied Behavioral Science*, 32(1), pp.5–28. doi:10.1177/0021886396321001.

6 Whitmore, J. (2009). *Coaching for Performance: Growing Human Potential and Purpose.* 4th ed. London: Nicholas Brealey. Source: *Administrative Science Quarterly*, 44(2) (June, 1999), pp.350–383. Published by: Johnson Graduate School of Management, Cornell University Stable URL: http://www.jstor.org/stable/2666999

7 Mark Solomons, M. (n.d.). *Help centre.* [online] knowledge.welbee.co.uk. Available at: https://knowledge.welbee.co.uk/developing-coaching-skills [Accessed 14 December 2022].

8 Welbee (n.d.). *Fourteen proven ways to transform staff wellbeing in your school.* [online] Welbee. Available at: https://welbee.co.uk/wp-content/downloads/14_Proven_Ways_to_Transform_Staff_Wellbeing_in_Your_School.pdf.

9 Tucker, A. and Singer, S. (2014). The effectiveness of management-by-walking-around: A randomized field study. *Production and Operations Management*, 24. doi:10.1111/poms.12226.

10 Acas (2020). *Fear and trust in the evolving world of work | Acas.* [online] www.acas.org.uk. Available at: https://www.acas.org.uk/fear-and-trust-in-the-evolving-world-of-work.

11 CIO (2021). *Sir Clive Woodward's four steps to creating a winning culture.* [online] CIO. Available at: https://www.cio.com/article/199790/sir-clive-woodward-s-four-steps-to-creating-a-winning-culture.html [Accessed 15 December 2022].

12 Dr Alma Harris, Teacher magazine: https://www.teachermagazine.com/au_en/articles/distributed-leadership

13 Leithwood, K. and Mascall, B. (2008). Collective leadership effects on student achievement. *Educational Administration Quarterly*, 44(4), pp.529–561. doi:10.1177/0013161x08321221.

9 Managing workload

Schools are busy places, of course, and you're not going to change that fundamental fact. But you can cut out extraneous work and at the same time give staff the sense that they have a role in asking decisions about what really matters and what can be ditched. You will probably have reviewed things such as lesson planning, marking, data collection and report writing, as well as other areas that have a high impact.

You may already have reviewed England's Department for Education Workload Reduction Toolkit[1] and other resources. If your school is in a sector or country that is not covered by this, it may still provide a useful framework for you.

We've visited the Health and Safety Executive (HSE) Management Standards a few times now: they form a useful structure to remind us of the primary sources of stress at work. The first two are Demands and Control.[2] Both of these are central to ensuring workload is manageable; the processes we'll discuss here should help you to reduce the demands on staff as well as increasing their sense of Control.

We know from research by the UCL Institute of Education in London, which we covered in Chapter 1[3] that teachers' average working hours have remained at a similar level for at least 20 years. The research suggested that pre-Covid those hours were dropping slightly. But more recently there have been signs that progress has stalled: the National Foundation for Educational Research looked at the picture in

 DOI: 10.4324/9781003315766-12

2020–21[4] and found teachers continued to work longer hours than those in other professions and were more likely to want to reduce those hours.

Full-time teachers and middle leaders in primary and secondary schools reported working just shy of 53 hours in their most recent working week; a reduction of more than 4 hours on average compared with the previous survey in 2016.

Let's just recap on why this matters (if we need to): when ex-teachers are asked why they left, workload is the reason most commonly cited. If you can get those hours down and give your staff a sense of agency in their working lives, you'll be much more likely to hold on to them. More than half of full-time teachers still feel they work too many hours.

Where to start? Hopefully by this point in your school's journey, you'll have talked regularly with staff about their work and run a staff survey. So you should have a pretty good idea of how staff in your institution feel about their workload, and about how it's managed by the senior leadership team and other line managers. Below there are some tips on areas you might explore.

Digging deeper

One recommended next step is to organise some conversations with staff, if you have not done this effectively, in which managers can add to this picture. Again, the HSE can help.[5] Its 'Talking Toolkit' provides templates for such conversations, along with prompt questions and suggestions for follow-ups to explore what's being said. There are separate conversations for 'demands' and for 'controls' and we have adapted these slightly below. The areas to cover in relation to 'demands' might include:

– How well do you feel you are able to cope with the demands of your job?

– To what degree are you given achievable demands which relate to the hours you work?

– Which tasks take most time, and how does your department cope at busy times?

– Are you affected by any hazards, violence or harassment from pupils or parents? How does this impact you?

– What changes and support could be put in place to help you cope with the issues you've talked about?

In relation to 'Control,' you might ask:

– To what degree do you feel you are consulted over the way your work is organised and undertaken, through regular meetings, one-to-ones or performance reviews?

– Do you have regular opportunities for discussion and input at the start of projects or new pieces of work?

- How are you encouraged to use your skills and initiative to do your work?

- Are you encouraged to develop new skills and undertake new and challenging pieces of work?

- To what degree do you feel involved in how decisions are made?

- What changes and support could be put in place to help you to cope with any of the issues you have talked about?

A workshop

Running a workshop may possibly prove a quicker and more efficient way to get this job done – or you may wish to follow up on your one-to-ones with a whole-school review, as a way of engaging everyone and coming up with some more detailed proposals.

The Department for Education's workload reduction kit has a useful outline for such a workshop. Its aim should be to ensure that everyone – support staff, teachers, leaders, governors, trustees, and parents – understands the key things that happen within a school year and contributes to reviewing when the pinch points will come. This way, you should be able to get everyone on board and invested in the process. It's important to emphasise that any changes shouldn't just be about improving the lives of staff, but also about what works for pupils, and about improving their outcomes.

This is where the findings from your survey and your one-to-one discussions and meetings can come in. In groups, the participants are asked to consider which tasks take up more time than they're worth. Using key points from the survey findings, the DfE suggests the groups could be asked to answer the following:

- What could we stop doing to reduce workload without affecting pupils, and what could we streamline?

- Are there areas which are not covered in the survey results but which could be addressed? These might include:

  ○ Classroom or office organisation – access to resources, workstations, physical layout, time management.

  ○ Planning – use of time, productive collaboration and sharing, prioritising, timekeeping.

  ○ Feedback and marking – policy, impact, outcomes, understanding expectations.

  ○ Assessment and reporting – use of varied practices, purpose and impact, frequency.

○ Data collection – duplication, purpose, audience, frequency, systems (technology), analysis.

○ Pinch Points – calendar planning.

You might also consider what you can do differently.

The toolkit also provides a range of resources to help you take this forward, and the groups should consider which will be useful as well as thinking about how staff will be supported to feel confident with any necessary changes.

Inspection

One of the key drivers of workload and stress in schools is inspections, so you may wish to consider the views of the inspectorate on managing workload. Let's face it, some points which emerge from these school discussions might *not* be acceptable to the inspectorate. So it's a good idea to be armed with a clear list of what will and won't be required when the inspectors call. Ofsted's handbook[6] for those it inspects contains a 'myth-busting' list of the documents its teams can ask for, and which they won't ask for.

For instance, inspectors won't ask to see past or future lesson plans. They won't ask to see predictions of pupils' progress or attainment scores. They don't expect schools to carry out any specified amount of lesson observation. And they don't specify the frequency, type or volume of marking and feedback. If you want to change your practice in these areas, or in a whole range of other areas, you may do so.

Unfortunately, it is often not as simple as that – leaders and staff often don't believe such assurances and are understandably anxious.

Whether you are inspected by Ofsted, Estyn, Education Scotland or the Independent Schools' Inspectorate, you can easily filter the latest inspection reports from their website if you want to gain insights into what is being highlighted.

Following up

None of this is likely to work if it's a bolt-on to what you do every day: it has to become central to the life of your school. So think about how you can systematise what you've learned through these processes.

Once the responses from surveys, workshops and/or one-to-ones have been assimilated, draw up an action plan with a timeline and provision for reviews of how each item is working. The HSE's Talking Toolkit has a manager's action plan:

● Set a date to revisit the proposed changes.

● Hold regular meetings to discuss anticipated workloads (and to deal with any predicted busy times).

● Provide training to help staff prioritise.

- Develop a system to notify employees of unplanned tight deadlines and any exceptional need to work long hours.

- Identify blocks of time to allow for proper collaborative planning.

- Make high-quality resources and curriculum plans easily accessible.

- Clearly explain why data is being collected and how it will help improve the quality of teaching.

- Make sure that marking is meaningful, manageable and linked directly to its impact on pupil progress.

- Consider the workload impact of each new initiative before it is introduced.

- Consider introducing a work-life balance policy.

- Review the Department for Education's Workload Reduction Toolkit.

The team at Goldsmiths', University of London – we met them in Chapter 1[7] – also have useful insights about how to move forward.

They also provide templates for you to fill in. So a worked example might look like this:

Workload:

1. Aims: the organisation provides employees with adequate and achievable demands in relation to the agreed hours of work.

2. Issue: workloads are not planned effectively, meaning some weeks have excessive work expectations.

3. Solution: plan work using the school calendar to ensure this is balanced with other commitments and spread throughout the school year.

4. Who will lead: line managers to ensure work is planned for their department or function, supported by a senior leader to coordinate activities and suggest the idea to senior leaders.

5. What will they do: solutions to be raised at the next senior leadership meeting.

6. How will they follow up: via monthly meetings and supported through staff bulletins.

Tips to improve Demands and Control

We know from school leaders and staff that the school environment will always have a high workload – this includes schools with good wellbeing scores.

Current structures and demands make this inevitable. Identifying areas where workload can be reduced simply tends to support staff to manage workload better.

Offer personal development opportunities to help staff recognise unhealthy behaviour habits that are contributing to workload pressures, and help them to focus on improving personal effectiveness – for example, prioritising and learning to say 'no.'

Help staff to understand the importance of 'chunking' activities, for example creating specific times for emails and important work and to communicate to others when they are not available. This will prevent them from feeling overwhelmed and will provide time to digest information as well as preventing distractions that come from interruptions or focusing on multiple tasks.

Where possible, offer staff opportunities for regular check-in time with other members of their team: this can prevent situations from building and escalating over longer periods of time.

Encourage staff to reward themselves for completing tasks by creating a list of non-work-related things to do – this links to developing social prescriptions.

Remember to remind staff of the importance of rest time, especially at particularly busy times.

Ask leaders and staff to focus on what they have achieved and what has been completed, rather than what hasn't, and to accept that everything can't be done. It's important to be comfortable living with unfinished work and with picking up tasks the next day. The way in which line managers are able to coach and lead this effectively is key.

Encourage staff to make a daily/weekly list on a notepad, diary, calendar or even the Notes app on their phone to keep track of the tasks that keep being moved or not getting done. It's important staff reflect on why they aren't achieving what they set out to do and how they might create dedicated time. Can tasks be delegated?

Break tasks down into manageable steps and plan for them – we often put off tasks when they seem too large or difficult.

Ask staff, where possible, to decide what their working pattern will be and then make the work they do fit it. Letting workload dictate working hours will always lead to them being too long. Challenge staff to set specific goals to reduce the hours they work, share efficient working practices and celebrate successes.

Whole school approach

You will already prioritise and review workload and assess changes you want to make. You may also follow a process, such as the one we recommend below.

Before changing or implementing any new policies, procedures or practices, ask the question: "What impact will this have on the wellbeing of colleagues?"

Before adopting anything make sure it passes the test of what is important. Is it:

1. High effort for staff and low impact for pupils or staff? Ditch these.

2. Low effort for staff and low impact for pupils or staff? Not a priority.

3. Low effort for staff and high impact for pupils or staff? Make these a priority.

4. High effort for staff and high impact for pupils or staff? Review which are worth doing.

You can use the same process with existing work to identify things that have higher staff workload and lower pupil and school impact. Apply this test to all work to ensure the value provided is greater than the effort needed to deliver it.

You should also apply an in/out rule, if you aren't already. If you are going to add something new to what is an already too high workload, then you will need to remove something of at least an equal load. Use technology, where possible, to support this approach.

School calendar

Make sure that deadlines and other events are planned to minimise 'hot spots,' where workload is much greater than in a usual week. Coordinate deadlines to ensure staff who have demands from different leaders and sources (for example, data collection, student reports and pastoral support) are spread.

When setting deadlines, ensure staff feel confident to feed back when they might struggle and teach them to say 'no.' This includes to themselves and others. It is best to know when work is being set that deadlines will be challenging, rather than being let down when they are not delivered.

Map out the whole school year to avoid calendar congestion and ask yourself these reflective questions before committing an item to your school calendar: 'what will this feel like for a teacher with 23 contact hours a week, playground duties, planning, marking, phase meetings and staff meetings'? Highlight the pinch points within the school year and look to provide extra support for those under the greatest stress or at times of greatest stress.

Line managers

Having distributed leadership and encouraging line managers to coach and support their team is important. This is particularly true when it comes to workload. Celebrating when work is achieved and done well, making sure staff ask for help where needed, and developing personal effectiveness for themselves and their team will all make a big difference.

Leaders have to act as role models, e.g., working sensible hours, taking breaks, meeting deadlines and demonstrating good planning and practice (including making sure things are good enough rather than always having to be perfect).

This includes making sure line managers are effective in delegation and consider workload and removing tasks when distributing new ones. Given how busy senior and middle leaders are, this is often very hard for them to deliver but is important for their own and their team members' benefit.

Openly discuss this as a management team and identify small steps to start and then build on them as a group. It will be much easier to deliver with leaders supporting each other than individually.

To reduce demands, you should also ensure breaks are long enough for staff to be able to walk to the staff room and back and have the opportunity for refreshments and the time to switch tasks. It is very easy for staff to continue to work through breaks or to fit in extra work activity. Research has shown this is a false economy, leading to lower productivity and performance, as well as health issues.

Create the right staff room environment, where possible, to encourage more people to visit it during breaks. The way a staffroom is arranged and how it is used often sends a clear message about its culture. Is furniture arranged to allow staff to mingle and converse easily and does your staffroom encourage people to develop their relationships with one another?

Consider undertaking a staffroom audit to explore how this space is utilised and what needs to change that will support improving the culture.

Another way of encouraging staff to take a break is to find a way to have drinks ready and prepared for staff, as well as making sure the clearing up is done for them. This is likely to be more difficult in smaller schools and while finances and resources are tight, schools that find a way to do this see a fuller and more vibrant staff room, and realise significant improvements in morale and wellbeing, with all their associated benefits.

Outside the staff room and the idea of traditional breaks, you can also consider introducing learning around the science of brain breaks. These are quick refreshing activities to decrease tension from testing, long days or stressful times. Staff, and many leaders and teachers in particular, battle tiredness, and in some cases burnout and struggle to keep their head up each day.

By taking short brain breaks and switching tasks, they can improve how they feel and their productivity. Examples include forms of physical movement, breathing exercises, listening to calming music, reading for pleasure, watching a short video for pleasure, puzzles, colouring, arts and crafts and more. Doing this for just 2–5 minutes is optimal and makes a difference.

Meetings

School meetings can also add significantly to demands. Make sure meetings that are held are necessary and effective and as a result add value and don't impinge on staff time that could be used in other ways. This will also have an impact on the control (autonomy) staff feel they have.

Review the meetings that are held in your school. Below are some good practices you can use:

- Think about the purpose of the meeting – why does it need to happen, what's the main objective and the intended outcome?

- Is this the best way to communicate information or could this be distributed in other ways?

- Consider who the meeting is for, does everyone who is attending a meeting need to be there?

- Is there a clear agenda and will this deliver the outcome we want from the meeting?

- Is the agenda realistic, and can it be covered effectively in the time available? Because specific meetings may happen infrequently there is often a tendency to overfill the agenda – more is often less.

- Review after – were you able to stick to the agenda and deliver the intended outcome? Asking this is often a good way to finish and to take any learning into the next meeting.

- Did the meeting start and finish on time? As well as being good manners, this is important for people who have planned their workload or have other plans.

- Is everyone prepared for the meeting? This means that any important information needs to be distributed in advance and in a succinct but effective way and staff need the time to review it.

- After the meeting, circulate any actions agreed digitally and have a plan to follow up, so that you know how well they were delivered.

Emails

Finally, emails are another area often discussed and where staff members would welcome a reduction. There are a number of actions you might take, and you will probably have done some of these already.

- Set expectations with parents on the timescales for responding to emails and other communication – people are used to organisations asking them to wait 48 hours (or other timeline) for a response, unless urgent.

- Use out of office messages to effectively communicate to external and internal senders about when you will receive and respond to them.

- Agree protocols, for example, not to copy people in and add them to the address list if they need to receive the email – and indicate any action needed in the subject line and at the start of the email, including any deadline.

- Agree rules when emails can be sent – some schools ask for them to not be sent outside agreed hours as they know staff may read them, even if told not to. The challenge with this is a staff member might then receive a significant number at one time, for example, 7.30 or 8.00 a.m. on a Monday morning. Using email footers you can be clear that you do not expect a response, except in an agreed time.

Chapter 9: Key points

Revisit the Health and Safety Executive (HSE) Management Standards,[8] particularly Demands and Control, which are central to keeping workload manageable. Teachers report working an average of 53 hours a week in term time, and workload is the most common reason they cite for leaving the profession.

- **On Demands**, you might wish to ask if colleagues feel able to cope with their job, if their demands are achievable in working hours, which tasks are most onerous and time-consuming, if there are any particular hazards, such as behaviour issues which make the job more burdensome and what changes could be put in place to help.

- **On Control**, ask if staff feel consulted on the organisation and allocation of work tasks, if there are enough opportunities for discussion, if they are encouraged to use their skills and initiative, if they feel stretched to acquire new skills, and what changes might help.

- **You might ask these questions** in one-to-ones or group meetings, or you might organise a series of workshops – the Department for Education provides a useful toolkit for the latter.[9] You could use such workshops to discuss your school's staff survey findings.

- **The dreaded inspection:** inspections are a key driver of workload and stress; be clear what is and isn't required. Ofsted's handbook contains a 'myth-busting' list of the documents its teams can ask for, and which they won't ask for. Other inspectorates also provide information through their frameworks.

- **Following up:** the results of these discussions should become central to the life of your school. Think about how you can systematise what you've learned through these processes.

Notes

1 Department for Education (2018). *School workload reduction toolkit.* [online] gov.uk. Available at: https://www.gov.uk/guidance/school-workload-reduction-toolkit [Accessed 14 December 2022].
2 Great Britain: Health and Safety Executive (2019). *Tackling work-related stress using the Management Standards approach: A step-by-step workbook.* London: HSE [online] Hse. gov.uk. Available at: https://www.hse.gov.uk/pubns/wbk01.htm [Accessed 14 December 2022].
3 Allen, R., Benhenda, A., Jerrim, J. and Sims, S. (2019). *New evidence on teachers' working hours in England. An empirical analysis of four datasets.* [online] Available at: https://johnjerrim.files.wordpress.com/2019/09/working_paper_teacher_hours.pdf.
4 Jack Worth and Henry Faulkner-Ellis, Teacher Labour Market in England Annual Report 2022, NFER 2022: https://www.nfer.ac.uk/media/4885/teacher_labour_market_in_england_annual_report_2022.pdf

5 Talking Toolkit: Go Home Healthy. Preventing Work-related Stress in Schools, HSE 2018: https://www.hse.gov.uk/gohomehealthy/assets/docs/EducationTalkingToolkit.pdf

6 Ofsted (2022). *School inspection handbook.* [online] gov.uk. Available at: https://www.gov.uk/government/publications/school-inspection-handbook-eif/school-inspection-handbook [Accessed 14 December 2022].

7 HSE (2008). *Executive health and safety management competencies for preventing and reducing stress at work identifying and developing the management behaviours necessary to implement the HSE management Standards: Phase Two.* [online] Available at: https://www.hse.gov.uk/research/rrpdf/rr633.pdf.

8 Her Majesty's Stationery Office (2007). *Managing the causes of work-related stress: A step-by-step approach using the management standards.* [online] Great Britain: HMSO. Available at: https://www.hse.gov.uk/pubns/wbk01.htm

9 Department for Education (2018). *School workload reduction toolkit.* [online] gov.uk. Available at: https://www.gov.uk/guidance/school-workload-reduction-toolkit [Accessed 14 December 2022]. Includes workshop facilitation notes.

10 Looking after your support staff

At this point, we might take a step back. If you have done some work on wellbeing in your school – talking to staff members, workshops or running a survey – how did the responses and needs of your non-teaching workforce differ from those of the teaching staff, and how did the school react to their specific needs?

Did you include all staff members? The grounds maintenance staff, the catering staff, the lunchtime supervisors, the admin and finance team, the technicians? It's important to understand the needs of everyone across the school, particularly as we are seeing increasing challenges in recruiting support staff. Opportunities for flexible working that came during lockdown, together with often low comparative pay, have seen people move from the sector.

Non-teaching staff make up the majority of those working in schools – it's why they deserve their own chapter. The latest figures from the English Department for

Education[1] (DfE) show 52 per cent of the school workforce are not teachers. Just under 3 in 10 are teaching assistants; 1 in 11 has an administrative role; 1 in 12 does an auxiliary job such as cleaning, catering or grounds maintenance.

And that's taking the full-time equivalent figure. The proportion of support staff who are part-time is greater than that of the teaching workforce, so in headcount terms – and let's face it, that's what matters when you're considering the wellbeing of individuals – there are around 500,000 teachers and 800,000 support staff in England.

School support staff aren't one homogeneous group, of course. But it's hard to break down their characteristics using official data because the DfE doesn't go into detail in its official surveys. We know what teachers get paid, but we don't have that information about the majority of the school workforce. We do know from the official data that 9 out of 10 support staff are female. The only type of support staff which has a gender balance is technicians. This affects their needs in terms of wellbeing. That's a relatively easy one, as the teaching workforce is largely female too, so you should already be thinking about issues such as work-life balance, maternity cover, the need to look after children or older relatives and support through the menopause. We also know in 2021 the average teacher salary was £42,358. But the government didn't ask what support staff were paid, so Unison, the union to which many of them belong, did its own survey.[2] Unsurprisingly, given that pay scales for full-time teaching assistants started at £17,000, it found one of the major issues affecting the wellbeing of this group was low pay.

More than half the 7000 who responded to Unison's survey said they were on term-time only contracts. Two-fifths earned a full-time equivalent of £15,000 or less. Their comments reflected on the effects of this:

"At present I am renting a tiny two-bed for £1,100 a month with my husband who has cancer and cannot work full time. If he is unable to contribute, my monthly wage does not even pay our rent."

"As a single person, I am just over the threshold for any financial help from the government and struggle to keep on top of bills. I panic when I have to visit the dentist or optician."

"Once all the bills are paid there's hardly anything to live off for the rest of the month, especially with children and the rising cost of petrol and council tax. It's always a struggle."

"We seem to do one of the hardest jobs, yet we're on low pay. After fighting a pay freeze, especially during a scary pandemic and being on the frontline with no choice, we never feel valued. Even if we get a cost-of-living increase, because of the rise in utility bills, food and cost of living, we are still taking a pay cut."

One in five have at least one additional job; these include working in bars, nail bars, care homes, call centres, cafés and supermarkets. That means they are juggling the multiple roles and timetables of sometimes-competing workplaces along with family needs, which takes its toll.

One respondent commented:

I have taken on jobs in the gig economy, primarily food delivery. Often I can spend all weekend working to earn about an additional £100, without which I cannot sustain my family. The knock-on effect of that has been me neglecting my child and their needs. It has put strains on my relationship and is having a heavy impact on my mental health.

Many of those who responded didn't feel their school employers really appreciated what they had to put into their roles, let alone the effect it had on them. Many said they were expected to work additional hours without additional pay, for instance, particularly during the pandemic. These included extra cleaning, covering for absent staff and Covid data reporting.

And here's a sobering figure: more than two-fifths said they were actively looking for better jobs elsewhere. The wellbeing of support staff is a major recruitment and retention issue for schools, and while it may not be possible to increase their pay to compete with other sectors, there is so much more that schools could do to help them feel part of the community.

Unison found only half its respondents felt valued at work – much of this related to pay, with many saying they did feel personally valued but didn't feel adequately rewarded financially for what they did.

Others felt it wasn't just the low pay that was at issue: "Sometimes higher levels of management and governors lose sight of the work that goes on behind the scenes," said one. "Support staff are very much treated as second-class citizens when it comes to things like training, etc. Teaching staff are given coaching and other types of professional development whilst support staff are given little or none," commented another.

Many of them said a little appreciation would go a long way. Just an acknowledgement, an occasional 'thank you,' would do. While the demands of these under-paid and under-regarded workers were minimal, there's much more schools and colleges could be doing to address their needs. As we mentioned above, these are likely to be around work-life balance and family commitments as well as pay. But beyond that, we don't know much because the official data doesn't tell us much and research evidence has tended to focus on teaching staff.

What little we do know about the wellbeing of support staff in schools tends to raise more questions than it answers. For instance,[3] those in non-teaching roles seem to be more likely than their teaching colleagues to be aware of school policies on mental health and wellbeing, though we don't know why this would be the case.

The DfE Education Staff Wellbeing Charter[4] doesn't specifically mention non-teaching staff, though it does refer to 'staff' rather than to teachers. So we don't have a very clear set of guidance on how to support this group, though of course much of what applies to teachers applies to them too. There is a better body of work on this in the health sector, where similar issues arise. The Health Foundation[5] has been looking into what can be done to support low-paid staff in the NHS, for instance.

The foundation's work has shown that in the health service, lower paid workers have higher rates of workplace stress, sickness absence and are at increased risk of long-term conditions such as diabetes and heart disease. They are also more likely to retire early through ill-health. Other factors affecting the health and wellbeing of lower paid staff in the NHS included increased exposure to racial discrimination, being involved in physically demanding work and working with potentially hazardous materials in cleaning, laundry and catering roles. Those workers were less likely to be able to access health and wellbeing interventions, and more likely to be working through outsourced contracts.

The foundation suggested the starting point for improvement of wellbeing at work should be clear communication channels, strong representation and a voice within the organisation for *all* staff. While financial incentives to promote physical health and wellbeing, such as discounts on gym membership, were possible ways forward, it said, it is the impact of pay, career progression and job autonomy, as well as cultural issues around value, respect and support, that are all crucial.

So if you haven't already included your support staff in your wellbeing work, what should you do? Here's a handy checklist[6]:

1. Keep support staff involved in all discussions to identify priorities for their development and wellbeing. Leaders often find this difficult for those supporting in the classroom, such as teaching assistants – they usually work set hours, have little flexibility, are not paid overtime and may not be given the opportunity to attend staff meetings. Yet they need to be included in school events and meetings on a regular basis and kept in the know.

   This can mean taking extra steps to communicate, both centrally and through line managers, to ensure they are kept fully informed and to make sure they know who they can speak to if they have issues. They should also, as much as possible, be included in school processes and systems for talent management, development and succession.

2. Review line-management and pastoral arrangements to ensure all groups of staff are supported. This also means making sure their leaders and line managers benefit from the things we have already covered in earlier chapters, for example, exposure to the competencies proven to prevent and reduce staff stress, coaching, training and more.

3. Ensure support staff are included when collecting feedback – one-to-one meetings, workshops and surveys. Respond to them so they feel listened to and valued.

4. Include support staff in wellbeing opportunities and be mindful many of them aren't paid to work extra hours and may not be there on any given day, if they

are part-time. Think about how best to include them. Are there times when you can make these paid?

5. There may be different needs within groups of support staff and as well as including them in whole school meetings and events where possible, you might also plan specific sessions for some groups. These should be advertised well in advance.

6. Grow your own talent – build support staff career paths into your people strategy and include them in devising wellbeing support within your available resources. You can also ask them to lead sessions for teaching staff, too, as well as the other way round. Teachers will have something to learn from them and it will help remove any divide.

7. Look to give greater control to those carrying out specialist support roles. In Welbee surveys, teaching assistants (TAs) in particular often indicate they have little say in what they do at work and how they do it. Teachers indicate they have greater autonomy and control but a higher workload. There is an opportunity to help by agreeing outcomes to be achieved and asking TAs to take more of a lead in how they are delivered.

   Not always easy, as many teachers are perfectionists and like things done a certain way and we have already covered the challenges of the hours and time they work, making it difficult to meet and talk with them – support staff are not always in at key times.

   Think about these and other opportunities across all your support staff and steps you can take to empower them and give them responsibility. Use effective questioning, listening and coaching.

8. Finally, fully include them in performance management and appraisals. In some schools support staff are not included or do not have effective processes for self and line-management feedback on performance and career aspirations. This is a missed opportunity for greater engagement and to improve outcomes.

If you're now struggling to recruit and to retain staff in support roles, as many schools have for some time in key teaching roles, you can use the above and the tips shared throughout this book. You get out what you put in: make sure you do not overlook opportunities to support the wellbeing of non-teaching staff.

Chapter 10: Key points

All support staff – grounds maintenance staff, catering staff, lunchtime supervisors, admin and finance team members and technicians should be included in staff surveys: consider how their responses differ from those of the teaching staff and leaders. Just recognising that they're there and do valuable work will reap rewards. Here are some tips:

- Keep support staff involved in all discussions to identify priorities for their development and wellbeing. Make sure they feel they are listened to.

- Review line-management and pastoral arrangements to ensure all groups of staff are supported.

- Communicate – make sure everyone knows who they can speak to if there are issues.

- Include support staff in staff meetings and events where possible – but be mindful that they aren't paid to work extra hours and won't all be there on any given day. Can you make these activities paid?

- Plan specific sessions for different groups of support staff. These should be advertised well in advance.

- Explore how they can have more say in how they go about their job, even if outcomes are set. For example, TAs reducing teacher workload through being given more say in how work is delivered.

- Grow your own talent – build support staff career paths into your people strategy and include them in devising wellbeing support within your available resources. And ask them to lead sessions for teaching staff, too, as teachers will learn from them.

- Include support staff in performance development and appraisals.

Notes

1 Gov.uk (2022). *School workforce in England, reporting year 2021*. [online] explore-education-statistics.service.gov.uk. Available at: https://explore-education-statistics.service.gov.uk/find-statistics/school-workforce-in-england [Accessed 14 December 2022].

2 Richards, J. (2021). *Schools risk support staff exodus over pay, warns UNISON | news, press release | news*. [Online] UNISON National. Available at: https://www.unison.org.uk/news/press-release/2021/11/schools-risk-support-staff-exodus-over-pay-warns-unison/.

3 Cooper Gibson (2019). *School and college staff wellbeing: Evidence from England, the UK and comparable sectors CooperGibson Research 2*. [online] Available at: https://assets.publishing.service.gov.uk/government/uploads/system/uploads/attachment_data/file/937601/Wellbeing-literature-review_final18052020_ap.pdf.

4 Department for Education (2021). *Education staff wellbeing charter*. [online] gov.uk. Available at: https://www.gov.uk/guidance/education-staff-wellbeing-charter.

5 The Health Foundation (2021). *Five things we learnt from our work on the health and wellbeing of lower paid NHS staff*. [online] www.health.org.uk. Available at: https://www.health.org.uk/news-and-comment/newsletter-features/five-things-we-learnt-from-our-work-on-the-health-and-wellbe.

6 @TeacherToolkit (2016). *Support Staff in Schools*. [online] TeacherToolkit. Available at: https://www.teachertoolkit.co.uk/2016/03/10/support-staff [Accessed 14 December 2022].

Don't forget the senior leadership team

How often do trustees and governors check in with their CEOs and principals and how often do CEOs and principals check in with their leadership teams about their wellbeing?

We've talked in Chapter 5 about individual strategies all of us – and that means you too – can take to help relieve stress: stress management strategies, taking exercise, staying hydrated and getting enough sleep. And it's surely clear by now that what leaders do affects everyone around them.

This section is about recruitment and retention, and nowhere is that more important than in the senior leadership team – once you have the right team around you, you want them to stay, to be fulfilled and supported and to avoid the stresses that can lead to long-term sickness.

So, what are the key strategies to ensure that this crucial group are not overlooked while you're building a whole-school culture of wellbeing?

The evidence is clear on this: leadership stress cascades down, and so this step isn't an indulgence, it's a foundation stone. A Nuffield Foundation study[1] looked at this issue. Using data from the 2018 Teaching and Learning International Survey (TALIS), in which teachers from more than 40 countries were asked about work-related stress and its impact on their mental health, the researchers found supportive leadership was just about the most important factor in determining how teachers felt.

DOI: 10.4324/9781003315766-14

The study looked at leadership, workload, collaboration, preparation and disciplinary climate as key aspects of the working environment which could affect three key indicators: retention, job satisfaction and workplace wellbeing. It found that while discipline in a school was important, supportive leadership was the single biggest factor in determining each of those three things.

Specifically, supportive leaders are likely to retain staff via improving job satisfaction and through reduced workplace stress, the research showed – and this was also consistent with earlier studies. If you want to keep your senior team, as well as your wider workforce, you need to pay attention to their wellbeing too.

DAVID BIGNELL, FORMER PRIMARY SCHOOL PRINCIPAL AND MINDFULNESS TEACHER

Some people might call it a mental health crisis. I call it 'the wall' – you don't know it's there until you hit it.

I did four years at my first school, then going on seven years at a very popular, very successful middle-class school, and towards the end of that period I started to really struggle with being a leader, and with that sense of responsibility.

The build-up was just that feeling of being weighed down by that sense of responsibility. We'd actually had a successful Ofsted so it wasn't rational in that sense. I think it was almost just a sense of burnout, of not having the resources. It's a bit like if you ask the caterpillar, 'how is it you're doing this? How are you walking?,' the caterpillar just gets confused and falls over. I think in leadership, you ride a wave of confidence and self-esteem and if for whatever reason that collapses on you, you start to think 'how am I doing this?' And then quite quickly after that, 'I can't do this.' And then you fall into a negative spiral.

In my experience, the children were always the easy part. There were a number of tricky situations, some to do with staffing, some to do with parents. It was a demanding school, a high performing school, so even when you get to where you want to be, you've got to maintain it or even improve on it. It was just this relentless pursuit of something else.

There were a couple of touch points. One was a visit from the school improvement partner from the local authority, which is basically like an interrogation. And if you're not feeling on top of your game, all of a sudden the answers don't come and then you start to doubt yourself. And a couple of other tricky situations were going on.

I've dealt with most of these things before in one form or another, but when they all come together, it can be quite overwhelming. And I think probably because I'd been successful, I didn't really have much of a toolkit. I never felt this way before and it was just like, 'what is happening to me?'

All of a sudden, it just wasn't really working for me anymore. I needed to take a step back. I learnt a lot from that experience and one of the most important things I learned was I needed to look after myself more. It may sound odd, but I actually realised I needed more male company: I have three daughters and I work in primary education and I didn't have any other outlets, so I actually took up golf as part of my rehabilitation. I really enjoyed going out with the guys on a weekend and hitting a ball as hard and as far as I could, not being caught up in any other stuff. You enter a state of concentration, which was of great benefit to me.

I went to see the doctor and I got signed off for about six weeks. I took some medication, which I found really helpful. Twenty-one years into my teaching career and I hadn't had any time away from it, really. I was really fortunate; my school was very supportive. I got some counselling; people were kind and helpful.

I got it back together. And I put it all back together in a different way: I started to run cricket clubs at school, for example, which I hadn't done for a long time. And I loved it. And what it meant was, there was a point during the day I'm really looking forward to. And that was a very conscious thing.

I think what I did go back with was maybe just a sense of not thinking it was all about me. Because that seems to me to be the fundamental mistake of leadership, particularly headship, is when you actually start to think you are personally responsible for every outcome, every child, every family, every member of staff.

Managing your leadership team for a low-stress, high-support culture

Take a look at the colleagues with whom you work most closely; the ones you probably see every day, or at least every week. What is causing them stress? Bear in mind that the things which cause you the greatest stress, probably won't be the same things that get to them. Do you know your team well enough to understand their individual tolerance levels for certain things? Are you managing their workloads in a way which plays to their strengths and minimises their vulnerabilities?

If you aren't doing this, you may well be seeing:

- More regular instances of disputes and disaffection within your team.

- An increase in staff turnover.

- An increase in complaints and grievances.

- An increase in sickness and absence.

- Reduced team performance.

- An increase in parent dissatisfaction or complaints.

By now you are likely to have spent time thinking about the factors in your own working life that cause stress, and how to manage those. Maybe there are others in the leadership team who can take some of the stresses off you, and vice versa? Are there things you find hard – dealing with parental complaints, for instance – which someone else can handle with confidence and with minimal stress?

Look out, in particular, for those driving themselves beyond reasonable limits, those team members who withdraw and seem to reject offers of help and those who might feel excluded from the team. Look for others within your team who have different or complementary skills; try to ensure you all collaborate and delegate effectively. School leaders often think they have to be seen to have all the answers but giving direction and using all the resources available is a far better option. On a personal level, make sure you have people you can rely on for advice and support. It really does matter who you surround yourself with.

Action: Build your own 'mastermind' group with a combined set of skills that adds to what you can do as an individual. Find people who share your values, who have a positive outlook and who will also be critical friends. This means they have to be able to challenge your ideas and actions, though.

While those closest to you are crucial, your network might also include a range of remote 'advisers' who may not work inside your organisation every day – those writing blogs, making videos, coaching – anyone who has experience and is prepared to share it.

List all the members of your immediate and wider team and set out clear responsibilities for everyone. Some team members may focus on managing changes while others run business-as-usual activities. If you can eliminate uncertainty, those around you will quickly begin to concentrate on what needs to be done. Make sure roles can be rotated so that everyone can have quieter periods; it's easy to allow certain 'go-to' individuals to take the strain off others at the expense of their own needs.

When asking for advice from your team, remember to listen to answers. Where you do not take on what is suggested, clearly explain why – this way you are much more likely to build trust. This is so important in difficult times, when it is inevitable you will make mistakes.

Leaders also need to understand and demonstrate cabinet responsibility. It is OK to challenge and disagree prior to decisions being made, but from then on you must all stand behind them and communicate as one. Ultimately, all members of the leadership team need to take an executive role on behalf of the school or trust.

Focus on outcomes and make sure you have clarity about what you need to achieve. Create short-term goals to generate wins and keep them simple. Explain why they are important and the part that each person has to play in meeting them.

We've said this before, but don't forget communication is key. Build in regular meetings at which concerns can be aired and workload can be apportioned. Provide regular updates and briefings where appropriate, but don't overload.

Keeping your team together in tough times

All schools have been through challenges in the past few years, and school leaders have learned a lot about adversity. It's worth taking a step back now to reflect on those lessons: how will you organise differently during the next crisis? What are the things you had to do during the pandemic that you would actually like to incorporate into daily life?

The National Health Service has some interesting reflections on team organisation in a crisis.[2] In order to manage different people's reactions to pressure, its guidance suggests, it's vital to have a system that monitors for early warning signs. When things get tough, some people will react emotionally while others will withdraw and tend not to ask for help when they need it.

So what can you do now, to prepare for the next rocky patch?

If you make it a habit to check in daily with each member of your immediate team – and for them to do so with others – you'll be building a solid basis for dealing with future adversity.

Ask yourself:

- Do you have a clear and up-to-date picture of the issues each team member faces?

- Have you given your team permission, clearly and explicitly, to prioritise their own mental health?

- Does everyone recognise they have a shared responsibility to be aware of and to look out for each other's wellbeing?

Do you know who might be affected by:

- Past traumatic experiences which can affect resilience.

- Health conditions.

- Faith issues – for example, Muslim colleagues observing Ramadan may have their energy levels affected by the cycle of fasting.

- Family or caring issues which need to be addressed.

- Neurodiversity – for example, a team member who has dyspraxia may find rapid change stressful.

Where to start: some practical steps

Ask yourself:

- Have we got a consistent approach across all parts of our school or college, so that everyone is getting the same messages about wellbeing, from pupils to senior leaders?

- Do we need to revisit any core policies, such as safeguarding or behaviour, to ensure consistency of message and practice?

– How can we build in expertise to our senior team about mental health, so that the initiative is led from the top and is supported at all levels? (Just 13 per cent of managers in the United Kingdom have had specific mental health training).[3]

– Do we praise staff enough for what they do? One way of celebrating success is to set a daily goal for each member of your team to notice and praise someone who's doing something right. This needs to be specific and authentic. There might be different levels of praise – immediate, when you observe something good happening; public, in a meeting with other colleagues; or even as a specific congratulatory one-to-one. Try to offer praise in line with clear goals you've set, so that this becomes a means of achieving specific things you want to see.

– Do we provide support to develop personal effectiveness so leaders (and others) are better able to manage the heavy workload – we covered ways you might work more effectively in Chapter 5.

Further reading

The King's Fund has put together an overview of steps you can take to foster team spirit and cohesion:
https://www.kingsfund.org.uk/audio-video/stress-hospital-staff-covid-19
Management Today has a list of tips on how leaders can look after their own mental health:
https://www.managementtoday.co.uk/leaders-tips-looking-own-mental-health/leadership-lessons/article/1696910
For further research on links between stress and health, see: Keller, A., Litzelman, K., Wisk, L.E., Maddox, T., Cheng, E.R., Creswell, P.D. and Witt, W.P. (2012). Does the perception that stress affects health matter? The association with health and mortality. *Health Psychology*, [online] 31(5), pp.677–684. doi:10.1037/a0026743.

Chapter 11: Key points

● Do you understand each individual's tolerance levels for certain things? Are you managing workloads to play to their strengths and minimise their vulnerabilities? Early warning signs that there may be issues include increases in disputes and disaffection, turnover, staff complaints, absences and parent complaints. Team performance overall is likely to suffer.

● Think about how you might take some of the stress off other team members, and vice versa: who finds certain things harder, or easier, than others? Is someone particularly strong on dealing with parents, for instance, while others struggle? Who provides your support system; who does that for each team member? Watch out for team members driving themselves too hard or becoming withdrawn.

● Set out clear responsibilities for everyone. Some team members could focus on managing changes while others run business-as-usual activities. Focus on outcomes and make sure you have clarity about what you need to achieve. Create short-term goals and keep them simple.

- Consult your team but also remember to listen to answers. Where you do not take on what is suggested, clearly explain why. It is OK to challenge and disagree prior to decisions being made, but from then on everyone must stand behind them.

- Leaders also need to understand and demonstrate cabinet responsibility and communicate as one. Ultimately, all members of the leadership team need to take an executive role on behalf of the school or trust.

- Build resilience before the next crisis hits. Ask yourselves if you understand each other's experience and vulnerabilities.

- Ask yourselves:
  - Does everyone in the school get the same messages about wellbeing?
  - Do we need to revisit core policies such as safeguarding or behaviour to ensure consistency?
  - How can we build expertise about mental health into our senior team?
  - Do we thank staff enough for what they do?

Develop your own and all leaders' personal effectiveness – refer back to Chapter 5, which contains a list of tips and actions you can take.

Notes

1 Jerrim, J., Sims, S. and Allen, R. (April 2021). *The Mental Health and Wellbeing of Teachers in England.* London: Nuffield Foundation.
2 NHS Learning Hub (n.d.). *Support for leaders through COVID-19 – Leadership Academy.* [online] learninghub.leadershipacademy.nhs.uk. Available at: https://learninghub.leadershipacademy.nhs.uk/support-for-leaders/ [Accessed 14 December 2022]
3 BITC (2019). *Mental health at work 2019: Time to take ownership.* [online] Business in the Community. Available at: https://www.bitc.org.uk/report/mental-health-at-work-2019-time-to-take-ownership/ [Accessed 14 December 2022].

SECTION 4
School culture

12 Culture, cake and yoga

MARK EAGER, PRINCIPAL, BRIXHAM COLLEGE

I am a good collaborator: I feel leadership is about consultation and involving people in decision-making. The head teacher I took over from was more traditional than me. I changed things and made it more of a community focus – one of the things about our school is its sense of community. We are quite isolated, and that brings some community benefits, but we didn't really reflect on that. I didn't think anything was broken, but we just didn't know.

Like most schools, we did things like, donut Fridays. We had a staff management group and I listened to what they had to say. We set up a social committee of staff to pull things together, but none of it really worked.

Donut Fridays worked really well until people started to take them as being an entitlement. They were about once a month, out of my own pocket and I tended to do them if there'd been a hard week, or a parents' evening. People would say, 'We haven't had a donut Friday for a while.' The social committee of staff began to fizzle out because they had great ideas but they were the only people who wanted to do them: everyone said, 'Yes, great, I would love to do that.' Then it would come to being involved and people weren't that keen to come forward. The management group became hijacked by colleagues who had their own agenda and wanted to bring their own issues, and it was difficult to differentiate between those people and the whole school. When the senior leader group leadership group reflected, there was no real top-down strategy sitting underneath it.

At that point we were finding it really difficult to recruit teachers – the sea is on three sides of us. It was really about, 'How do we make the recruitment strategy about this being a vibrant place to build your career.'?

I saw a well-being seminar advertised and I thought, 'I'll go for that. The dates worked, so I rocked up. It was absolutely fantastic and we decided to do an anonymous survey. The results were horrific. It was low scores across the board for all the things in the survey. It was really negative from staff, and a real divide between senior leadership and the rest of the school. It was a real moment where I had to sit and take stock. It could have knocked our confidence; I had to be very careful what I put out to the senior leadership team because it would have destroyed some of them.

It was quite a moment for us. We could have looked at it and thought 'Oh Jesus. How do we respond? Is it all nonsense?' Or, 'That will be the last time we ask them.' Or do we actually try to take on board what this thing is telling us?

I eventually shared the data report with the senior leadership team, over a four-week period. We were in the bottom one per cent in every category. And then there were the anonymous comments. We decided once we had got over the pain of it to say, 'OK. Let's ask what this is telling us.'

When I stripped it back, what wasn't working was the relationships between staff and between leaders. We had people who were leaders that weren't leading. We had people that were being led, that didn't necessarily understand what that meant. People saying they would do things and not delivering.

We all had to go back to basics about what it means to be part of a college. Just with those with responsibilities in the first instance, but it was shared with everybody. I took the stance that we had to be very transparent. We had leadership and behaviour training with staff about what it meant to be a leader and what came with leadership.

There were quick fixes on communicating values and what it meant, as a school. We talked about education, what it meant to work here and to be part of it. That was really enjoyable. People really welcomed it. We did the survey again, one year later and the impact was massive. We were in the top 25 per cent, lots of the feedback saying it had been positive. That almost gave us a shot in the arm to really engage further.

We went back to one of the reasons for starting this – we wanted to look at what well-being was about, at engagement of staff and getting the best staff. From that we developed a people strategy of which well-being is part. It was about onboarding, induction, support, and identifying people who were future leaders. We introduced a pathway for people to progress and develop themselves in the school. We put everything that well-being exercise had told us into one strategy. It was almost a life cycle of an individual: They travel through Brixham College to moving somewhere else for promotion, or deciding what they want is to be here for 20 years. And what does that mean?

In year one, it was about relationships and Leadership behaviours

In year 2 it was all about establishing a people strategy and about what it means to be part of a college. Going back to our values and going back to our commitment to you as an employee, making sure you are onboarded, giving you support in your career, whether you are here or elsewhere.

In year three – I would characterise that as being about talent spotting, about keeping the best people here. We introduced a leadership development programme with three different pathways. A group spent this year being part of the senior leadership team to give them that experience. One member of staff from that group is already an assistant principal elsewhere.

There were six in that cohort one got a job elsewhere, the others are working like Trojans in the school, committed to the school, sending messages out to others.

The programme was open to non-teaching staff in the same way. In September this year, we will have two or three non-teaching members who will have the opportunity to join the senior leadership team, and that has been really well received by support staff. We gave them the same entitlement to CPD. Then we also changed their performance management to match that of teachers; we wanted to break that divide. We changed the way they get paid to match the pay awards to those of teachers.

It's helped us get through Covid, because we have had that goodwill and people have trusted the decisions we have made. People were on our side, staff were going, 'How can we help?' I doubt that would have been the case before.

You have reviewed your school data, run a survey and explored the experiences and views of all your staff, including those supporting the running of the school, such as the site and cleaning team. You've held meetings and used an INSET day to discuss the way forward. Maybe even before that, you were trying to instil a culture of wellbeing in your school. Or maybe you were really just adding things piecemeal with the odd slice of cake or a word of praise here or there?

This chapter is about what a school can look like when it really puts wellbeing at its core.

Of course you will have other priorities. You must focus on outcomes and inspection, and you'll be worried about recruitment of staff and budgets. There'll still be some lingering after-effects from the pandemic, and the ongoing concerns about the mental health of both staff and pupils. But know this: the schools which are best able to tackle those challenges are the ones with a culture where staff come first and will do their best work and thrive.

While it will be challenging to keep all these plates spinning, it will work. Improved staff wellbeing will lead to lower costs, less time spent on recruitment, staff absence cover, grievances and counselling.

In the past few years, you may have had little time to focus on anyone but the students, and making them the priority was important in a crisis. But students need teachers who love their jobs, who feel positive and well-supported: we'll come back in the next chapter to the evidence on staff wellbeing and pupil results.

Your staff are your most expensive and valuable asset, and if you put their wellbeing at the forefront of everything you do, they will be better able to take care of your students and to help them to achieve. And then your other stakeholders will be satisfied and happy.

This philosophy was at the heart of Richard Branson's approach to business – love him or hate him, his commitment to putting his employees first is well documented. This quote summarises the impact this can have.

> It should go without saying...if they (your employees) are given the tools to do the job, if they are well looked after, if they're treated well, then they're going to be smiling, they're going to be happy, and therefore the customer will have a nice experience...If you can put your staff first, your customers second and your shareholders third, essentially in the end the shareholders do well, the customers do better and your staff are happy.[1]

Is this not true for educators? Put staff first, students second and other stakeholders third to deliver the best outcomes for all.

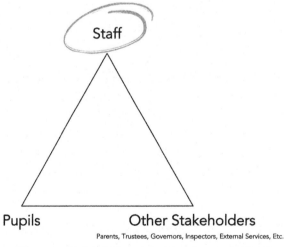

Illustration 12.1 Which stakeholders do you put first?

Where does it all go wrong?

Let's assume you're already part way down the road to creating a wellbeing culture in your school. You can be sure there are others nearby which aren't: more and more school leaders are aware of the need to tackle this area, but too many do not have a clear plan of how best to go about it, and they often start in the wrong place. They tend to look for quick fixes, and as a result are often dealing with symptoms, rather than causes or prevention.

As staff members, it's always good to see cakes on the table, when we are asked to attend after school staff meetings. Or perhaps it's free fruit in the staffroom, or the breakfast when we have an early morning start.

Staff may have the opportunity to take part in activities, for example a wellbeing day or even a wellbeing week. It might be yoga, other exercise, team building or some form of training on self-care.

There is nothing wrong with any of these. If your school or college already has the right climate and staff wellbeing foundations in place, and supports staff throughout the year, then these will add to what you are already doing. They are just not the place to start or to focus on first – they are unlikely to deliver significant long-term changes or benefits.

If staff do not feel supported or valued, do not have good relationships with their line manager or do not enjoy their work, then after they have eaten their cake, practised yoga or participated in a wellbeing day, what has changed?

Climate and staff wellbeing is all about the culture that leaders create.

Improving staff wellbeing is a bit like building a house – you need to build the right foundations first, and only then should you work on the ground and first floor. That way, you will build something that can stand tall and last the ravages of time.

We've already talked about some of the simple steps which can begin to improve staff wellbeing: things like the behaviours of leaders, which we looked at in Chapters 5 and 11. We've also talked about building teams, in Chapter 8.

These behaviours need to be supported with effective systems and processes. Performance management, appraisals, meeting practices, vision and values, data, finance and planning are all examples.

Everyday leadership behaviours and communication are the most important element, but systems change will also add to the mix and can help to embed those changes throughout the whole school.

It is important to talk openly about mental health and have additional support in place for those that need it: for example, an employee assistance scheme or access to counselling. This shows support is part of your culture – building the right foundations and creating an environment where people can thrive will reduce the need for these services.

Over a year, we have teacher's day, stress awareness week and world wellbeing week, among others. The purpose of these to raise awareness is clear, yet they add to the feeling that these are not part of everyday life – as they should be.

Awareness of stress, wellbeing and appreciating teachers and other school staff should be for 365 days a year. It is about creating psychological safety as a long-term approach – we briefly covered this in Chapter 8.

Improving wellbeing and performance is not a quick fix. It is about consistent practice and embedding behaviours and systems into the school culture. Then, this will just become part of what you do each day.

So, how might your staff wellbeing policy look? Hopefully by now, if you're in England, you'll have signed up to the DfE's Education Staff Wellbeing Charter[2] – or if you're not, at least taken a look – as this will help you to put some meat on those bones.

Let's return one more time to those HSE Management Standards, which cover the primary sources of stress at work and which if not properly managed are associated with poor health and wellbeing, lower productivity and increased sickness absence.

A quick reminder – they cover:

- **Demands**: workload, work patterns and anything within the work environment that adds to the demands that staff face, including deadlines, student behaviour and parents.

- **Control**: how much say a staff member has in what they do and how they are able to do their work.

- **Support**: including the sponsorship and resources provided by the school, and encouragement of leaders, line managers and colleagues.

- **Relationships**: including how positive working behaviours are promoted to avoid conflict and effectively dealing with unacceptable behaviour.

- **Role**: the extent to which staff understand their role within the school, how this fits with that of their department or function and the aims of the school, and whether leaders ensure roles do not conflict.

- **Change**: includes how well organisational change (large or small) is managed and communicated within the school.

As an employer, your school has a duty to ensure the health, safety and welfare of its staff as far as reasonably practicable. It is also required to have in place steps to manage those factors that could harm staff members' physical and mental wellbeing, which include work-related stress. This duty extends only to those factors which are work related and within the school's control. You should therefore consider putting the HSE standards at the forefront of your wellbeing policy and commit to being judged against them.

The HSE definition of work-related stress is: "The adverse reaction a person has to excessive pressure or other types of demand placed on them." There is an important distinction between 'reasonable pressures' which stimulate and motivate and 'stress' where an individual feels they are unable to cope with excessive pressures or demands.

You are likely to have a staff wellbeing policy in place: below is a draft you can adapt for your needs.

Draft wellbeing policy[3]

The sections of your wellbeing policy could include:

1. Statement of Intent

The governing body and school's senior managers acknowledge the potential impact that work has on an individual's physical and mental health, and that there is a persuasive business case, as well as a moral and legal duty for taking steps to promote staff wellbeing as far as reasonably practicable.

We are committed to fostering a culture of cooperation, trust and mutual respect, where all individuals are treated with fairness and dignity, and can work at their optimum level. We also recognise that work-related stress has a negative impact on staff wellbeing and that it can take many forms and so needs to be carefully analysed and addressed at an organisational level.

This staff wellbeing policy expands upon the school's health and safety policy, setting out how the school will promote the wellbeing of staff by:

- Creating a working environment where potential work-related stressors are understood and mitigated as far as practically possible through good management practices, effective human resources policies and staff development.

- Increasing managers' and staff members' awareness of the causes and effects of stress.

- Developing a culture that is open and supportive of people experiencing stress or other forms of mental ill-health.

- Developing the competence of managers through introducing them to the competencies proven to prevent and reduce staff stress.

- Engaging with staff to create constructive and effective working partnerships, both within teams and across the school.

- Establishing working arrangements whereby staff feel they are able to maintain an appropriate work-life balance.

- Encouraging staff to take responsibility for their own health and wellbeing through effective health promotion programmes and initiatives.

- Encouraging staff to take responsibility for their own work effectiveness as a means of reducing their own stress and that of their colleagues.

2. **Arrangements for wellbeing and stress prevention through good management practices**

- Having clear job descriptions and person specifications to ensure staff members are clear on what is expected in their role and the right person is recruited where vacancies exist.

- Ensuring training and development procedures are in place so individuals have the necessary skills and competencies to undertake the tasks and duties required of them.

- Ensuring managers are aware of those behaviours proven to prevent and reduce staff stress and providing opportunities for them to self-assess against them and undertake training where appropriate.

- Having effective processes and procedures for:Promoting staff appropriately.

  ○ Reward and recognition.

  ○ Managing performance and capability.

  ○ Absence management and return to work to ensure that individuals are supported following illness.

  ○ Harassment and anti-bullying.

  ○ Communicating with staff on the work of the school and issues affecting their work.

  ○ Seeking staff feedback, including use of anonymous staff surveys.

  ○ Flexible working arrangements and keep in touch days with staff on maternity leave.

  Suitable adaptations will be made for disability and accessibility.

  These arrangements will be updated and augmented as required and when deemed necessary by the findings of stress risk assessments.

3. **Consultation and Communication**

- The school will consult with staff on the staff wellbeing policy and measures taken to implement the policy through the operation of the (insert relevant committees, e.g., health and safety, staff wellbeing, school council).

- Staff surveys and other tools will be used to gather feedback on staff wellbeing.

- The views of individuals will be sought in areas or teams subject to local stress risk assessments.

- In those areas where safety representatives have been appointed by recognised trades unions under the provisions of the Safety Representatives and Safety Committees Regulations 1977, these safety representatives will also be consulted on the development of local stress risk assessments.

- The staff wellbeing policy and measures taken by the school to manage work-related stress will be communicated and promoted in school.

- The staff wellbeing policy will be published on the school website (specify where).

- Leaflets (or a summary document) will be produced for staff who do not have easy access to a computer. The contents of the policy will be covered during general induction training sessions for staff and through specific training on stress awareness.

4. **Responsibilities for implementing the staff wellbeing policy**

   Headteacher and the school's senior managers will:

- Support steps taken to develop a culture of cooperation, trust and mutual respect within the school.

- Champion good management behaviours as set out in the competencies proven to prevent and reduce staff stress and the establishment of a work ethos within the school. They will discourage assumptions about long-term commitment to working hours of a kind likely to cause stress and should encourage staff to maintain a reasonable work-life balance.

- Promote effective communication and ensure that there are procedures in place for consulting and supporting staff on any changes in the school, to management structures and working arrangements at both a school wide and departmental/year group level.

Managers and supervisors will:

- Treat individuals reporting to them with consideration and will promote a culture of mutual respect in the teams they manage. They will quickly and effectively deal with unacceptable behaviour and will take decisive action when issues are brought to their attention.

- Ensure that there is good communication within their teams and that there are opportunities for individuals to raise concerns about their work, and to seek advice at an early stage where concerns are raised. (Insert details here of those available to offer such advice, for instance human resources, wellbeing committee or health and safety team.)

- Adhere to the management principles set out in school policies and procedures, and the competencies proven to prevent or reduce staff stress.

- Ensure workload is distributed equitably and fairly among the team and that when work is delegated, team members have the necessary knowledge and skills to deliver it.

- Regularly check in with team members, thank and encourage them and offer praise when it is due.

- Take action in the interests of all team members, other colleagues and students to manage the underperformance of any individual staff member.

- Attend training as appropriate in order to increase their awareness of the causes and effects of work-related stress.

- Cooperate with others (insert specifics where appropriate) to ensure that risk assessments are undertaken for roles or working practices that may give rise to work-related stress and poor wellbeing.

- Encourage their staff to participate in activities undertaken by the school to promote wellbeing and more effective working.

Staff must:

- Treat colleagues and others they interact with during the course of their work with fairness, consideration and respect.

- Cooperate with the school's efforts to implement the staff wellbeing policy, attend briefings and raise their own awareness of the causes and effects of stress and poor wellbeing.

- Raise concerns with their line manager if they feel there are work issues that are causing them stress and having a negative impact on their wellbeing.

- Be liable for their own health and wellbeing as far as is practically possible.

- Take ownership of setting out their own development plan and discussing this as appropriate with their line manager, as one of the means to enable them to work effectively in their team and reduce the risk of stress.

- Take responsibility for working effectively in their assigned roles, supporting others as appropriate and helping to avoid causing stress to their colleagues.

Human resources will:

- Provide advice to managers and staff members on best practice in relation to human resource management, developing policies and procedures as required.

- Ensure that there are arrangements in place for communicating the content of the school's human resource management policies, procedures and toolkits to managers and staff.

- Develop arrangements to enable managers and staff to achieve the necessary competencies needed in relation to managing work-related stress and improving wellbeing.

- Ensure there are arrangements in place to support individuals experiencing stress, for example referring them to the school's occupational health advisers where appropriate.

- Ensure there are arrangements in place to support managers experiencing problems with employee performance, including managing capability.

- Seek the views of staff on the effectiveness of the school's staff wellbeing policy and stress management arrangements using evidence-backed staff surveys and other appropriate tools.

- Collate management information which will enable the school to measure its performance in relation to stress management and employee wellbeing, such as:

  ○ Sickness absence data.

  ○ Staff turnover and exit interviews.

  ○ Cover periods provided.

  ○ Numbers of self-referrals to a counsellor/staff assistance scheme.

  ○ Numbers of referrals to the occupational health adviser.

  ○ Numbers of grievance and harassment cases.

Staff/health and safety/wellbeing committee (as appropriate) will:

- Determine the staff wellbeing policy and recommend its adoption.

- Monitor the implementation of the staff wellbeing policy and the operation of associated arrangements such as the staff counselling service.

- Ensure the staff wellbeing policy is kept under review and updated as appropriate.

- Develop a school-level risk assessment based on the Health and Safety Executive's "Management Standards for Work-Related Stress."

- Coordinate and deliver appropriate training and briefings to increase awareness of the causes and effects of work-related stress among managers and other staff.

- Assist and support managers to undertake local stress risk assessments where required.

- Organise appropriate activities to promote health and wellbeing.

- Consult with staff voice/union representatives on the development and implementation of the staff wellbeing policy.

- Act as the main focus group for consulting on the effectiveness of the staff wellbeing policy and the measures taken to implement it, including organising staff questionnaires in relation to wellbeing and work-related stress and validating findings of school-level risk assessments.

- Review the policy every two years following feedback from staff surveys, reviewing management information and the findings of stress risk assessments, and in consultation with the senior management team.

5. **Risk Assessment**

At whole-school level, a risk assessment will be developed to establish whether the school's policies and procedures are sufficient to enable compliance with the HSE's Management Standards in relation to the management of work-related stress. Where gaps in arrangements are identified, the relevant (insert people/groups/committees) and senior management team will consult so that the necessary action can be taken to address any gaps identified in the school's policies and procedures.

- Where problems arise at a department or local level, a risk assessment will be undertaken by the relevant manager.

- When risk assessments are undertaken at a departmental level, the staff working in the area which is subject to the risk assessment will be consulted. Any safety representative appointed by recognised trade unions under the provisions of the Safety Representatives and Safety Committee Regulations 1977, representing staff working in the area covered by the risk assessment will also be consulted.

6. **Monitoring and reviewing the Wellbeing Policy**

The staff wellbeing policy will be reviewed every two years by (insert as appropriate – health and safety committee, wellbeing committee/staff council/senior management team/governing body/appropriate named individuals with the seniority and experience required). This will take into account all relevant collected data and risk assessments as outlined in this policy.

Chapter 12: Key points

This chapter is about what a school can look like when it really puts wellbeing at its core.

- There's nothing wrong with free cake or fruit, staff social events, resilience or mindfulness training or wellbeing days. However, they are not the place to start and won't deliver significant benefits or long-term change. Afterwards your staff will go back to their classroom or place of work and face all the same underlying issues that were there before.

- Focus on building wellbeing foundations so they become part of your climate and culture and of the leadership behaviours and systems that support it.

- Have a clear wellbeing policy in place – what might your school's look like? First remind yourself of those HSE standards: Demands, Control, Support, Relationships, Role, Change.

The sections of your wellbeing policy will reflect those standards and should include:

- **Statement of Intent**: to include a mission statement, details of how it builds on existing policies by creating a culture and environment in which wellbeing is central. Key points on how this will be achieved.

- **Arrangements for wellbeing and stress prevention** through good management practices: to include human resources processes, management of performance, absences, bullying and disputes, flexible working arrangements and disability.

- **Consultation and communication**: to include staff surveys and feedback, trades union consultation, how the school community will be kept informed, plans for training on the policy and on specific areas such as stress management.

- **Responsibilities for implementing** the staff wellbeing policy; to include the roles of head and senior leadership team, of managers and supervisors, of all staff, of the human resources team, of the school wellbeing committee or similar. Plan for a whole-school risk assessment, and give details of how the policy will be reviewed regularly.

Notes

1 Branson, R. (2016). Put your staff 1st, customers 2nd, & shareholders 3rd | Inc. Magazine. YouTube. Available at: https://www.youtube.com/watch?v=NPiCYoX-S_I.
2 Department for Education (2021). The education staff wellbeing charter. [online] Department for Education. Available at: https://assets.publishing.service.gov.uk/government/uploads/system/uploads/attachment_data/file/1034032/DfE_Education_Workforce_Welbeing_Charter_Nov21.pdf [Accessed 14 December 2022].
3 From Welbee – https://welbee.co.uk/draft-wellbeing-policy

Wellbeing and your students

This is a book about teacher wellbeing. And yet every school leader who sets out to improve staff morale will have to face a fundamental question: what's this doing for the students? Schools and colleges are, after all, there for those who need educating, not for those who do the educating.

We've talked about how a happier workforce is a more effective workforce, and about how good staff wellbeing practices should aid retention and recruitment. But if at any stage you need a persuasive argument for a radical change in the culture of your institution, surely that argument will need to be about what, ultimately, all this is doing for the pupils.

The first answer to this question is that all those who spend their days in a school which has wellbeing at its heart – including the pupils – should have a strong sense of belonging and a common identity which promotes positive,

DOI: 10.4324/9781003315766-17

inclusive attitudes to one another. That has to be good for everyone; especially those being educated, who hopefully will absorb a set of values they can take with them through life.

Refer back to the words of John Maher, the Headteacher of Ashfield School, in Chapter 5. He is constantly visible; he picks up litter; he talks to everyone, staff and student alike. That's all about building a strong culture in which everyone feels included and in which there are shared values which everyone recognises. Some of those pupils may be causing anti-social disruption at the weekend, he tells us – but they aren't doing it in school, because they understand that isn't how things are done inside the school gates.

The second answer perhaps requires more empirical evidence. Schools aren't just about shared values: they're also about getting results. And the latter is often the measure by which they're judged: by inspectors, by prospective parents, by the wider community. Like it or not, results matter. So will all this work you're about to put into building a culture of wellbeing make any difference to the SAT scores or the GCSE results? Good news – the short answer is "yes." If you look after your staff, they will be better able to look after your students, and that will give you the best possible chance of satisfying your other stakeholders, too.

The evidence

The evidence for making wellbeing a part of every-day behaviours and activities is compelling. In 2007, researchers at Birkbeck College, London, carried out a major study[1] which involved 24,100 staff in 246 primary schools and 182 secondary schools. It demonstrated that improvements in staff wellbeing could be linked to a statistically significant increase in SAT results in primary schools and an increase in the percentage of pupils gaining five or more good GCSEs. The researchers could also link teacher wellbeing with the amount of progress pupils made between the ages of 11 and 16.

Of course, there are lots of things involved in getting the right results. But staff wellbeing is an important factor. The researchers found that while 92 per cent of variation in SAT scores could be accounted for by other factors, eight per cent could be attributed to teacher wellbeing. They didn't find a link between scores and the wellbeing of non-teaching staff, however.

The researchers found their results particularly exciting because teacher wellbeing is a variable which can be altered: a large part of the variation in performance between schools is due to children's home circumstances, and that isn't so easy to shift.

The major implication of these findings is that if we want to improve school performance, we *must* pay attention to teacher wellbeing – it isn't an add-on. How teachers feel on an everyday basis is likely to affect their performance and so, in turn, the performance of the pupils they teach.

How does this happen? That's less clear, though at one level it seems obvious: happier, more motivated teachers are likely to make pupils feel happier, more motivated and more confident. Happier teachers may be better able to concentrate on the job of teaching and may be more motivated to help pupils who need special attention.

The Birkbeck study couldn't establish cause and effect, and maybe the better results led to better wellbeing, rather than wellbeing leading to results. It's complicated: both virtuous circles and downward spirals are possible. Maybe improvements in teacher wellbeing can lead to improved pupil performance, which in turn leads to a further rise in teacher wellbeing, and so on.

There isn't a wealth of evidence on the links between better pupil performance and teacher wellbeing. But there is lots of evidence of the reverse effect: that teacher stress, burnout, depression and anxiety are linked in pupils to poorer academic achievement, lower levels of concentration, low satisfaction rates, lack of motivation and behaviour issues.

A global review of the evidence[2] uncovered five quantitative studies, four of which associated teacher stress with lower standard test scores in reading, literacy and mathematics.

A qualitative study highlighted possible mechanisms by which this occurred: pupils reported that when they felt their teacher was stressed, their concentration was affected. They would often work in silence so as not to upset the teacher, they said, refrain from asking questions, or feel the need to rush through their work, if the teacher was in a bad mood.

This study did not find a causal link, and a review on the same subject by the Work Foundation[3] concluded more research was needed before a conclusion could be drawn. However, a separate 2021 report from the Teacher Development Trust has found a link.

There are also studies from other sectors which can help if you need to make the case for cultural change. In 2014, the Department of Business Innovation and Skills published a report on how worker wellbeing affects workplace performance.[4] It found that in a wide range of businesses, staff wellbeing was strongly linked with improved profitability and productivity, as well as with enhanced outputs and services. Why would education be any different from other sectors?

This study said factors such as training, skills development opportunities, the level of autonomy staff had in their role, how much scope they had to use their own initiative and the extent to which they could influence decisions were key to improving job satisfaction (you may remember we talked about these in Chapter 2).

It also pointed to three mechanisms through which a sense of wellbeing could lead to higher job performance:

● By affecting employees' cognitive abilities and processes, enabling them to think more creatively and to be more effective at problem-solving.

- By affecting employees' attitudes to work – raising their propensity to be cooperative and collaborative.

- By improving employees' physiology and general health, boosting cardiovascular function and immunity, enabling speedier recovery from illness and therefore securing greater levels of energy and effort.

Dame Carol Black's 2008 review of the health of Britain's working-age population, 'Working for a healthier tomorrow,'[5] also found considerable evidence that health and wellbeing programmes produced economic benefits across all sectors and all sizes of business: in other words, good health is good business. She concluded the benefits of wellbeing went beyond the quality of life of staff and extended to increasing an organisation's productivity and profitability.

Teaching styles for wellbeing

Much of what we've already said about creating a wellbeing culture will feed into the classroom, of course. It's about being crystal clear what your school's values are and applying them at all times and in all situations.

But in more specific terms, some advice from the University of British Columbia might be useful to digest. The university has a 'Teaching and Learning Enhancement Fund' which trials different approaches, and it's come up with a synthesis of methods it believes work in promoting student wellbeing.[6]

Here's its advice, in summary. It was developed with university students but could equally apply with younger children:

- Foster connections: introduce yourself, use students' names, have short informal conversations with individuals, smile.

- Support peer relationships: start a session with an icebreaker, incorporate group work and discussion, keep the same groups throughout a term, encourage students to attend community events and run field trips where relevant.

- Help students to feel motivated: explain why a topic is important or relevant to their world, offer choices in assignments where possible, use hands-on learning, provide opportunities for them to explore a topic further alone, encourage students to ask questions, use multi-media, incorporate humour.

- Active teaching methods: simple language, clear examples; moving at a pace that's appropriate.

- Supporting structure: set out assignment and exam dates early, provide a detailed syllabus, share your course material in one place; be flexible on deadlines so that one bad day doesn't ruin a student's chances.

- Avoid group marks, provide timely feedback.

- Share general information about mental health and wellbeing, ask how they're doing, check in with students who may be struggling.

- A safe classroom environment: students shouldn't feel judged for making mistakes or holding opinions which are different from others,' establish relationships based on trust, use inclusive language and examples.

Practical steps

Here are some useful resources to help include your pupils in your planning for greater wellbeing:

The National Children's Bureau has produced a useful whole school framework for emotional wellbeing and mental health, with supporting resources for school leaders.[7] It suggests you might start by asking the following question: 'Are our ethos, mission statement and aims being effectively translated into meaningful learning experiences for all pupils, and what factors might impact on this?' From these discussions, you might go on to develop learning attributes which you can share with children, staff and parents.

Supplementary questions for discussion might include:

- Can our pupils identify the core values our school has in terms of wellbeing for all?

- Are those values integrated with the understanding and skills we teach on emotional development?

- Are pupils aware of the support available for them in the school, and do they believe it to be safe and confidential?

- What peer support systems are in place? These may be friendship groups as well as more formal systems.

- Who are your pupils' trusted adults, and are they always open and clear about their roles when having difficult conversations?

Here are some of the ways in which groups of schools in the NCB project went about developing a whole school approach to wellbeing and mental health.

Primary schools

Overall aim: 'To equip children with the knowledge and skills to allow them to successfully navigate the complexities of the social world that they are part of.'

The schools used a common framework comprising:

- Ethos: establishing children as partners in the process of learning.

- Community: creating and exploring spaces to enable learners to develop a range of personal and social skills.

- Lead: creating opportunities for both staff and pupils to lead on action research and the implementation of a range of innovative initiatives.

- Speak: opportunities for the development of a shared and common language for social engagement.

- Act: provide opportunities for effective practice. Once the ethos had been explored, schools then chose which other aspects of the framework for promoting the 'social learning agenda.'

Secondary schools

Secondary schools in the project, comprising all those in a single district, developed a whole school approach to their emotional wellbeing practice.

They used four stages:

1. Discover

2. Dream

3. Design

4. Destiny

In the discover part of the process, the schools:

- Built a dialogue with other forums, groups and decision-makers through a subgroup of heads from the secondary heads' forum.

- Established a Community of Practice across the 14 schools to share knowledge, experience and offer support.

Four specific lessons emerged:
Lesson one – staff wellbeing

- Leadership and senior level commitment is essential.

- Recognition is needed of the stress and strain on staff arising from external demands on schools and the increasingly complex problems and challenges students present.

- Teaching is about relationships and teachers see where young people are at risk.

The project identified three dilemmas for teachers:

- Supporting students' problems without the skills, time or credibility to do anything can affect staff emotional wellbeing.

- To be caring is to risk being out of your depth and can be damaging.

- There is a link between how you are treated and how able you are to treat others.

Through staff team sessions on how to protect and promote their own wellbeing, they strengthened their sense of efficacy and confidence. In the longer term, building this into the school culture as a normal part of practice could be transformative, they felt. They listed the following ways forward:

- The solution is change in school culture, not a stand-alone project.

- A whole school view of what is possible, building on what is happening now to avoid the sense this is another 'do more with less,' is needed.

- It's important to recognise the good practice that already exists. It may not be acknowledged or joined up. Using and building on these strengths helps to implement change.

- Develop small solutions, build on what you have as a route into engaging staff and senior leadership teams.

Much of the solution to integrating children's welfare into your staff wellbeing plan has already been discussed: as the NCB project identified, it's about building a culture across the whole school. Do that right, and the rest will largely work itself out.

Chapter 13: Key points

So, what is all this doing for the pupils? There are two answers.

One, a wellbeing culture should embrace everyone in the school community. Pupils should absorb positive, inclusive attitudes and values that they can take through life. Two, there's some evidence that happier staff get better results.

This chapter includes some suggestions on producing a whole school framework for emotional wellbeing, questions for discussion on pupils' involvement and links to further resources.

If you want to improve pupil wellbeing and outcomes:

- Follow the evidence – staff first

- Build the right wellbeing foundations, focusing on leaders' behaviours and processes that support these

- Role model the agreed values and don't pass on your stress (much easier to do in a safe and supportive culture)

- Use tried and tested methods to directly support pupils – the NCB provides a framework you can follow (there are others and you may have created your own). This is will only deliver the needed outcomes when built on the right staff wellbeing foundations.

Notes

1 House, H. and Dewberry, C. (2007). *Staff wellbeing is key to school success.* [online] Available at: https://clickweb.lancashire.gov.uk/modules/clicksuite/clickweb/media/doc.asp?id=44615.

2 Gibson, S. (2021). *Stress, burnout, anxiety and depression: How they impact on the mental health and wellbeing of teachers and on learner outcomes literature review October 2021.* [online] Available at: https://www.educationsupport.org.uk/media/qeupkgep/literature-review-stress-anxiety-burnout-and-depression-impact-on-teachers-and-on-learner-outcomes.pdf.

3 Bajorek, Z. and Gulliford, J. (2014). *Healthy teachers, higher marks? Establishing a link between teacher health & wellbeing, and student outcomes.* [online] Available at: https://f.hubspotusercontent10.net/hubfs/7792519/healthy_teachers_higher_marks_report.pdf [Accessed 14 December 2022].

4 Bryson, A., Forth, J. and Stokes, L. (2014). *Does worker wellbeing affect workplace performance?* [online] Available at: https://assets.publishing.service.gov.uk/government/uploads/system/uploads/attachment_data/file/366637/bis-14-1120-does-worker-wellbeing-affect-workplace-performance-final.pdf [Accessed 14 December 2022].

5 Hulshof, C.T.J. (2009). Working for a healthier tomorrow. *Occupational and Environmental Medicine,* [online] 66(1), pp.1–2. doi:10.1136/oem.2008.040899.

6 University of British Columbia, Teaching Strategies to Promote Student Wellbeing. (n.d.). [online] Available at: https://blogs.ubc.ca/teachingandwellbeing/files/2016/09/Science-Symposium-Handout-V2.pdf [Accessed 14 December 2022].

7 Stirling, S. and Emery, H. (2016). *A whole school framework for emotional well-being and mental health.* [online] *Partnership for Well-being and Mental Health in Schools.* NCB. Available at: https://www.ncb.org.uk/sites/default/files/uploads/files/NCB%20School%20Well%20Being%20Framework%20Leaders%20Resources_0.pdf.

SECTION 5
Overseeing change

14 The role of governors and trustees

If you're a trustee or governor, how do you fit into the wellbeing journey of your school or schools?

There are two things to think about: the things you should do; and the things you shouldn't.

We know from talking with CEOs and headteachers how important governors and trustees are; particularly those chairing the board: they can provide a sounding board and a confidential 'critical friend' on issues, some of which school leaders may not feel ready to address with their immediate team. They provide oversight and can provide reassurance that an eye is being cast over the school's strategic aims and that its sense of direction is the right one.

But when governance goes wrong, it can place extra and unnecessary burdens on already stretched school leaders and staff. It's a delicate balance, and one which needs constant thought and review. Governors are there to support, but they're also there to challenge, and that challenge can be stressful and burdensome at times.

So, where to start? The National Governance Association (NGA), with the Schools Advisory Service, has dug deep into this issue and has come up with detailed advice both for boards of governors in local schools, and for the boards of

DOI: 10.4324/9781003315766-19

MATs – we'll refer to them collectively here as 'boards.'[1] We've drawn heavily on their material in compiling this list of dos and don'ts:

Do:

- Respect the difference between strategic governance and operational management. The board's job is to support the delivery of core strategic functions; the CEO or headteacher is expected to implement them.

- Ensure that there are robust policies and practices in key areas such as behaviour, anti-bullying and diversity, including tackling prejudice and stigma around mental health.[2]

- Make sure you are compliant with employment and equalities legislation, promoting safeguarding, transparency and equality of opportunity and avoiding discriminatory practice.

- Monitor the impact of strategies and initiatives that promote a positive and sustainable workplace culture.

- Check HR policies are applied consistently and promote a positive culture.

- Set out a clear vision of where the governing or trust board wants the school to be in three to five years' time, in terms of creating a culture of wellbeing. The board and the CEO or headteacher share responsibility for creating a climate in which the school is seen to be a great place to work.

- Try to make sure all kinds of stakeholders are represented on the board – see below for information on recruiting a wellbeing governor.

- Engage with a wider range of stakeholders, including pupils, parents, staff and the wider community, to help you to make informed decisions about wellbeing policies. Building and maintaining key relationships is a shared responsibility between the board and the CEO or headteacher, so this should be undertaken collaboratively.

- Agree priorities to ensure that progress is made within available resources.

- Monitor progress on an annual cycle, with termly update, clearly set out and categorised.

- Treat the CEOs or headteacher's annual appraisal as an opportunity to provide support as well as a mechanism for accountability.

- Try to ensure the whole governing body or trust board embodies and reflects the school's culture of wellbeing in all its activities. All governors and trustees should feel supported to participate actively and equally.

- Ensure the relationship between chair and CEO or headteacher is based on trust, mutual respect and a full appreciation by each of the other's role and remit.

- Remember clerks to the board are also a part of your school community and deserve to have the same respect paid to their wellbeing as anyone else.

- Recognise the demands on leaders and treat them with compassion, even when there are difficult conversations to be had.

- Agree protocols with the CEO or headteacher to ensure visits are effective, conducted in the right spirit (i.e. not perceived as inspections) and convenient to all parties.

- Self-assess governor or trustee skills and governance. The NGA recommends boards and senior leaders self-evaluate annually and undertake an external review every three years or: before any significant change; when there is no previous history of board evaluation and so a starting point is required; when there is a new chair, new trustees or governors, or new leadership of the trust or school; and when there are specific issues with standards, financial management or complaints.

Don't:

- Get involved in day-to-day management or try to do other people's jobs for them. You may think you're helping, but this is likely to lead to confusion and stress on both sides.

- Overload CEOs or headteachers with strategies, initiatives and monitoring activities – as a board, you have a duty of care to support their work-life balance.

- Expect school leaders to be available on tap, or without notice – you have a responsibility to ensure they have time set aside for strategic thinking, including time spent off site if needed.

- Forget to regularly evaluate the impact of the board on the school and its staff – including in terms of workload.

Meetings

The timing of meetings is a key consideration. These should take place at appropriate intervals, should have manageable agendas and should be at a time which is manageable for all concerned. Think about whether some board members and staff attendees might be better able to manage their work-life balance if they were able to attend via an online platform rather than in person.

Data and information

As a board you will need key data in order to ensure you fulfil your duty to monitor what's happening in the school. However, the workload involved can be much reduced through careful planning, and by ensuring there isn't duplication. Before you ask for information, think about whether the material may be already available in an existing format. Monitoring visits are desirable, and the CEO or headteacher should encourage such visits. But they should take place under agreed protocols so that they are not seen as threatening and that they are at times convenient to everyone.

Information that will help boards understand the situation with regard to staff wellbeing include:

● Staff absences and changes in them.

● Staff retention and reasons, for example, from stay and exit interviews.

● Details of any grievances or disputes between staff.

● Pupil behaviour statistics.

● Information from surveys and other staff feedback.

This is in addition to anything governors or trustees pick up when visiting the school or from their meetings or papers they read. It is important to share this information in the way it is collected for the school, where possible, and not create another collection method, which will add to workload.

Leave implementation and day-to-day management to the executive team in the school or trust and make sure it is part of the school development plan so staff wellbeing is part of the mainstream and not something to the side. It also makes sure that progress is likely to be tracked more effectively.

Do we need a formal wellbeing policy?

As we've discussed elsewhere, it's good practice for a school to have a staff wellbeing policy. But if there isn't one, there's no need for governors to impose one. The NCB suggests appointing a wellbeing link governor or trustee, who can liaise with the CEO or headteacher and other senior leaders – see below for help with appointing such a governor if you don't have an obvious candidate for the role. Governors should be there as a support for staff wellbeing, and by absorbing the values and practices which form part of the school's wider culture, they should be able to reinforce and strengthen it.

Practical steps to take

We suggested a staff wellbeing policy in Chapter 11 based on the HSE management standards, but you may also want to look at this template from the London Grid for

Learning: https://wbc.lgfl.org.uk/documents/Staff%20Wellbeing/Template%20Staff%20Wellbeing%20Evaluation.pdf.[3]

Governors for Schools has a programme to help match governing bodies with wellbeing governors. Find out more here: https://governorsforschools.org.uk/wellbeing-governors/the-role-of-the-wellbeing-link-governor/

Governors for Schools has also run a wellbeing webinar on how and why governors should support staff mental health and wellbeing, and a summary of key points is available here:

https://governorsforschools.org.uk/app/uploads/2021/01/Health-Wellbeing-Webinar-Summary.pdf

In this video, Sinéad Mc Brearty, CEO of Education Support, talks with school governor Adam Thomas and Hannah Stolten, CEO of Governors for Schools about how governors can support staff mental health and wellbeing: https://youtu.be/OOIbyVoU6j4;

The DfE's workload reduction resources can be useful for governing bodies: https://www.gov.uk/guidance/school-workload-reduction-toolkit#support-for-governing-boards-and-trustees

Chapter 14: Key points

How do governors and trustees fit into the wellbeing journeys of schools (and multi-academy trusts)? Again there are two answers: there are the things they should do, and things they shouldn't.

They should:

- Provide a sounding board on ideas and issues.
- Make sure the strategic direction is right.
- Respect the difference between governance and operational management.
- Manage the meetings schedule to ensure work-life balance for governors, trustees and staff.
- Make sure the right policies are in place.
- Oversee compliance with employment and equalities legislation.
- Monitor the impact of strategies and initiatives for wellbeing.
- Make sure policies are applied consistently.
- Set out a clear vision of where the school is going.
- Bring in a wide range of stakeholders.
- Embody the school's values and act with compassion, even when difficult conversations are necessary.

- Remember they have a duty of care to school leaders.

- Carry out an annual internal evaluation and consider external validation every three years.

They shouldn't:

- Get involved in day-to-day management or try to do other people's jobs for them.

- Overload the headteacher with strategies, initiatives and monitoring activities.

- Expect school leaders to be available on tap or without notice.

- Forget to regularly evaluate the impact of the board on the school and its staff.

- Impose a staff wellbeing policy if it isn't in place – a link governor for wellbeing is an alternative. There is guidance on appointing one in the chapter.

This chapter also has hints on practical steps to take, and links to further reading.

Notes

1 NGA: Promoting a culture of wellbeing in schools and trusts: An evaluation tool for governing boards and school leaders. https://www.nga.org.uk/Knowledge-Centre/Staffing/Workload-and-wellbeing/School-leader-wellbeing.aspx
2 https://wbc.lgfl.org.uk/documents/Staff%20We LGFL (2022). *Staff wellbeing policy.* [online] Lgfl.org.uk. Available at: https://wbc.lgfl.org.uk/documents/Staff%20Wellbeing/Template%20Wellbeing%20Policy%20for%20shools.docx [Accessed 14 December 2022].
3 National Governance Association (2014). *Promoting school leaders' wellbeing.* [online] Nga.org.uk. Available at: https://www.nga.org.uk/Knowledge-Centre/Staffing/Workload-and-wellbeing/School-leader-wellbeing.aspx [Accessed 14 December 2022].

15 Bringing the outside in

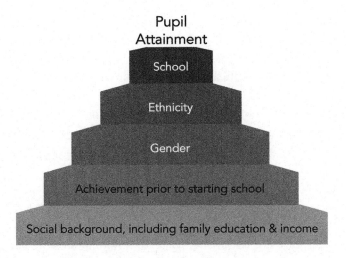

Pupil
Attainment

School

Ethnicity

Gender

Achievement prior to starting school

Social background, including family education & income

Let's return for a moment to John Maher, the principal of Ashfield School – we met him in Section 2:

> Some of our students may be causing disruption in the community at the weekend but they're not behaving that way in school. … We are the size of a village here; we have 3000 individuals crammed together in a small space 39 weeks of the year and that can go massively wrong or right.
>
> When the students walk in this door they can leave all the troubles, all the clashes they are having outside… they can just come in, follow the behaviour codes of the school, relax and be their safe and real selves.

Effective school leaders like John Maher create a culture within their school walls that is recognised and accepted by everyone, by and large. But they also recognise that children – and staff – have much more going on outside the school and will inevitably bring some of this with them every day.

There's a wealth of research which tells us the effectiveness of schools is not only due to what they do, and that more of it is down to the attributes the pupils have when they arrive. The late, great Professor of Social Statistics, Harvey Goldstein, believed that once you took into account all the social factors affecting schools, there was a limited amount they *could* actually do, in terms of improving exam results:

> After you've adjusted for the achievements of children when they start school, there are further effects related to their social background, whether they're a boy or girl, their ethnic background. Other background factors – social class, income; all these have a very important effect, very early on in childhood.
>
> The school effect tends to be rather small. Once you've taken account of all this, maybe it accounts for 10 per cent of what's left, which is not enormous.[1]

Other researchers have come up with similar results: a major study in the United States[2] found classroom behaviour was significantly influenced by factors such as homelessness, abuse, being the child of a teen mother or of one who didn't do well in education. The more of these risks a child faced outside the school gate, the higher the likelihood that he or she might have behavioural or attendance problems.

So, schools aren't islands. It would be a counsel of despair, though, to simply say there isn't much they can do to change things. The best schools, and their leaders, are the ones who plough on regardless, doing what they *can* do. John Maher is among them, and he and his peers have seen the changes that can take place when you do the right things and keep on doing them every day.

And there is good news. There's significant evidence that by building relationships with parents, carers, families and other outside stakeholders, a school can bring them into its vision and culture so that they understand and bolster it.[3] The National Children's Bureau, in its review of the evidence on promoting wellbeing in schools,[4] advises that involving parents, carers and families can strengthen schools' efforts by reinforcing their own strengths and by enabling them to reflect back the messages of the school to their offspring.

This can be done informally, through conversations with individual parents or carers, or it can be done more formally through a presentation at a parents' evening, through printed information, through parenting education courses or through work with dedicated family link workers.

Informal contacts

Several of the headteachers featured in the book, in talking about the situations that cause stress in their daily lives, mentioned that real flash points can come in dealing with parents. One said his moment of breakdown, after which he had to take time out and to re-evaluate his practice, was accompanied by a lengthy complaint involving an ombudsman. Others talked about tricky meetings which played on their mind before and after they took place.

These aren't always easy relationships. Parents don't always have the same values and aims as schools; maybe they've had terrible experiences of education themselves and are at risk of transmitting those feelings to their children. Those who have had good experiences may expect their children's education to be a carbon copy. Others may be very vocal in their determination that their offspring should do well; should be in the top sets and should never be held back – even when their grades aren't supporting this.

Most schools will be well aware, then, that it's helpful to build strong foundations before any issues arise. Meeting parents before their children start at the school, for instance, and being visible at the school gates each day so that parents can stop and chat, can be good ways of strengthening relationships.

On a slightly more formal note, it's helpful – if sometimes impractical – to let parents know you are available to them and that they can speak to you about any concerns. Use these contacts to reinforce the schools' values, where appropriate.

The next step

Advice from the Anna Freud National Centre for Children and Families suggests[5] schools might wish to develop a differentiated approach to parental engagement; with different strategies for those who have the greatest needs. The centre points out that these relationships will improve – and the school's values will be more likely to be adopted – if the school ethos recognises the importance of a child's home environment, family situation and key relationships.

Strategies it suggests include:

● Invite parents and carers into school to celebrate achievements.

● Be sensitive to children's and families' social context and the difficulties they may be facing.

● Try to build a sense of belonging and teamwork by regular, positive messaging. Make sure parents know you're in it together and can make things work.

● Identify your ten most challenging students; have regular conversations with those around them and have a senior leader text positive feedback at least once a week.

Spotting the signs

Mentally Healthy Schools, a collaboration between three of the United Kingdom's leading child mental health and education charities, has a useful checklist of things that might indicate a child is struggling with issues at home.[6] These might include:

● Becoming withdrawn.

● Sleeplessness and nightmares.

● Behavioural problems and anger.

- School refusal.

- Regressing or acting suddenly younger than their years – for example, clinginess or baby talk.

The organisation suggests that as a first step, classroom teachers should involve their school's designated safeguarding lead if they spot these signs. They should be able to advise on suitable next steps, which should include being there to provide continuity, comfort and a sense of belonging for children who are going through changes in their personal lives.

Its checklist, which reflects much of what we covered when discussing building a whole school culture, includes:

- Helping children and young people develop resilience through teaching and embodying social and emotional skills.

- Building that sense of belonging and positive relationships based on trust, safety and security.

- Promoting acceptance and understanding and demonstrating what healthy relationships with adults can be.

- Noticing when a student is struggling: some may benefit from seeing a school nurse or accessing one-to-one or group-based counselling. Community-based support groups include community counselling, specialist Children's Mental Health Services, voluntary sector organisations, family support or children's services.

- Creating a school atmosphere that welcomes and celebrates all types of families.

- Working in partnership with parents and carers to find the best strategy for supporting their child. Being aware that parents and carers may also be under pressure and providing signposting to appropriate support.

Questions for the whole school

- How does the board of governors approach parental engagement? Are parents and carers represented in decision-making?

- Are there opportunities for parents and carers to come into school and attend events alongside their children? Are parents and carers aware of how they can best support their child's learning, both in school and at home? Are there opportunities for parents and carers to talk about mental health and wellbeing?

- Are staff and parents and carers given the opportunity to learn about mental health and wellbeing? Are they aware of local partnerships who could support parents and families?

● Are there other stakeholders that you could engage with in order to support parents and carers: MAT, local education authority, faith groups, community organisations, national helplines and websites?

Further resources

Use this link for guidance from the Anna Freud Centre on engaging parents and carers on the topic of mental health and wellbeing: https://www.annafreud.org/media/9165/supporting-schools-to-engage-with-all-parents-and-carers-booklet.pdf

Or for advice and information on understanding mental health problems: https://mindedforfamilies.org.uk/

Chapter 15: Key points

● Schools aren't islands. No matter how strong the school's culture is, pupils and staff will bring in their baggage, their stresses and their crises from other parts of their lives. But there's plenty of evidence that by building relationships with parents, carers, families and other outside stakeholders, a school can bring stakeholders into its vision and culture so that they understand and bolster it.

● This can be done informally, through conversations with individual parents or carers, or more formally at a parents' evening, through printed information, through parent courses or through family link workers.

● The Anna Freud National Centre for Children and Families suggests[7] different strategies depending on a family's level and type of engagement. You might invite parents and carers into school to celebrate achievements, use positive messaging to make sure parents know you're in this together, identify your ten most challenging students and organise regular conversations along with positive feedback. Try to be sensitive to each family's needs and issues.

● Mentally Healthy Schools has a useful checklist of things to look out for.[8] Children struggling at home might be withdrawn, tired, angry, absent or act younger than their years. Your school's safeguarding lead should be involved and may be able to help families to get appropriate support. Key tips include being clear and open about the problem, positioning the parent or carer as the expert, highlighting the child's strengths, using reflective listening, focusing on opportunities to work together and trying to imagine how they feel.

● Whole school questions include reflecting on how governors and trustees engage with parents, whether parents have enough opportunities to be in school, whether everyone is aware of resources to learn about mental health and wellbeing, and whether other outside organisations could help.

Notes

1 Abrams, F. BBC Radio 4 analysis: Do schools make a difference? October 2012: https://www.bbc.co.uk/programmes/b01b9hjs

2 Rouse, H.L., Fantuzzo, J.W. and LeBoeuf, W. (2011). Comprehensive Challenges for the Well Being of Young Children: A Population-based Study of Publicly Monitored Risks in a Large Urban Center. *Child Youth Care Forum*, 40, pp.281–302. doi:10.1007/s10566-010-9138-y

3 Demkowicz, O. & Humphrey, N. (2019). *Whole School Approaches to Promoting Mental Health: What Does the Evidence Say?* London: EBPU. https://www.ucl.ac.uk/evidence-based-practice-unit/sites/evidence-based-practice-unit/files/evidencebriefing5_v1d7_completed_06.01.20.pdf

4 Stirling, S. and Emery, H. (2016). *A whole school framework for emotional well-being and mental health.* [online] NCB. Available at: https://www.ncb.org.uk/sites/default/files/uploads/files/NCB%20School%20Well%20Being%20Framework%20Leaders%20Resources_0.pdf.

5 Anna Freud National Centre for Children and Families, Supporting mental health & well-being in schools: Engaging with all parents and carers, undated, https://www.annafreud.org/media/9165/supporting-schools-to-engage-with-all-parents-and-carers-booklet.pdf.

6 Mentally Healthy Schools (n.d.). *Home environment: Mentally healthy schools.* [online] mentallyhealthyschools.org.uk. Available at: https://www.mentallyhealthyschools.org.uk/risks-and-protective-factors/home-based-risk-factors/home-environment [Accessed 14 December 2022].

7 Anna Freud National Centre for Children and Families, Supporting mental health & well-being in schools: Engaging with all parents and carers, undated, https://www.annafreud.org/media/9165/supporting-schools-to-engage-with-all-parents-and-carers-booklet.pdf.

8 Identifying the signs, Mentally Healthy Schools, https://www.mentallyhealthyschools.org.uk/risks-and-protective-factors/home-based-risk-factors/home-environment/

SECTION 6
Rethinking education for wellbeing

16 Rewriting the book

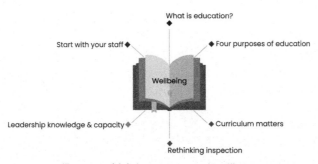

Illustration 16.1 Inspections and wellbeing

So what if we could start again, with a blank sheet? What would education look like for most young people? Would we put wellbeing at the heart of the system, or not? If we did, how might it look?

We can't do it, can we? Education isn't only about wellbeing, and neither is adult life. There's a natural and sometimes creative tension which should be inherent in study or work, in which we need to push ourselves outside our comfort zone. But we do know from the evidence set out in the preceding chapters that a happy school is more likely to be a successful school.

In this chapter, we're taking a step back to look at the bigger picture. If we *could* start from scratch and put the wellbeing of staff (and pupils) front and centre of education systems around the world, what would change? Would we teach the same subjects? Would we teach differently? How would schools be inspected, and would management structures be altered?

What *is* education, anyway? Do we even want it to always be comfortable and nurturing, or is that idea sometimes at odds with the discipline and rigour that is necessary in order to create an ordered and high-achieving environment?

DOI: 10.4324/9781003315766-22

What is education?

There are so many answers to this question that we certainly can't visit them all. But here are a few which might help point to ways in which wellbeing could be made more central. Education is nothing if it isn't about what societies need now, so of course it needs to change with the times. And this is something that's recognised by the United Nations' education agency, UNESCO.

UNESCO was founded in 1945 with an aim that very strongly reflected the time: to use culture and education to promote justice, liberty and world peace – a job which it said could clearly not be left to governments. And while it hasn't revised this view, it has come up with a new angle in recent years:

> We commit with a sense of urgency to a single, renewed education agenda that is holistic, ambitious and aspirational, leaving no one behind. This new vision [should] 'ensure inclusive and equitable quality education and promote lifelong learning opportunities for all.[1]

Surely there should be room in there somewhere for creating cultures based on a sense of wellbeing. Indeed there is. "A good quality education is the foundation of health and wellbeing," UNESCO says on its website – pointing out, as a corollary, that for many children, wellbeing starts with being adequately fed and vaccinated, being able to survive childhood and to do so with both parents alive and well.[2]

A good quality of education is a foundation stone to which every human being should have a right. So far, so good. But what *is* it? Perhaps we should turn for answers to the late Sir Ken Robinson, whose TedTalks on education and creativity have been viewed more than 80 million times.[3]

In a posthumously published book,[4] he set out a vision of what it should mean to be educated now:

> I believe that education should expand our consciousness, capabilities, sensitivities, and cultural understanding. It should enlarge our worldview. As we all live in two worlds—the world within you that exists only because you do, and the world around you—the core purpose of education is to enable students to understand both worlds. In today's climate, there is also a new and urgent challenge: to provide forms of education that engage young people with the global-economic issues of environmental wellbeing.

He sets out four purposes of education:

- Personal: education is deeply personal and is about cultivating the minds and hearts of people as individuals – many of the deepest problems in current systems of education result from losing sight of this basic principle.

- Cultural: schools should help students understand their own cultures, understand other cultures and promote a sense of cultural tolerance and coexistence.

- Economic: education should enable students to become economically responsible and independent. With the world of work changing at an ever-quickening pace, that means connecting them with their own unique talents and interests, dissolving the division between academic and vocational programmes and ensuring young people experience working environments long before it is time for them to enter the labour market.

- Social: education should enable young people to become active and compassionate citizens. It is essential to give young people real-life democratic experiences long before they come of age to vote.

These four purposes suggest eight core competencies, he says:

> Curiosity, creativity, criticism, communication, collaboration, compassion, composure, and citizenship.

Now, ask yourself a question: could these competencies be learned in an educational environment that didn't have a culture of wellbeing – the sort of supportive culture suggested by leaders from successful schools who are quoted in this book?

There's an alternative view, of course: that young people should be raised in an atmosphere that's disciplined; where there's a focus on rigour, and possibly also on tradition. Maybe it isn't incompatible? As Sir Ken points out, there's plenty of room in a modern education system for diversity and for different pathways towards a common end.

Take this, from the British Army's Chief of the General Staff, in the introduction to a document setting out what soldiers must be in future[5]:

> Today in the Army it's not just the outcome that's important. It's increasingly the manner in which that outcome is achieved; this is about common decency and courtesy. It's about mutual respect, and the moral courage to do not just the right thing, but the best thing, and not to tolerate anything less. There's nothing politically correct or woke about it. It's about improving how we treat each other and how we behave around one another.

Armies aren't known for their political correctness, or for their willingness to nurture individuality. Yet this one is placing a 'values and standards-based character and resilience grounding' at the heart of its basic training, to 'maintain our advantage by outperforming our adversaries physically, cognitively, and socially,' and supported by a dedicated team to support mental health and wellbeing. If they can do it, maybe it isn't a controversial notion?

What's the evidence for an education system built for wellbeing?

So, an education system which values individuality, yet which is based on mutual respect and compassion, is a desirable thing. But will it fulfil its other basic purpose, which is to ensure young people have the economic, cultural and social capital they need to lead fulfilled and useful lives?

Here's a recap on what the evidence tells us about putting wellbeing at the heart of education, based on a review conducted for the National Children's Bureau (NCB).[6]

Taken together, well-conducted reviews demonstrate there is a solid group of approaches, programmes and interventions which show repeated and clear evidence of positive impacts on:

- Academic learning, motivation, sense of commitment and connectedness with learning and with school.

- Staff wellbeing, reduced stress, sickness and absence, improved teaching ability and performance.

- Pupil wellbeing including happiness, a sense of purpose, connectedness and meaning.

- The development of the social and emotional skills and attitudes that promote learning, success, wellbeing and mental health, in school and throughout life.

- The prevention and reduction of mental health problems such as depression, anxiety and stress.

- Improving school behaviour, including reductions in low-level disruption, incidents, fights, bullying, exclusions and absence.

- Reductions in risky behaviour – such as impulsiveness, uncontrolled anger, violence, bullying and crime, early sexual experience, alcohol and drug use.

What's not to like? Follow the evidence, consistently and with a sense of purpose, and you should see positive effects on learning, pupil wellbeing, social skills and behaviour, along with a happier workforce.

The NCB report comes up with a list of approaches which will, when done right, yield results:

- Wellbeing in schools starts with the staff: they need to feel motivated and able to promote emotional and social wellbeing in others, and they can't do that if they're stressed and burned-out.

- Take a whole-school approach and implement it carefully. Start with a positive and universal focus on wellbeing, emphasising strengths and capacities rather than focusing on problems and weaknesses.

- Develop a supportive ethos which fosters a sense of 'connectedness.'

- Intervene early, if you can: the most effective interventions are those that target the preschool and early primary years.

- Think long term: a major reason why interventions fail is that they aren't long enough or intense enough to make a difference. Brief interventions don't tend to have a sustained impact.

- Your initiatives will work better if you involve parents, carers and families.

- Remember that mental health issues and stress are normal, particularly for young people who are going through rapid changes while growing up.

- Use expert intervention, for example, from psychologists for specific projects such as teaching about stress, or to help young people with problems. Refer to outside agencies where necessary.

- Teach social and emotional skills, which can provide protection against mental health problems or risky behaviour.

- Set clear boundaries for discipline and apply them consistently. Everyone needs to know what's acceptable and what's not acceptable, and to understand the consequences of transgression.

- Understand the causes of behaviour: responses based solely on punishment, which see behaviour in isolation, tend not to work well.

Curriculum matters?

Would we need to rethink the curriculum if we wanted an education system built for wellbeing? There isn't really a consensus on this one, and in any case, maybe this needs to be a separate conversation about equipping young people with knowledge and skills relevant to the world they're growing up in. This means ensuring teachers and support staff are also fully equipped to manage the challenges they face in being role models, as well as being able to teach others. Maybe we could build the list of proven approaches into a traditional curriculum just as easily as we could make it happen in a different, modernised one.

There is one curriculum-related piece of information that is useful – according to a review[7] of the evidence, there's a strong correlation between the quality of personal, social and health education in a school and its overall effectiveness.

The review suggests some common themes which can help – many of them reflect the wider evidence about how to build a culture of wellbeing.

- Remember this isn't just about PSHE lessons but about fostering good relationships and wellbeing across the whole curriculum.

- Include lessons which are participative and interactive; allow pupils to be involved in developing them.

- Make sure lessons have clear objectives and are taught by people who are trained and comfortable in the role.

- Be inclusive of different cultures, ethnicities, sexual orientations, faiths and ages.

- Start early but make sure content is age-appropriate.

- Involve outside agencies.

- Ensure there's buy-in from the senior management team.

- Evaluate and monitor so that goals and outcomes are clear.

Rethinking inspection

The key document for inspections in England, the Ofsted framework, doesn't specifically use the word 'wellbeing.' The equivalent document for Scotland uses it 63 times. To be fair, its teams should ask whether school leaders are working to ensure there aren't unnecessary burdens on school staff in terms of workload, whether they engage well with staff and take account of the pressures on them, and whether they protect them from bullying and harassment. They also ask whether relationships among learners and staff reflect a positive and respectful culture.

However, it is interesting to note that in the questionnaire issued by Ofsted to staff during an inspection, it is not until question 13 that a question directly asks how they are motivated or led effectively, and workload is not mentioned until question 19. Some of the earlier questions do cover areas that will impact staff wellbeing, such as pupil behaviour – this speaks to the focus on inspections being very much pupil focused.

The framework[8] also reads as if staff and pupil wellbeing has been shoehorned in as an afterthought. Read this:

> The resources and materials teachers select – *in a way that does not create unnecessary workload for staff* (our emphasis) – reflect the provider's ambitious intentions for the course of study and clearly support the intent of a coherently planned curriculum, sequenced towards cumulatively sufficient knowledge and skills for future learning and employment.

It matters because in the United Kingdom all state schools must face inspection, and they know it matters: their reputation and even their future depend on it. Poor inspection results are often a driver to schools becoming academies or being moved to different academy trusts. So inspection frameworks really do drive the way in which schools operate.

The Independent Schools Inspectorate (ISI) has attempted to address this in the form of a new inspection framework to be launched in September 2023. ISI is appointed by the government to check on non-state schools which are associated with the Independent Schools' Council as well as some overseas schools and independent further education colleges – educating around half a million young people.

Its first principle reads: "This inspection framework places the responsibility of the school's leadership and management and governance to actively promote the wellbeing of pupils at the centre of ISI's evaluation of the school."

The inspectorate says explicitly that it intends to focus on the impact of school leadership on pupil wellbeing. It names four key values which it believes will put children's wellbeing at the heart of a school's life: children first, diversity, integrity, transparency. It defines pupils' wellbeing as meaning their physical and mental health and emotional wellbeing, protection from harm or neglect, education, training and recreation, contribution to society and social and economic wellbeing.

However, this is a missed opportunity – there is no explicit mention of the wellbeing of staff.In its response to consultation on its new framework, ISI set out the following.[9]

The focus on wellbeing:

- ISI will continue to emphasise that the framework does not place any additional responsibility on schools or introduce additional requirements that are not already contained in the Standards.

- School leaders are already required to 'actively promote the wellbeing of pupils.' The definition of 'wellbeing' is clearly articulated by statute and incorporated in the Standards. Evidence of effective provision can be clearly demonstrated as stated in the framework across many aspects of school life which are covered by the Standards.

- The proposed framework supports school leaders in articulating the impact of their leadership by providing a structured approach to demonstrating how they meet this existing requirement.

- Hearing the views of pupils continues to be an important aspect of inspection practice and is triangulated with other inspection evidence. Inspectors will continue to be interested to hear from school leaders how pupil voice is heard and acted upon by the school.

We know there is good intention; most school leaders want to support their staff and build a culture where they can do their best work. Yet in such a busy environment what gets measured will take priority.

Should this be the case? It is clear that structures within education in many countries are not consistently delivering the outcomes we all want to see. Demands (workload) placed on staff and the lack of control many of them feel are usually cited as reasons behind high stress levels and poor wellbeing. Yet it is how well these are led and managed that is both the real problem and a big opportunity.

Without creating capacity for leaders to lead, and without giving them the right tools to enable them to be people experts alongside their subject expertise, significant change is unlikely. There are many CEOs, principals and other leaders who do great work in building wellbeing foundations and a climate and culture where staff can do their best work. This is in spite of the current system, resources and capacity.

The big opportunity is in providing leaders, both those newly appointed and those that are more experienced, with more time to lead. Education is one of only a handful of sectors where those promoted often have to carry on with a significant part of their previous job – for example, classroom teaching. Elsewhere, a majority of a leader's time is spent leading, supporting, coaching and developing team members.

It's important to have experienced teachers in the classroom, but how do we ensure newly appointed middle leaders, particularly those with large teams, have time to learn the new skills they need as well as to practise and improve them?

If we want to make schools and other education organisations more attractive places to work, to reduce staff attrition, to improve recruitment and to further raise and sustain pupil outcomes, we need a change. One that requires a significant financial investment, increased teacher numbers, improved continuing professional development (CPD) and better succession planning. We need to ensure all leaders have the skills they need and time available to use them.

Unfortunately, it does not look like there is the political or financial will to deliver this and the current economic situation makes it even more unlikely. That is why this book has been written – to provide practical help to support the delivery of staff wellbeing improvement, with all the benefits this brings, despite the current challenges.

Chapter 16: Key points

- Let's start again with a blank sheet. Can education really be about wellbeing, or do we need to accept we sometimes need to be pushed outside our comfort zone to meet life's challenges?

- These days even the British Army believes that need for stretch and challenge must be accompanied by mutual respect and the moral courage to do 'not just the right thing, but the best thing.' So surely we can have a culture of wellbeing in schools without their core purpose being compromised.

- What is education, anyway? The United Nations started out with the view it should be about engendering world peace, but now it believes it's also the foundation of health and wellbeing.

- The late Sir Ken Robinson believed education had four purposes: personal, cultural, economic and social. He added eight core competencies: curiosity, creativity, criticism, communication, collaboration, compassion, composure and citizenship. These competencies could only be learned in a supportive, compassionate institution.

- Does curriculum matter? Possibly not, in the wider sense – but there is evidence that really good Personal, Social and Health Education does make a difference in terms of wellbeing. It needs to be taught with a whole-school focus, involving all pupils and with clear objectives. It needs to start early but to be age-appropriate, to have buy-in from senior leaders and to be monitored properly to ensure its goals are met.

- The inspection framework of the government's inspection service for England, Ofsted, doesn't mention wellbeing, though it does look at workload, bullying and other wellbeing issues. A new inspection framework to be introduced in September 2023, developed by the United Kingdom's ISI, puts pupil wellbeing up front and centre – it's worth a read. Its inspectors focus on key values which should put children's wellbeing at the heart of school life. However, it fails to mention staff wellbeing. What gets measured gets done and this is a missed opportunity – leaders need to choose to make staff wellbeing central to what they do.

- Communicate, communicate, communicate.

Notes

1 UNESCO, 2 UNESCO (2013). *Education for health and well-being.* [online] UNESCO. Available at: https://en.unesco.org/themes/education-health-and-well-being#:~:text=UNESCO [Accessed 14 December 2022]. UNESCO (2016). *Education 2030: Incheon declaration and framework for action,* https://unesdoc.unesco.org/ark:/48223/pf0000245656

2 UNESCO (2019). *Education 2030: Incheon declaration and framework for action.* [Online] Unesco.org. Available at: https://unesdoc.unesco.org/ark:/48223/pf0000245656. Education for Health and Wellbeing, UNESCO website: https://en.unesco.org/themes/education-health-and-wellbeing

3 TED (2006). *Do schools kill creativity? | Sir Ken Robinson. YouTube.* Available at: https://www.youtube.com/watch?v=iG9CE55wbtY.

4 Sir Robinson, K. and Robinson, K. (2022). *Imagine if: Creating a future for us all.* London: Penguin Books.

5 UK Government (2021). *Future soldier guide | 1.* [online] Available at: https://assets.publishing.service.gov.uk/government/uploads/system/uploads/attachment_data/file/1037759/ADR010310-FutureSoldierGuide_30Nov.pdf.

6 Professor Weare, K. (2015).What works in promoting social and emotional wellbeing and responding to mental health problems in schools? National Children's Bureau, 2015, https://www.ncb.org.uk/sites/default/files/uploads/files/ncb_framework_for_promoting_wellbeing_and_responding_to_mental_health_in_schools_0.pdf

7 Department for Education (2015). *PSHE education: A review of impact and effective practice.* [online] gov.uk. Available at: https://www.gov.uk/government/publications/pshe-education-a-review-of-impact-and-effective-practice.

8 Ofsted (2022). *Education inspection framework.* [online] gov.uk. Available at: https://www.gov.uk/government/publications/education-inspection-framework/education-inspection-framework.

9 Independent Schools Inspectorate (2022). *Consultation response summary consultation and pupil feedback on proposed changes to how association independent schools in England are inspected from September 2023 Feedback table and modifications 2.* [online] Available at: https://static1.squarespace.com/static/624881de604b217e86768672/t/6384865a21635d43d069a3ce/1669629531131/consultation_response_summary.pdf [Accessed 2 January 2023].

17 Getting physical

We've spent a lot of time discussing things you have to dig into to be able to see – culture, management systems, ways of behaving. But there are also more tangible, physical ways in which schools can promote wellbeing, both for staff and for pupils.

Look around you – maybe you're sitting in a calm, quiet, leafy environment, in a school with large playing fields and lovely gardens where members of your community can take a break and recharge batteries. And maybe you aren't. Maybe you're close to a six-lane highway, with minimal outside space and buildings which frankly should have been knocked down in the 1970s.

Some of those things can't easily be changed. You can't move your school easily from the inner city to the leafy shires, and nor would you necessarily want to. But there are changes many schools can make to ensure their physical environment is as healthy as it can be. And if at this point you're already shaking your head and muttering 'capital budget,' take heart. Probably you haven't got a spare couple of million in your back pocket just itching to be spent on a Zen garden, but maybe this chapter will arm you with some useful ammunition when you make a bid for capital funding.

DOI: 10.4324/9781003315766-23

Where does it go wrong?

Temperature

It possibly won't come as a surprise that room temperature is a key factor in basic welfare for pupils and staff alike. Older school buildings are likely to be draughty in winter and overheated in summer – not to mention the risks of stepping around receptacles placed to catch drips from leaking roofs.

A study of 75,000 high school students in New York City[1] found they were 12.3 per cent more likely to fail an exam on a 30-degree day than on a 20-degree day. Why? Poor ventilation has to be a factor, as we have to assume exams are taken indoors. Researchers at the Harvard TH Chan School of Public Health[2] reviewed more than 200 different scientific studies and found:

- Poor ventilation in schools caused loss of concentration, low attention spans and fatigue.

- Increased classroom noise was associated with lower test scores in primary schools.

- In the United States, it was estimated that almost half of all schools were dealing with environmental issues that contributed to poor air quality.

We must assume, of course, that if an issue affects pupils, it also affects staff – so problems are magnified as pupils and teachers all struggle to produce their best work. The researchers called for standardised health performance indicators for schools, and a national school infrastructure assessment: "investing in school buildings is an investment in our collective future," they wrote. They didn't add, but could, that it is also an investment in a happy, productive teaching force.

It isn't just the indoor environment that can make people ill – those same researchers used satellite imaging to judge how green the landscapes were around school buildings, and found those with greener space around them had lower rates of absenteeism. Even after controlling for factors such as household incomes and race in the schools' areas – after all, attendance is likely to be lower in poorer areas which are also less green – they found the same. And they also looked at air quality in those areas, with a similar result: where there are higher levels of particulates in the atmosphere, absenteeism is higher – in fact, the effect sizes for greenness and pollution levels are as big as those for either racial mix or incomes in the area.

What can be done?

The Harvard researchers have spent years looking at the ways in which school buildings and their surroundings can affect both physical health and academic performance. They recognise schools don't have much control over these things, but they suggest there are some solutions which might be affordable even for the most cash-strapped.

For example, they say, improved ventilation systems can reduce the levels of particulates in the air – as well as helping to control the spread of infectious diseases. Planting trees and investing in landscaping can also help, as can access to parks and nature: we'll come on to that one but suffice to say if you really can't add green spaces to your school estate, you might think about other ways to give both pupils and staff access to them.

You might also want to think about items such as the floor coverings you use: other research from the same team, which looked at office workers, found those in certified 'green buildings'[3] where there were lower levels of the volatile organic compounds emitted by furniture and carpets suffered 30 per cent fewer 'sick building' symptoms such as headaches, eye and respiratory complaints. Ventilation, they said, is another way to mitigate this and increase productivity by thousands of dollars per worker per year, for a cost of just tens.[4] Light levels tended to be better, too, in greener buildings – and that contributed to performance.

There are other ways you can improve your school's indoor environment to boost performance and wellbeing. A study at the University of Salford[5] identified seven design features that together could explain 16 per cent of variation in pupils' progress. Three of these we've already discussed: light, temperature and air quality. The other four were:

- **Ownership**: Adding originality or novelty character which make a room unique can make its users feel more connected and can improve performance. For children, personalised lockers or coat hooks, good quality or ergonomic and comfortable furniture, even a unique location can help improve the experiences of both staff and pupils. Intimate corners and even distinctive ceiling patterns can strengthen this sense of ownership.

- **Flexibility**: This pointed to the idea of 'horses for courses,' with larger rooms with simpler shapes for older pupils and more complex ones for younger pupils. Breakout spaces and rooms, clever storage solutions, different learning zones and display areas were helpful, though more of these were needed for younger than for older children.

- **Complexity**: The study found balance was needed here – too sterile and the room wouldn't provide enough visual stimulation; too complex and attention would start to wander.

- **Colour**: White walls plus a feature wall with vivid and or light colour was found to produce a good level of stimulation, as did brightly coloured furniture and displays. According to the Salford team, room colour had an effect on both emotions and physiology, causing mood swings that could affect performance.

The researchers said they'd found support for the idea of 'inside out' design, which focuses on the user's needs rather than on the design *per se*. So, they said, in design terms, there was no such thing as a bad school, just bad classrooms which didn't meet their users' needs.

Going outdoors

There's a wealth of evidence, then, that being in greener, cleaner spaces helps both productivity and wellbeing. And there's more. Taking learning outdoors, where possible, can also be helpful for all concerned.[6] Learning in natural settings can boost social and collaborative skills, self-confidence, engagement and even academic attainment.

This isn't controversial – its' widely accepted now that being outdoors is good for your physical health and your mental wellbeing. There's even an Outdoor Classroom Day movement,[7] dedicated to inspiring and celebrating outdoor play and learning. There are two such days each year, so why not get involved and go outside, perhaps with a trip into the countryside, especially if your school doesn't have much green space of its own?

The organisation suggests teachers can boost their own sense of wellbeing, on any day of the year, by:

- Taking a moment or two every day during playtime to walk around outside – even if just for 10 minutes.

- Experiment with taking lessons outdoors when appropriate.

- Launch a 'daily mile' and join in yourself.

- Set outdoor homework and do it yourself too.

Harnessing technology for wellbeing – the good, the bad and the ugly?

We hear a lot about the effects of technology on our lives; most of it bad. But there are both positives and negatives to using IT effectively, particularly in terms of teacher wellbeing. The pandemic has brought us to a much greater acceptance of the idea that meetings and teaching sessions don't have to be face to face. While schools struggled with the loss of learning time in the classroom with pupils, and while the effects of that, particularly on the most vulnerable pupils, were real, there are good legacies from it too.

We talked in detail in Chapter 9 about managing workload: one suggestion there was that teachers don't always have to be physically present at twilight sessions, for instance. The way is open now to much more flexible ways of working. So if staff members want to head off to collect children from school or do other domestic duties before logging in from home for a meeting, it can help to ease the pressure on them.

The Digital Wellbeing Educators project sets out seven ways teachers can use digital tools to make their lives – and their pupils' learning – easier.

- Course creation and e-learning tools, to create courses, simulations or other educational experiences.

- Presentation software and animation tools, to display information in the form of a slide show.

- Webinar and meeting tools to facilitate staff interaction without always being face to face. These need to be deployed judiciously – while one staff member may relish the idea of logging in from home after the school day rather than staying in school for an extra hour, others may not. Be respectful of the individual needs of staff members and be flexible in how you use online meetings.

- Screen casting, audio and capture tools, to share screens directly from a browser.

- Collaboration and file sharing tools, to help people involved in a common task achieve their goals.

- Bookmarking and curation tools, to collaboratively underline, highlight and annotate an electronic text.

- Project management tools, to assist team working among staff members.

Researchers have found[8] that a range of online strategies can help ease teacher stress – in addition to those above, a further example is using online sessions to engage with parents. This can include parent evenings and can improve home-school relationships.

Doing it all safely

But… back to the bad bit. All school staff need to feel safe using online technology. They need to know they won't be subjected to cyber-bullying, and they need to know exactly what to do to avoid any question of inappropriate behaviour in online interactions with pupils and families.

And there's more bad news. The Safer Internet Centre says UK schools are falling far short of what's needed in terms of staff awareness and training around online safety. The centre, which is appointed to oversee the issues in the United Kingdom, says the best practice is to embed safety in everything you do, through a framework of policies and routes for reporting concerns. Both staff and pupils need to be protected, it says.

But it's reported[9] while most schools have policies and systems in place to tackle issues such as keeping children safe and monitoring inappropriate images, more than 4 in 10 had no staff training in place for internet safety, and just under 3 in 10 were not dealing properly with data protection issues. This lack of professional development was shown to have had a negative effect on schools' performance overall. The Centre's Professionals Online Safety Helpline had seen an increase in calls about issues such as privacy while teaching from home, and about employers' expectations that teachers should use personal devices at home.

So, there's much to be done when it comes to online safety – just one of the many environmental factors which can affect teachers' wellbeing. And there's much that *can* be done when it comes to improving the physical environment in which your staff have to work – both inside the school buildings and outside them. Neither has to cost a fortune, yet it's possible that they could save you one if they can help in building a happier, healthier and more committed workforce.

A design brief for wellbeing

In May 2020, the international design practice Scott Brownrigg collaborated with The Learning Crowd to consider how school design might support the health and wellbeing of teachers and pupils in a post-Covid world.[10] It drew together panellists and audience members from the worlds of both design and education at a roundtable to discuss how the built environment impacts our wellbeing and mental health. As a result, a report was published which asked: 'What should the brief for wellbeing include if we want every child to flourish?'

Here are the answers the roundtable put forward:

Outdoor Environment Brief

- Provide a framework for future development – forest schools, food-growing areas, harvest communities and orchard projects, farms and animals.

- Connect indoor and outdoor space for play and outdoor learning – bring the fresh air in.

- Encourage physical activity – link physical activity and healthy eating.

- Enable and encourage children to explore – different areas for sensory engagement, opportunity to connect with our natural world and ecology.

Community Connectivity Brief

- Incorporate "little bit of extra" space to meet local needs.

- Enable the school to build the community and the community to develop a sense of pride around the school, feel ownership. Integrate the school into its local environment.

- Buildings and external areas should be a continuation of, and connect with, the community.

- Incorporate children's centres, adult education and youth clubs.
- Showcase spaces for food and culture as key avenues for outreach to local families. Cooking and food encourage healthy eating and provide links to communities.

Inclusion Brief

- Incorporate a true variety of spaces inside and out – discrete, private, purpose designed, protected spaces for specialist activities and learning support as well as general multi-use spaces.
- Give every child a chance to shine.
- Provide good acoustics in every space, not just designated teaching spaces.

What are the post-occupancy wellbeing indicators?

- Healthy and productive
- Safe, secure and sustainable
- Functional

While these recommendations are focused on helping pupils to flourish, by definition, they also create a physical environment where everyone will do their best work.

ANNE-LOUISE PAYNE, THREE RIVERS ACADEMY:

When I took over as head in April 2016, they literally had just broken ground. Luckily, we were able to stay in the old buildings, which was actually quite exciting. From a well-being point of view, for students and staff and parents, for the whole community really, to be able to see a brighter future literally, from the ground up, was quite a big thing.

The school officially required improvement at the time, and as part of the due diligence process it became clear it was likely to be worse than that. Six weeks after I arrived, Ofsted told us the inevitable – the school was put into serious weaknesses.

I think the issues boiled down to a few key aspects, I would say lack of aspiration, lack of high expectations for children, actually believing the children can do better and raising academic targets. Another thing was the revolving door of teaching staff – one of the things that's very important to children in any school is trust in adults, being able to build positive relationships. Any big school will have a turnover but people came and went, if you came back after a holiday the kids would say, 'OK, you said you were going to come back and you did, I'll give you that.'

The old school was ugly, it was old-fashioned, it was falling apart, it looked unloved. There were lots of different buildings and that meant there were lots of places that could be hidey hole places, so children didn't feel safe.

But a building is just a building; in terms of welfare what matters most is that sense of children feeling safe and well cared for in a place they can be proud of. The building helps but you have to have the culture and the ethos to go with that.

There were some tough conversations, but the Ofsted judgement was very much a line in the sand. I was very much of the mindset that it doesn't matter what building you're in, you have to get the culture and ethos right and take that with you – then the shiny new building is the icing on the cake. By June 2019 the school was graded good in every category. So that was the journey, it was just under three years.

With a new school you get to consider every aspect, not just from an academic point of view but from a welfare point of view as well. We looked at it from the perspective of every member of the school community, students, staff, parents, the sense of community which is very, very strong here.

In the new build from a community point of view, everyone is under one roof including the sixth form, so the younger children see the older students as role models around the school. Staff would say that by all being under one roof they see each other more. In secondary schools the staffroom is often the most under-used room in the school. In the busy day people either stay in their classrooms to work, prepare and plan, or they'll be with their teams in smaller offices. Whilst we do have faculty work rooms, just by the nature of everyone being able to walk through the building it doesn't feel as big, so there's a lot more daily contact.

Another key aspect is the glass. There is so much glass in this building internally, and the students have said right from the beginning that they feel safe because of that passive supervision. There's always somebody there and there are lots of open spaces as well. On the first floor there's are four areas which are kitted out with computers so it's a place that children can go to be before and after school, or at break and lunchtime. For some its part of their wellbeing that at lunch time they want to do some of their homework there and chat to their friends.

Then on the ground floor we have this huge area called the mall. There's lots of seating and the canteen pods are there; I arrived this morning at twenty past seven and two boys came in with me to go to breakfast club. They sit there with their friends; they feel safe there and there are none of the hiding places which you get in a lot of big secondary schools. I've worked in a lot of secondary schools with narrow corridors, and you don't have that here – there are open spaces, so it feels airy.

At the far end is sports, and performing arts, drama, music, dance. That's deliberately designed so that it can be separated from the rest of the school for community letting. So in terms of wellbeing, a lot of our students and parents of prospective students who will come here to use the community part of the school even before they might come to the main school -what is great is when students come up into year six they've been here to play football, or to see a drama performance. It really helps in terms of reaching out into the community.

Externally, I know anecdotally from staff who were here before that it was an absolute nightmare to supervise because it was a huge site with hiding places. There were trees, there was a ditch. Now it's very open and visible. At the front of the school is the piazza. It's got benching so you'll see children sitting there before and after school waiting for their friends, but during the day it's used by the sixth form. And then on the other side you've got the huge field, there's hard surface areas, there's football and the multi-use games area (MUGA).

Children are like adults; they find their tribe. There are the ones who want to chat with their friends, and then you'll have the kids who just want to go out there and hoof a ball around. It's a lovely atmosphere because its big enough for some to be playing football and others to just sit and chat.

When children are in a school where they know the school isn't doing well they feel let down, they feel unloved, and so I suppose when we moved in they felt invested in just by the nature of the fact it was a brand-new building. When we moved in I remember saying to a younger child, 'What do you really think of the building then?' He said 'Miss, I feel like I'm going to university every day. I don't know what that means but that's what it feels like.' For me that was the best quote, because it feels like it's about aspiration. The building is a grown-up space. It feels grown up, it doesn't look like a typical school, so the children felt special and invested in as students.

In terms of recruitment things are really tough now, particularly in recruiting support staff. We are having to be a lot more flexible in HR. But since we had our good Ofsted, I knew that if I could get people over the threshold the children would sell the school. The children are the best ambassadors – people don't want to hear from us. When they're proud of their school, that's the best marketing you can get.

Chapter 17: Key points

How can you adapt your school's physical environment to facilitate a wellbeing culture? There are things you can't change, but there are many things you can change, including:

- Temperature and air quality: poor ventilation leads to loss of concentration, fatigue and reduced performance, not to mention increased risk of infection.

- Noise levels – associated with lower test scores. Different floor coverings can help.

- Outdoor environment: research shows schools with green space around them have lower rates of absenteeism.

- Light levels: can you improve areas where lighting may be too dull or too harsh?

- Colour: White walls plus feature walls with colour are thought to improve stimulation, along with bright furniture and displays.

You may also want to think about:

- Ownership: personalisation – something as simple as a coat hook – can enable users of a room to feel a sense of belonging.

- Flexibility: different spaces for different groups and activities; clever solutions for enabling different activities and group sizes.

- Complexity: too sterile and the room won't provide enough visual stimulation; too complex and attention will wander.

- Taking your learning outdoors: learning in natural settings can improve wellbeing, social and collaborative skills, self-confidence, engagement and even academic attainment.

- Harnessing technology for wellbeing: think about ways in which you can use digital tools to make everyone's lives easier. This can include course creation and e-learning tools, presentation software, webinar and meeting platforms, screen sharing, file sharing and project management. But… make sure you do it safely. Too many schools are falling behind in ensuring staff are fully trained in internet safety and safeguarding.

Further resources

Creating the right work spaces: tips from Education Support: https://teachershub.education support.org.uk/school-culture/physical-environments-support-staff-mental-health-and-wellbeing
Outdoor classroom day resources library: https://outdoorclassroomday.org.uk/resources/
How changing things like air quality, lighting, acoustics can cut absenteeism and improve productivity: https://www.ncbi.nlm.nih.gov/pmc/articles/PMC2920980/
Green buildings: https://www.rateitgreen.com/green-building-articles/green-schools-enhancing-health-wellness-and-academic-performance/111
Resources library for outdoor classroom day: https://outdoorclassroomday.org.uk/resources/

Notes

1 MacNaughton, P., Eitland, E., Kloog, I., Schwartz, J. and Allen, J. (2017). Impact of Particulate Matter Exposure and Surrounding 'Greenness' on Chronic Absenteeism in Massachusetts Public Schools. *International Journal of Environmental Research and Public Health*, 14(2), p.207. doi:10.3390/ijerph14020207.
2 For Health (2017). *MA SMART – schools for health*. [online] Research. Available at: https://research.forhealth.org/2017/03/06/ma-smart/ [Accessed 15 December 2022].
The Massachusetts' School Metrics and Research Tool (MA SMART), Harvard TH Chan School of Public Health, https://research.forhealth.org/2017/03/06/ma-smart/

3 Singh, A., Syal, M., Grady, S.C. and Korkmaz, S. (2010). Effects of Green Buildings on Employee Health and Productivity. *American Journal of Public Health*, [online] 100(9), pp.1665–1668. doi:10.2105/ajph.2009.180687.

4 Carrington, D. (2016). Green buildings make you work smarter and sleep sounder, study reveals. *The Guardian*. [online] 16 December Available at: https://www.theguardian.com/environment/2016/dec/16/green-buildings-make-you-work-smarter-and-sleep-sounder-study-reveals.

5 Barrett, P., Davies, F., Zhang, Y. and Barrett, L. (2015). The Impact of Classroom Design on Pupils' Learning: Final Results of a Holistic, Multi-Level Analysis. *Building and Environment*, [online] 89(89), pp.118–133. doi:10.1016/j.buildenv.2015.02.013.

6 Mann, J., Gray, T., Truong, S., Brymer, E., Passy, R., Ho, S., Sahlberg, P., Ward, K., Bentsen, P., Curry, C. and Cowper, R. (2022). Getting out of the Classroom and into Nature: A Systematic Review of Nature-Specific Outdoor Learning on School Children's Learning and Development. *Frontiers in Public Health*, 10. doi:10.3389/fpubh.2022.877058.

7 Outdoor Classroom Day (n.d.). *Find out about outdoor classroom day and why you should get involved!* [online] Outdoor Classroom Day. Available at: https://outdoorclassroomday.com/about/.

8 Passey, D. (2021). Digital Technologies – and Teacher Wellbeing? *Education Sciences*, 11, p.117. doi:10.3390/educsci11030117 https://files.eric.ed.gov/fulltext/EJ1290364.pdf

9 Phippen, A. (2021). *UK schools online safety policy & practice assessment 2021 Annual analysis of 360-degree safe self-review data covering schools and colleges in England.* [online] Available at: https://swgfl.org.uk/assets/documents/uk-schools-online-safety-policy-and-practice-assessment-2021.pdf [Accessed 15 December 2022].

10 Taylor, H. (2020). *What if schools were designed for wellbeing?* Scott Brownrigg. Available at: https://scottbrownrigg.b-cdn.net/media/4734/report-what-if-schools-were-designed-for-wellbeing.pdf

18 The policy picture

Throughout this book, we've aimed to focus on the practical steps school leaders and their teams can take to safeguard and improve staff wellbeing. But we all know that isn't the whole picture: the external demands on schools are to some extent a necessary evil – most educators accept they work in a highly regulated sector where scrutiny and a legislative framework are important elements. So, to some extent, this chapter is about the scale of those demands, and about how policymakers can do more to enable schools to alleviate them in order to foster healthier schools.

What's in this chapter applies mainly to the United Kingdom, though similar policy issues exist elsewhere. We've covered the concerns raised about workload in the United States by the teachers' union, the NEA. Inspection plays a greater or lesser part in different countries – much greater in Europe than in the United States.

What do we know? A reminder

Here's a run-down of some of the key points from Welbee's staff survey, which was covered in detail in Chapter 1. The survey, which drew responses from almost 8000 teachers and other school staff, was mapped against the Health and

DOI: 10.4324/9781003315766-24

Safety Executive's six Management Standards: Demands, Control, Support, Relationships, Role and Change.

There was good news: school staff scored well on three of the six standards: role, support and relationships. It seems that internally, schools are doing well on building supportive and communicative ways of working. Staff also felt, on the whole, that they were consulted about change, though they didn't feel they had enough influence over when change was made. But they scored themselves less highly on the final two standards – Control and Demands. Put briefly, schools are still trying to do too much with too few resources, leading to stress and burnout. And to a large extent, this is driven by external factors: legislative demands and funding. While there is more that schools can do to cut workload and increase flexibility in working practices, external policy needs to address these issues more seriously and consistently too.

The picture wasn't consistent across all parts of the education world, nor across different types of staff. Non-teaching staff tended to score more highly on wellbeing than those in teaching roles, while those in SEN schools scored more highly than those in all other schools. Senior leaders had the lowest scores, followed by middle leaders.

There wasn't a significant difference between local authority and academy schools in the survey, but independent schools scored higher than state schools on control and lower in most other standards.

There is a clear need for demands on staff to be reduced across all sectors and phases and this has to be an area of focus, particularly as Covid catch-up initiatives continue and we enter a further period of cost challenges. Ways of enabling greater internal control of schools' working lives and practices should be another key focus.

Similar issues relating to overwork, burnout and stress caused by high demands on teachers have been reported elsewhere, too. In the United States, for example, the main teaching union has called for system-wide responses to recruitment issues and overwork as staff report increased levels of stress.

What government promises

The English Department for Education (DfE) is well aware of the issues, of course, and its Education Staff Wellbeing Charter spells that out: "We recognise that the DfE shapes the policy environment that state funded schools and colleges operate in, and that our policies can have both direct and indirect impacts on the wellbeing of staff."[1]

The department promises to work in partnership with the sector and to show leadership in protecting and promoting wellbeing. The charter also recognises that the government has a different relationship with the further education sector.

It promises to:

– 'Design-in' wellbeing by integrating it into its school workload policy test and by considering the impact of policy changes on staff wellbeing.

– Measure and respond to changes in staff wellbeing over time, focusing on levels of anxiety, happiness, worthwhileness, life satisfaction and job satisfaction across the sector, and to build this evidence into policymaking.

– Continue to take the advice of sector experts on wellbeing and mental health and to build wider wellbeing evidence into policymaking, including measures of mental health stigma reduction.

– Support the sector to drive down unnecessary workload and to remove unnecessary burdens – this will include improvements in how the DfE collects data.

– Ensure government guidance covers staff wellbeing and is published only during working hours where possible.

– Champion flexible working and diversity in all settings and at all career stages.

– Break down stigma by building staff wellbeing and mental health into communications on recruitment and retention.

– Embed wellbeing in training and professional development, and continue to ensure professional development and initial training covers managing pupil behaviour.

– Improve high-quality mental health and wellbeing resources online, focusing on those that help employers and staff deliver their organisational commitments, and to review progress in 2023.

Inspection

The school inspectorate makes its own contribution to the government's wellbeing charter, recognising it has a dual role to play, in making clear its requirements on wellbeing and also in reducing the stress and workload associated with the inspection process.

It promises to:

– Ensure inspectors take staff wellbeing into account in coming to judgements.

– Review whether inspections are impacting staff wellbeing, for example, by creating unnecessary workload and to act on the findings.

– Continue to try to reduce the administrative workload created by inspections.

– Be clear that it does not grade individual lessons or people, or require evidence that could be used for performance management. It does not require lesson plans or information to be provided which would not already be available.

However, the charter also requires commitments from school leaders, some of which may require substantial change, for example, the requirements to champion flexible working and to give staff a greater voice in decision-making. We covered this in Chapter 4.

The built environment

As we've noted in Chapter 17, school buildings are key to ensuring the wellbeing of all those who work and learn in them. The DfE recognises this in its climate change strategy for schools, though it focuses on the needs of pupils rather than staff: "By improving the physical environment in and around education settings, we can impact positively on both the physical and mental wellbeing of children and young people," it says, promising to act on necessary improvements to the country's vast education estate.

The department has already begun the work of piloting different technologies and approaches to sustainable building and estate management and suggests that after 2025, this phase will end and resulting knowledge will be rolled out. The main focus of this will be on achieving net zero in new buildings and blocks, but there is also ongoing work on a 'biophilic' primary school which should provide evidence of how a greater connection to nature should impact on the health and wellbeing of children and young people.

The department also plans to pilot the use of smart air and environmental quality monitors in schools and to feed that into school building design in the future.

Physical activity and outdoor learning

The DfE's climate strategy[2] also mentions looking into nature-based classroom design to provide better access to the outdoors and opportunities for outdoor learning – and it specifically mentions that this should impact positively on physical and mental wellbeing. There's also a promise to link school grounds as a single 'National Education Nature Park' which can provide more green spaces, shading and flood resistance.

And finally, there's support for initiatives to increase active and safe travel to school –again, the beneficiaries are listed as children, families and carers, but we may assume better bike routes could also be helpful for staff health and wellbeing, too.

The gaps

All this talk of physical improvement points to a major stumbling block: resources. It all costs money, and without major additional resources, the notion of making schools into physically healthy places will be a rather limited one. The same goes for dealing with workload issues, too, of course.

And while there are well-meaning statements on the burden of legislation, there are pressures in the other direction, too. Barely a year goes by without a major bill on Education, and the amount of new law which education institutions must absorb and deal with on a regular basis must often seem overwhelming. For instance, the 2022 Schools Bill[3] for England contained no fewer than 15 different measures covering issues as diverse as the establishment of new multi-academy trusts, truancy powers, investigation of illegal schools and the means by which a grammar school could become a comprehensive. Other parts of the United Kingdom aren't immune to blizzards of legislation, either. The Education (Scotland) Act 2016[4] covered a similarly diverse range of topics including the Gaelic language, reducing inequality in outcomes, school meals, the appointment of chief education officers, early learning and headteacher training.

Schools' and headteachers' organisations have been saying for years that resourcing needs to improve, and recent inflationary pressures have pushed the issue to crisis point. Geoff Barton, General Secretary of the Association of School and College Leaders, had this to say about the 2023–24 funding settlement for English schools:

> The squeeze on education funding over the past decade has resulted in schools and colleges having to make very significant cutbacks to provision. Furthermore, the settlement for 2023–24 does not remotely take into account the huge inflationary pressures which schools and colleges are now experiencing. We are hearing reports of energy bills being increased by 300% or more. Many settings have also continued to face Covid cost pressures in using supply staff to cover for absence. They also face the prospect of having to absorb the cost of pay awards from existing budgets. It is increasingly inevitable that many will have to make further cutbacks to provision.

So here are some recommendations for government and for others responsible for system change, based on the findings of the Welbee staff survey and other information gathered from Welbee's work with schools:

● We need to address the need for Covid catch-up, but too much of this is being done through additional lessons after school, in the holidays or by reducing breaks. The limited funding provided won't provide the capacity needed so existing staff have been forced to take up much of the additional work at a time when they are bound to be exhausted. A long-term plan should set out how schools will deliver the outcomes needed in a way which is not detrimental to staff and student wellbeing.

● Longer holidays and an earlier finish are seen as perks of a teaching job, but the fact is most teachers work evenings, weekends and holidays. If we want to support schools in improving the wellbeing of staff, we have to make a change.

There's a saying: "If you keep doing what you've always done, you'll get what you've always got." We need to create greater capacity in the sector, give staff more autonomy and give leaders a better chance of leading effectively.

● We need more staff in schools, with more autonomous time and much better staff development at all career stages – simply revamping existing qualifications and Teaching Schools will not be enough. School staff need to have space in their day to grow and reflect.

● Schools should be asked to become more engaged in creating solutions, rather than simply being asked to implement plans which have been designed at the centre. Education staff badly need to feel a greater sense of agency and ownership over what they do. More broadly, a wider range of stakeholders should be consulted on changes to education policy and practice.

● In England, the DfE should be held to account on making changes and meeting the commitments of their Education Staff Wellbeing Charter. It is down to school leaders to challenge policymakers when they don't 'build in' staff wellbeing to their policy workload test.

Remember the challenges that all school leaders face, particularly when they are new to their role: a third of new teachers leave within five years, school recruitment targets have been missed since 2012, teacher job satisfaction in England is among the lowest in the world. Teachers faced high levels of stress and mental ill-health even before the twin blows of Covid and the cost-of-living crisis.

We need a national debate on how best to achieve this. How can we increase capacity and support those in education? Without far more focus on wellbeing than there is at present, some schools are inevitably going to slip backwards in this regard rather than moving forward.

Chapter 18: Key points

Key points from the Welbee Staff Survey: The good news: school and college staff scored well on three of the six standards: Role, Support and Relationships. Staff also felt consulted about change but wanted more influence over when it was made. The bad news: scores were lower for Control and Demands. Schools are still trying to do too much with too few resources, leading to stress and burnout.

The English DfE promises to:

● 'Design-in' wellbeing.

● Measure and respond to changes in staff wellbeing over time.

○ Continue to take the advice of sector experts on wellbeing and mental health.

- ○ Support the sector to drive down unnecessary workload.
- ○ Ensure government guidance covers staff wellbeing.
- ○ Champion flexible working and diversity.
- ○ Break down stigma.
- ○ Embed wellbeing in training and professional development.
- ○ Improve high-quality mental health and wellbeing resources online.
- ○ Ofsted promises to:
- ○ Ensure inspectors take staff wellbeing into account in coming to judgements.
- ○ Review whether inspections are impacting staff wellbeing, for example, by creating unnecessary workload, and to act on the findings.
- ○ Continue to try to reduce the administrative workload created by inspections.
- ○ Be clear that it does not grade individual lessons or people or require evidence that could be used for performance management, or require lesson plans or information to be provided which would not already be available.

The environment: School buildings are key to achieving a sense of wellbeing, and this will be a key part of the design of new schools in future. Nature-based and outdoor learning will be built in, and there will be support for safer travel to school.

The gaps: some recommendations for government:

- A long-term Covid recovery plan should consider how catch-up programmes affect staff and student wellbeing.
- Create capacity to give staff more autonomy and leaders a better chance of leading effectively.
- More staff in schools, with more autonomous time.
- Much better staff development at all career stages.
- Ask schools to help create solutions, rather than simply asking them to implement plans designed at the centre.
- Ministers should be held to account by school leaders if they don't 'build in' staff wellbeing to policy workload tests.
- A national debate on school staff wellbeing.

Notes

1 Department for Education (2021). *Education staff wellbeing charter.* [online] gov.uk. Available at: https://www.gov.uk/guidance/education-staff-wellbeing-charter.

2 Department for Education (2022). *Sustainability and climate change: A strategy for the education and children's services systems*. [online] gov.uk. Available at: https://www.gov.uk/government/publications/sustainability-and-climate-change-strategy/sustainability-and-climate-change-a-strategy-for-the-education-and-childrens-services-systems. Department for Education policy paper, Sustainability and climate change: a strategy fo r the education and children's services systems, April 2022, https://www.gov.uk/government/publications/sustainability-and-climate-change-strategy/sustainability-and-climate-change-a-strategy-for-the-education-and-childrens-services-systems

3 UK Parliament (2022). *Schools bill, 2022*. [online] Parliament UK. Available at: https://bills.parliament.uk/publications/46433/documents/1770 [Accessed 15 December 2022].

4 Scottish Parliament (2016). *Education (Scotland) Act 2016*. [online] Legislation.gov.uk. Available at: https://www.legislation.gov.uk/asp/2016/8/contents/enacted.

19 | The digested read

You're busy, so here's a 20-minute version of this book. If you want to delve deeper, you can go back to each individual chapter for more.

Chapter Summaries:

Chapter 1: Introduction

- Wellbeing is how staff feel, personally and socially: how they evaluate their life satisfaction, how they can develop and become fulfilled; how they function physically, mentally, emotionally and spiritually; their sense of positivity about their working lives.

- The key factors in achieving good levels of wellbeing can be viewed through the Health and Safety Executive's Management Standards. These are: Demands, Control, Support, Relationships, Role and Change.

- National teacher wellbeing surveys consistently show poor results, with many respondents reporting overwork, burnout and a desire to leave the profession. UK teachers work some of the longest hours in the OECD.

- Research shows the situation is more stable than the headlines suggest: more teachers are reporting mental health problems, but so are professionals in other walks of life. Similarly, teachers work long hours and are often working at weekends and in evenings, but this has always been the case.

- Stress is linked less to the hours teachers work than to *how* they spend their working hours: extra hours spent on teaching, working with colleagues or extra-curricular activities are generally OK; extra hours spent on paperwork, lesson planning and marking are stressful.

- Accountability is a factor in causing stress, and therefore in policy terms, it has drawbacks as well as benefits. Teachers are more likely to be stressed by

 DOI: 10.4324/9781003315766-25

accountability measures such as inspections and appraisals if their colleagues feel the same way. Whole-school approaches are vital in effecting change.

- A Welbee Staff Survey revealed teachers scored higher than other professions in terms of Role, Support and Relationships. They scored comparatively lower in terms of Demands, Control and Change. Staff in special schools scored higher than in other types but there was little difference between local authority, academy and independent schools – staff wellbeing is mostly about culture, driven by leaders. Support staff had the highest scores, followed by teaching staff, middle leaders and then senior leaders with the lowest.

- The benefits of building a strong wellbeing culture can include better staff recruitment and retention, better staff performance, higher student outcomes and improved financial performance.

- Leadership is crucial: do what you say, be open, be consistent, praise more than you criticise and ideally deliver feedback directly in a one-to-one situation.

- The first step in effecting whole-school change should be gathering data – first through what's available in school, such as staff turnover and absence and then using an effective staff survey.

Chapter 2: First steps to measuring staff wellbeing

- Start by looking at existing data: teacher retention levels (and why staff leave), absence rates, grievances and disputes, staff and student behaviour, feedback on performance and relationships.

- Effective exit interviews are a good way to identify key reasons why staff members leave, though they come too late to stop someone from leaving.

- Stay interviews are a way to identify what you might do to ensure staff members stay – focus first on asking questions of the staff members you value most.

- Use return to work interviews to support staff with absences and to better understand causes and whether there are trends that can be addressed.

- Move beyond data and use a staff survey to seek further feedback – while you can do this yourself, there are benefits from using a third party – increased participation, better analysis, even recommended actions – and reduced workload.

- Use an evidence-built survey and choose what will work for you – pulse, question set and annual survey with comprehensive reporting are all available.

- The Health and Safety Executive's (HSE) Indicator Tool is recommended, as this assesses risks against known stress factors to find out what is going well and where to focus energy and effort for improvement.

- Communicate, communicate, communicate. Let staff members know why you want their feedback and how important it is to you. Encourage participation and share results with staff and other key stakeholders.

- Celebrate successes along with recognising those areas that require focus and action.

- Set clear goals and a plan of how to deliver them. Focus on foundations first – behaviours of leaders and processes that support them so wellbeing is simply part of the culture.

Chapter 3: Having a clear plan

Once you have reviewed your school data and run a staff survey, you need a clear idea of what you want to do and what to focus on. Below are some tips for you to follow.

- Set clear goals with the aim of embedding wellbeing in everyday life so it is simply part of the culture

- Share your results with all staff – everyone needs to buy into and feel ownership of actions and changes that are agreed. Include governors, trustees and other stakeholders.

- Don't take on too much – take small and agreed steps and communicate about them regularly. As well as looking forward, remind people what has been achieved.

- Start with the foundations, for example, vision and values, leadership behaviours and processes that support them.

- Identify responsibilities for making sure each action is delivered (remembering everyone has to take ownership for their part) and be clear how success will be measured.

- Keep monitoring until it becomes part of everyday culture and business as usual for all staff.

- Don't organise activities, such as a wellbeing day as a means of starting – these should only be considered where you have built firm foundations.

- Don't move on too quickly; it is important you follow up and embed actions before going forward.

- Add actions and track progress as part of your school development plan, so staff wellbeing is seen as part of your current processes. This also makes sure you do not add any unnecessary workload.

- Repeat reviewing data and your staff survey so you can effectively track progress and better understand the actions that work and deliver improvements.

Chapter 4: Taking action

Questions to ask regularly:

- Is workload distributed and managed effectively to prevent and reduce stress?

- Do staff feel sufficiently involved, listened to and supported?

- Are leaders and colleagues treating each other with respect and compassion? Are interactions well managed and supported?

- Do leaders understand the impact of their behaviours, both positively and negatively?

For English state schools, the Department for Education (DfE) has introduced the Education Staff Wellbeing Charter – reviewing this may also be useful for those from other countries and other sectors. Should you sign up to it, if you are in England or follow its lead, if you aren't.

This means agreeing to the following 11 commitments, though you do not have to tackle everything at once. Numbers 3, 10 and 11 are the place to start.

1. Tackle mental health stigma.

2. Give staff support.

3. Provide managers with the right tools and resources.

4. Establish a clear communications policy.

5. Give staff a voice.

6. Drive down unnecessary workload.

7. Champion flexible working and diversity.

8. Create a good behaviour culture.

9. Support staff to progress.

10. Have a strategy for protecting leader wellbeing.

11. Measure staff wellbeing regularly.

Chapter 5: Leading for wellbeing

- **Principal wellbeing**. If you aren't managing your own wellbeing, you aren't managing the wellbeing of your staff or across your school. The wellbeing of principals has a clear impact on both staff and students. School leaders play a crucial role in creating healthy and caring schools.

- **Take a rain check**. Are you overstressed? Are you getting enough sleep, food, drink, exercise? Are you smoking or drinking more than previously, avoiding social contact, reacting angrily to small irritations? Are you tired all the time, experiencing repeated physical symptoms such as headaches, finding it hard to make decisions? Feeling inadequate, or suffering from memory loss? If so, stress may be affecting you. If you notice these signs, you may want to seek help – this might be from an employee assistance scheme, if your school has one, counselling, if available, or from your GP.

- **Avoid thinking traps**. Are you using unhelpful mental shortcuts to help you deal with problems? These may include jumping to conclusions, personalising, externalising, mind-reading, emotional reasoning, over-generalising, magnifying or minimising problems, catastrophising. When you face adversity, check and avoid these traps. The 'ABC' method can help: A is adversity; B is your belief about the reason for it, C is the consequence you expect. If you can find a more positive narrative about B, you can work towards more positive consequences.

- **Take time to reflect**. Do you tend to blame yourself, or others? Do you tend to think all problems are permanent or all-encompassing whereas maybe they are transient?

- **Be the change you want to see**. Take exercise, eat and drink regularly, take time out, try to form effective thinking habits.

- **Focus on your team**. Imagine their state of mind as an arc which runs from boredom to comfort, then to stretch, then to strain, then to crisis. Boredom will leave them unengaged; crisis will tip them over into burnout. Try to help them to get to stretch, but no further.

- **Stay calm**, make decisions, communicate well and be a good role model.

- **Manage yourself**. Understand that press and stress are normal and your beliefs about it matter. Working in a high stress role and knowing how to manage stress give the lowest risk of early death.

- **Learn how to manage your stressors**. The Mayo model of Avoid, Alter, Adapt and Accept is a framework you can use to make good choices.

- **Having a high level of self-awareness** allows you to make good decisions and it is also at the heart of emotional intelligence. Without this, it is impossible to make changes.

- **Your inner voice** is either your greatest cheer leader or biggest critic. Focus on what you have achieved and done well, not what you still have to do and mistakes you have made.

- **Don't multi-task**, chunk work, such as emails, and do your most important task or tasks first each day.

- **Manage interruptions** and your availability so that you are able to give people your full focus and deliver your most important work.

- **Manage workload** to ensure the task you undertake delivers an impact for staff, pupils or the school community and when introducing new work, ensure something is removed.

Chapter 6: Becoming a competent leader

- School leaders are getting younger, and those who are newly promoted particularly need support: they tend not to stay long, and that's a waste of valuable resources. How do you support your teams?

- Think about whether your responses to the following issues are positive or negative. So positive responses would include following through, finding solutions, while a negative one might include making unrealistic demands or failing to make decisions.

  ○ Workload

  ○ Employee problems, managing conflict

  ○ Planning

  ○ Empowering staff and including them in decisions

  ○ Facilitating staff development

  ○ Being accessible

  ○ Health and safety

  ○ Giving feedback

  ○ Managing your own emotions

  ○ Having a friendly style, displaying empathy

  ○ Communicating well

  ○ Taking responsibility

  ○ Knowing your job – and knowing when you should seek advice.

- Self-assess against the 12 competencies proven to prevent and reduce staff stress. Get the behaviours that underpin these right and watch staff members you lead flourish and do their best work.

Chapter 7: Getting the right staff and keeping them

What's the word on the street about your school? Chances are you're recruiting from the local area – people talk to each other, so reputation is key. Think about every stage in the 'lifecycle' of an employee:

- **Attraction:** See above: give out good vibes in every way, and the job's done for you. Think about using staff videos on your website and in your attraction and recruitment.

- **Recruiting:** Think about what will differentiate you from others and how you can stand out. Think how the best school in the world would look to a candidate, and what steps that school would take to recruit them, for example always providing feedback.

- **Onboarding:** New recruits need to have support so they can understand the culture and what's expected, so they feel they belong. This starts from the day they are appointed and is much more than their first day. It is how they meet senior leaders, their line manager, and colleagues and how they are managed and developed.

- **Performance:** Keep up a dialogue, don't wait for things to go wrong before engaging staff members – ensure this is an ongoing dialogue, as well as holding effective appraisals.

- **Development:** From day one, you should agree where this staff member is going in addition to discussing how they can support your school. What's their agenda; how can you help them meet it?

- **Retention:** This is not just about the rewards you can offer, although these are important. As well as delivering across the other six stages in the employee lifecycle, think about how you build wellbeing and other factors such as flexibility into the culture.

- **Farewell:** When someone moves on, make sure it's a positive experience: even where they move on through capability, how can you ensure this is dealt with effectively and with compassion? Where people move on through promotion, this should be a partnership, where you have supported their development. If working as part of a multi-academy trust or district, have a clear plan to manage career and promotions. Where people do leave unexpectedly, make sure you understand why – that's golden information. There's an exit interview template in Chapter 2. There is also a stay interview template – as it is even better to ask questions about what will encourage staff members to stay with you.

- **Putting a people strategy together:** These stages, together with the everyday experiences of staff, form part of your people strategy. If effective, they will support the reputation of your school as one where staff choose to work and stay. In developing this, think long-term and don't crisis-manage.

Chapter 8: Making staff feel valued

Good staff wellbeing is all about culture and climate. Putting staff first is the best way to ensure students achieve their best academic and all-round outcomes. Here are eight key techniques you may wish to consider:

- **Keep the conversation going:** Ensuring staff have a voice. Life is busy and school timetables are inflexible, but if you can schedule in regular one-to-ones with key colleagues, wider meetings and surveys, you will reap rewards. Build this into the life of your school so that everyone takes part, with senior and middle leaders seeing their team members regularly.

- **Build in teamwork:** Team members should share a sense of identity; common goals; successes and failures. They should work together and follow the same rules and should make decisions collectively. There should be rules which every-one buys into, and team members should have a variety of skills and backgrounds. A team will have more opportunities to be successful if it has clear objectives and sufficient time and skill and is supported by the organisational culture.

- **Create psychological safety:** Balance accountability with making sure peo-ple are not fearful of making mistakes, so they are able to deliver their best performance.

- **Embed coaching:** Coaching is designed to raise awareness and develop respon-sibility in others by using effective questioning and listening skills. It's usually non-directive, targets specific goals and forms the basis of a leadership style by raising awareness of both opportunities and responsibilities. It is different from mentoring, which tends to be a longer and more directive process.

- **Make praise part of every day:** Set a goal to catch people doing the right things every day, and ask other leaders to do the same. It builds morale and it builds your culture: it's contagious.

- **Manage by walking around:** Don't just walk about randomly, popping your head into classrooms: it makes staff anxious. Instead have a clear purpose and plan and build this into your own and organisational routines.

- **Don't avoid difficult conversations:** Identify when these conversations need to happen and prepare for them – use T-CUP (Thinking Clearly Under Pressure) and you will be ready for any eventuality. This process can be used for all situa-tions you might face – meaning you are more likely to make the right decisions and deliver an effective outcome.

- **Implement distributed leadership**: This is a model based on sharing responsi-bility and accountability as widely as possible and it can make a real difference. It takes pressure off the senior leadership team, and it builds esteem among middle managers and even more junior staff.

Chapter 9: Managing workload

Revisit the HSE Management Standards, particularly Demands and Control, which are central to keeping workload manageable.[1] Teachers report working an average of 53 hours a week in term time, and workload is the most common reason they cite for leaving the profession.

- **On demands**, you might wish to ask if colleagues feel able to cope with their job, if their demands are achievable in working hours, which tasks are most onerous and time-consuming, if there are any particular hazards, such as behaviour issues which make the job more burdensome, and what changes could be put in place to help.

- **On control**, ask if staff feel consulted on the organisation and allocation of work tasks, if they have some say in what and how they do things and there are enough opportunities for discussion, if they are encouraged to use their skills and initiative, if they feel stretched to acquire new skills, and what changes might help.

- **You might ask these questions** in one-to-ones or group meetings, or you might organise a one or more workshops – the DfE provides a useful toolkit for the latter.[2] You could use such workshops to discuss your school's staff survey findings too.

- **The dreaded inspection:** Inspections are a key driver of workload and stress; be clear what is and isn't required. Ofsted's handbook[3] contains a 'myth-busting' list of the documents its teams can ask for, and which they won't ask for. Other inspectorates also provide information through their frameworks.

- **Following up:** The results of these discussions should become central to the life of your school. Think about how you can systematise what you've learned through these processes.

Chapter 10: Support staff

All support staff – grounds maintenance staff, catering staff, lunchtime supervisors, admin and finance team members and technicians should be included in staff surveys: consider how their responses differ from those of the teaching staff and leaders. Just recognising that they're there and do valuable work will reap rewards. Here are some tips:

- Keep support staff involved in all discussions to identify priorities for their development and wellbeing. Make sure they feel they are listened to.

- Review line-management and pastoral arrangements to ensure all groups of staff are supported.

- Communicate – make sure everyone knows who they can speak to if there are issues.

- Include support staff in staff meetings and events where possible – but be mindful that they aren't paid to work extra hours and won't all be there on any given day. Can you make these activities paid?

- Plan specific sessions for different groups of support staff. These should be advertised well in advance.

- Explore how they can have more say in how they go about their job, even if outcomes are set. For example, teaching assistants reducing teacher workload through being given more say in how work is delivered.

- Grow your own talent – build support staff career paths into your people strategy and include them in devising wellbeing support within your available resources. And ask them to lead sessions for teaching staff, too, as teachers will learn from them.

- Include support staff in performance development and appraisals.

Chapter 11: Don't forget the senior leadership team

- Do you understand each individual's tolerance levels for certain things? Are you managing workloads to play to their strengths and minimise their vulnerabilities? Early warning signs that there may be issues include increases in disputes and disaffection, turnover, staff complaints, absences and parent complaints. Team performance overall is likely to suffer.

- Think about how you might take some of the stress off other team members, and vice versa: who finds certain things harder, or easier, than others? Is someone particularly strong on dealing with parents, for instance, while others struggle? Who provides your support system; who does that for each team member? Watch out for team members driving themselves too hard or becoming withdrawn.

- Set out clear responsibilities for everyone. Some team members could focus on managing changes while others run business-as-usual activities. Focus on outcomes and make sure you have clarity about what you need to achieve. Create short-term goals and keep them simple.

- Consult your team but also remember to listen to answers. Where you do not take on what is suggested, clearly explain why. It is OK to challenge and disagree prior to decisions being made, but from then on, everyone must stand behind them.

- Leaders also need to understand and demonstrate cabinet responsibility and communicate as one. Ultimately, all members of the leadership team need to take an executive role on behalf of the school or trust.

- Build resilience before the next crisis hits. Ask yourselves if you understand each other's experience and vulnerabilities.

- Ask yourselves:

  ○ Does everyone in the school get the same messages about wellbeing?

  ○ Do we need to revisit core policies such as safeguarding or behaviour to ensure consistency?

  ○ How can we build expertise about mental health into our senior team?

  ○ Do we thank staff enough for what they do?

- Develop your own and all leaders' personal effectiveness – refer back to Chapter 5, which contains a list of tips and actions you can take.

Chapter 12: Culture, cake and yoga

This chapter is about what a school can look like when it really puts wellbeing at its core.

- There's nothing wrong with free cake or fruit, staff social events, resilience or mindfulness training or wellbeing days. However, they are not the place to start and won't deliver significant benefits or long-term change. Afterwards, you staff will go back to their classroom or place of work and face all the same underlying issues that were there before.

- Focus on building wellbeing foundations so they become part of your climate and culture and of the leadership behaviours and systems that support it.

- Have a clear wellbeing policy in place – what might your school's look like? First remind yourself of those HSE standards: Demands, Control, Support, Relationships, Role, Change.

The sections of your wellbeing policy will reflect those standards and should include:

- **Statement of Intent**: to include a mission statement, details of how it builds on existing policies by creating a culture and environment in which wellbeing is central. Key points on how this will be achieved.

- **Arrangements for wellbeing and stress prevention** through good management practices; to include human resources processes, management of performance, absences, bullying and disputes, flexible working arrangements and disability.

- **Consultation and Communication**: to include staff surveys and feedback, trades union consultation, how the school community will be kept informed, plans for training on the policy and on specific areas such as stress management.

- **Responsibilities for implementing** the staff wellbeing policy; to include the roles of head and senior leadership team, of managers and supervisors, of all staff, of the human resources team, of the school wellbeing committee or similar. Plan for a whole-school risk assessment, and give details of how the policy will be reviewed regularly.

Chapter 13: Wellbeing and your students

So, what is all this doing for the pupils? There are two answers.

One, a wellbeing culture should embrace everyone in the school community. Pupils should absorb positive, inclusive attitudes and values that they can take through life. Two, there's some evidence that happier staff get better results.

This chapter includes some suggestions on producing a whole-school framework for emotional wellbeing, questions for discussion on pupils' involvement and links to further resources.

If you want to improve pupil wellbeing and outcomes:

- Follow the evidence.

- Build the right wellbeing foundations, focusing on leaders' behaviours and processes that support these.

- Role model the agreed values and don't pass on your stress (much easier to do in a psychologically safe and supportive culture).

- Use tried and tested methods to directly support pupils – the NCB provides a framework you can follow (there are others and you may have created your own). This will only deliver the needed outcomes when built on the right staff wellbeing foundations.

Chapter 14: The role of governors and trustees

How do governors and trustees fit into the wellbeing journeys of schools? Again there are two answers: there are the things they should do and things they shouldn't. They should:

- Provide a sounding board on ideas and issues.

- Make sure the strategic direction is right.

- Respect the difference between governance and operational management.

- Manage the meetings schedule to ensure work-life balance for governors, trustees and staff.

- Make sure the right policies are in place.

- Oversee compliance with employment and equalities legislation.

- Monitor the impact of strategies and initiatives for wellbeing.

- Make sure policies are applied consistently.

- Set out a clear vision of where the school is going.

- Bring in a wide range of stakeholders.

- Embody the school's values and act with compassion, even when difficult conversations are necessary.

- Remember they have a duty of care to school leaders.

- Carry out an annual internal evaluation and consider external validation every three years.

They shouldn't:

- Get involved in day-to-day management or try to do other people's jobs for them.

- Overload the headteacher with strategies, initiatives and monitoring activities.

- Expect school leaders to be available on tap or without notice.

- Forget to regularly evaluate the impact of the board on the school and its staff.

- Impose a staff wellbeing policy if it isn't in place – a link governor for wellbeing is an alternative. There is guidance on appointing one in the chapter.

This chapter also has hints on practical steps to take, and links to further reading.

Chapter 15: Bringing the outside in

- Schools aren't islands. No matter how strong the school's culture is, pupils and staff will bring in their baggage, their stresses and their crises from other parts of their lives. But there's plenty of evidence that by building relationships with parents, carers, families and other outside stakeholders, a school can bring stakeholders into its vision and culture so that they understand and bolster it.

- This can be done informally, through conversations with individual parents or carers, or more formally at a parents' evening, through printed information, through parent courses or through family link workers.

- The Anna Freud National Centre for Children and Families suggests[1] different strategies depending on a family's level and type of engagement. You might invite parents and carers into school to celebrate achievements, use positive messaging to make sure parents know you're in this together, identify your ten most challenging students and organise regular conversations along with positive feedback. Try to be sensitive to each family's needs and issues.

- Mentally Healthy Schools has a useful checklist of things to look out for.[2] Children struggling at home might be withdrawn, tired, angry, absent or act younger than their years. Your school's safeguarding lead should be involved and may be able to help families to get appropriate support. Key tips include being clear and open about the problem, positioning the parent or carer as the expert, highlighting the child's strengths, using reflective listening, focusing on opportunities to work together and trying to imagine how they feel.

- Whole-school questions include reflecting on how governors and trustees engage with parents, whether parents have enough opportunities to be in school, whether everyone is aware of resources to learn about mental health and wellbeing and whether other outside organisations could help.

Chapter 16: Rewriting the book

- Let's start again with a blank sheet. Can education really be about wellbeing, or do we need to accept we sometimes need to be pushed outside our comfort zone to meet life challenges?

- These days even the British Army believes that need for stretch and challenge must be accompanied by mutual respect and the moral courage to do 'not just the right thing, but the best thing.' So surely we can have a culture of wellbeing in schools without their core purpose being compromised.

- What is education, anyway? The United Nations started out with the view it should be about engendering world peace, but now it believes it's also the foundation of health and wellbeing.

- The late Sir Ken Robinson believed education had four purposes: personal, cultural, economic and social. He added eight core competencies: curiosity, creativity, criticism, communication, collaboration, compassion, composure, and citizenship. These competences could only be learned in a supportive, compassionate institution.

- Does curriculum matter? Possibly not, in the wider sense – but there is evidence that really good Personal, Social and Health Education does make a difference in terms of wellbeing. It needs to be taught with a whole-school focus, involving all pupils and with clear objectives. It needs to start early but to be age-appropriate, to have buy-in from senior leaders and to be monitored properly to ensure its goals are met.

- The inspection framework of the government's inspection service for England, Ofsted, doesn't mention wellbeing, though it does look at workload, bullying and other wellbeing issues. A new inspection framework to be introduced in September 2023, developed by the United Kingdom's Independent Schools Inspectorate (ISI), puts pupil wellbeing up front and centre – it's worth a read. Its inspectors focus on key values which should put children's wellbeing at the heart of school life. However, it fails to mention staff wellbeing. What gets measured gets done and this is a missed opportunity – leaders need to choose to make staff wellbeing central to what they do.

- Teaching styles for wellbeing: the University of British Columbia has trialled lots of different approaches and it suggests fostering connections, supporting peer relationships, helping students feel motivated, being active, setting out clear goals and plans, providing feedback, making sure the classroom environment feels safe… and smiling!

- Management style: we've talked about this already. Stay in touch with your staff, build teamwork into everyday life, embed coaching, make praise routine, distribute leadership, use the twelve competencies proven to prevent and reduce staff stress from Chapter 6.

- Communicate, communicate, communicate.

Chapter 17: Get physical

How can you adapt your school's physical environment to facilitate a wellbeing culture? There are things you can't change, but there are many things you can, including:

- Temperature and air quality: poor ventilation leads to loss of concentration, fatigue and reduced performance, not to mention increased risk of infection.

- Noise levels – associated with lower test scores. Different floor coverings can help.

- Outdoor environment: research shows schools with green space around them have lower rates of absenteeism.

- Light levels: can you improve areas where lighting may be too dull or too harsh?

- Colour: white walls plus feature walls with colour are thought to improve stimulation, along with bright furniture and displays.

You may also want to think about:

- Ownership: personalisation – something as simple as a coat hook – can enable users of a room to feel a sense of belonging.

- Flexibility: different spaces for different groups and activities; clever solutions for enabling different activities and group sizes.

- Complexity: too sterile and the room won't provide enough visual stimulation; too complex and attention will wander.

- Taking your learning outdoors: learning in natural settings can improve wellbeing, social and collaborative skills, self-confidence, engagement and even academic attainment.

- Harnessing technology for wellbeing: think about ways in which you can use digital tools to make everyone's lives easier. This can include course creation and e-learning tools, presentation software, webinar and meeting platforms, screen sharing, file sharing and project management. But… make sure you do it safely. Too many schools are falling behind in ensuring staff are fully trained in internet safety and safeguarding.

Chapter 18: The policy picture

Key points from the Welbee Staff Survey: the good news: school and college staff scored well on three of the six standards: Role, Support and Relationships. Staff also felt consulted about change, but wanted more influence over when it was made. The bad news: scores were lower for Control and Demands. Schools are still trying to do too much with too few resources, leading to stress and burnout.

The English DfE promises to:

- 'Design in' wellbeing.

- Measure and respond to changes in staff wellbeing over time.

  ○ Continue to take the advice of sector experts on wellbeing and mental health.

  ○ Support the sector to drive down unnecessary workload.

  ○ Ensure government guidance covers staff wellbeing.

  ○ Champion flexible working and diversity.

  ○ Break down stigma.

  ○ Embed wellbeing in training and professional development.

○ Improve high-quality mental health and wellbeing resources online.

○ Ofsted promises to:

○ Ensure inspectors take staff wellbeing into account in coming to judgements.

○ Review whether inspections are impacting staff wellbeing, for example, by creating unnecessary workload and to act on the findings.

○ Continue to try to reduce the administrative workload created by inspections.

○ Be clear that it does not grade individual lessons or people or require evidence that could be used for performance management, or require lesson plans or information to be provided which would not already be available.

The environment: school buildings are key to achieving a sense of wellbeing, and this will be a key part of the design of new schools in future. Nature-based and outdoor learning will be built in, and there will be support for safer travel to school.

The gaps: some recommendations for government:

- A long-term Covid recovery plan should consider how catch-up programmes affect staff and student wellbeing.

- Create capacity to give staff more autonomy and leaders a better chance of leading effectively.

- More staff in schools, with more autonomous time.

- Much better staff development at all career stages.

- Ask schools to help create solutions, rather than simply asking them to implement plans designed at the centre.

- Ministers should be held to account by school leaders if they don't 'build in' staff wellbeing to policy workload tests.

- A national debate on school staff wellbeing.

Notes

1 Her Majesty's Stationery Office (2007). *Managing the causes of work-related stress: A step-by-step approach using the management standards.* [online] Great Britain: HMSO. Available at: https://www.hse.gov.uk/pubns/wbk01.htm

2 Department for Education (2018). *School workload reduction toolkit.* [online] gov.uk. Available at: https://www.gov.uk/guidance/school-workload-reduction-toolkit [Accessed 14 December 2022]. Includes workshop facilitation notes.

3 Ofsted (2022). *School inspection handbook.* [online] gov.uk. Available at: https://www.gov.uk/government/publications/school-inspection-handbook-eif/school-inspection-handbook [Accessed 14 December 2022].

Index

Note: **Bold** page numbers refer to tables and *italic* page numbers refer to figures.

Printed in Great Britain
by Amazon

31126226R00145